God's Quest

"*God's Quest* is a welcome addition to complete the author's overarching review of humanity's quest for spiritual satisfaction and for God's quest to address the salvific need of humanity. In *The Quest*, Dr. Kulathungam focused on the human-initiated search for spiritual reality. In *God's Quest*, he describes the very distinct Judeo-Christian portrayal of the Almighty's pursuit of those created in his image. Distinctions are made between the two, especially as relates to the messianic and salvific nature of Jesus Christ's life, death, and resurrection. The chapter, 'Spiritual Revolution,' which focuses on the meaning of Pentecost and the purpose of Spirit baptism is especially stimulating. *God's Quest* is a highly recommended study for those desiring to engage the Judeo-Christian understanding of a God who pursues those he has created."

—DAVID WELLS
General Superintendent, Pentecostal Assemblies of Canada

"Building on his earlier work in theology of religions that re-oriented the question of religious pluralism from the human quest for God to God's quest for human beings, Dr. Kulathungam addresses the challenges of the differing visions of redemption among Jews and Christians. He turns to the sources of both religions—the narratives of the Bible. He argues that, despite differences, Jews and Christians share a common redemptive narrative—God's quest to redeem people. He argues that the revolutions in salvation and spirituality initiated by Jesus Christ and the Spirit of Pentecost, which distinguish Christians from Jews, nevertheless culminate in an eschatological revolution in the narrative of God's quest that promises a union and renewal that includes Jews and Christians."

—STEVEN M. STUDEBAKER
Associate Professor of Systematic and Historical Theology, Howard & Shirley Bentall Chair in Evangelical Thought, McMaster Divinity College

"People of all cultures and nationalities are looking for a path of redemption. *God's Quest* refers to this very topic and highlights God's quest to meet the human salvific quest. Dr. Lyman Kulathungam presents an excellent interdisciplinary study where philosophy, logic, theology, and religious studies intermingle. The chapters, written with passion and competence, address a wide spectrum of readers. For over twenty years, Lyman served as Visiting Professor at the Warsaw Theological Seminary, Poland, where he lectured on apologetics and world religions. . . . Dr. Kulathungam's experience and extensive qualifications predispose him to make a competent statement on *God's Quest*, a study beyond borders. I wholeheartedly recommend reading this extraordinary book."

—WŁODZIMIERZ RUDNICKI
Former President, Warsaw Theological Seminary, Poland, Senior Pastor, New Life Church, Warsaw, Poland

"Dr. Lyman Kulathungam provides an insightful, informative, and thorough look at the commonalities, differences, and the journey of Judaism and Christianity. He brings a logical, informed, objective, and experiential perspective in his presentation. I trust that as you travel through the content of this book, you find the experience to be both informative and spiritually enriching."

—DAVID SHEPHERD

> Former District Superintendent, Western Ontario District, Pentecostal Assemblies of Canada

"With his usual brilliance and insightfulness, Dr. Lyman Kulathungam invites the Judeo-Christian community to journey with him and to consider God's relentless quest of both the Jews and the Gentiles in this latest book: *God's Quest: The DNA of the Judeo-Christian Community*."

—TOM QUINN

> Regional Director, Western Ontario District, Regional Overseer and Liaison to Aboriginal Pentecostal Ministries, Pentecostal Assemblies of Canada

God's Quest

The DNA of the Judeo-Christian Community

Lyman C. D. Kulathungam

Foreword by Ronald A. N. Kydd

WIPF & STOCK · Eugene, Oregon

GOD'S QUEST
The DNA of the Judeo-Christian Community

Copyright © 2019 Lyman C. D. Kulathungam. All rights reserved. Except for brief quotations in critical publications or reviews, no part of this book may be reproduced in any manner without prior written permission from the publisher. Write: Permissions, Wipf and Stock Publishers, 199 W. 8th Ave., Suite 3, Eugene, OR 97401.

Wipf & Stock
An Imprint of Wipf and Stock Publishers
199 W. 8th Ave., Suite 3
Eugene, OR 97401

www.wipfandstock.com

PAPERBACK ISBN: 978-1-5326-4754-3
HARDCOVER ISBN: 978-1-5326-4755-0
EBOOK ISBN: 978-1-5326-4756-7

Manufactured in the U.S.A.   OCTOBER 21, 2019

For Sarojini
and Jaishan, Daniel, Mikayla, and Micah

Contents

List of Images and Illustrations | ix

Permissions | xi

Foreword by Ronald A. N. Kydd | xiii

Preface | xv

Acknowledgments | xxi

1. God's Quest Amidst Paradigm Shifts | 1
2. The Blunder in Bounty | 32
3. The Blunder of Babel | 47
4. The Silent Revolution | 65
5. The Salvific Revolution | 96
6. The Spiritual Revolution | 120
7. The Cross: Stumbling Block or Folly? | 148
8. Pentecost: Blasphemy or Off Track? | 170
9. Until Then | 192

Bibliography | 219

List of Images and Illustrations

Where there is no source indicated for an image, the material was located in the public domain.

Figure	With Permission of
Photograph of cross and menorah at church altar	Kishore Kuventhirarajah
Photograph of cross and menorah inscription on stone column from Laodicea	John W. Martens
Digital drawing of Egyptian Sun God Ra	Jaishan Kulathungam
Digital drawing of death mask of King Tutankhamun	Jaishan Kulathungam
Photograph of Adam's Peak, Sri Lanka	Palitha Ekanyake
Artwork of building of the Tower of Babel	The British Library Board
The Babel story in the broader narrative	Lyman C. D. Kulathungam
Painting of Nimrod	

List of Images and Illustrations

Mosaic of Alexander the Great meeting Jewish priests	Jim Hiberman and Jodi Magness
Rare Roman coin	Diana Miller, VCoins Support
Painting of the three crosses	Raheel Shakeel, Pixabay
Photograph of traditional site of the upper room	Ferrell Jenkins/BiblePlaces.com
Painting of Jesus and the rabbis	
Painting of Christ driving the money-changers from the Temple	National Galleries of Scotland
Photograph of the empty tomb	Loria Kulathungam
Painting of the death of Socrates	
Palatine graffito of Alexamenos	
Sketch of the tree of life (*Otz Chiim*)	Sarojini Kulathungam (adapted from Dedopulos, "The Tree of Life," in *Kabbalah*, 63.)
Transcendental meditation track	Lyman C. D. Kulathungam
Photograph of the Epicurean garden of death	Tim Whitmarsh
Antony Flew book cover	HarperCollins Publishers
Sketch of bird hovering over stormy waters	Daniel Kulathungam

Permissions

Barker, Kenneth L., and Donald W. Burdick. *The NIV Study Bible*. 10th Anniversary. Grand Rapids: Zondervan, 1995. Unless otherwise indicated, all Scripture quotations are from the New International Version (NIV).

British Library Board. *Building of the Tower of Babel*. Detail of a miniature from © British Library Board (MS 18850, folio 17v, the "Bedford Hours"), illumination on parchment, circa 1410 to 1430. Held and digitized by the British Library. This file has been provided by the British Library from its digital collections.

Flew, Antony, with Roy Abraham Varghese. *There is a God*. Copyright © 2007 by Antony Flew. Reprinted by permission of HarperCollins Publishers.

Levine, Amy-Jill, and Marc Zvi Brettler, eds. Excerpts from *The Jewish Annotated New Testament: New Revised Standard Version Bible Translation*. Second edition. Oxford: Oxford University Press, 2017. Reproduced with permission of the Licensor through PLSclear.

Martens, John W. Cross and menorah inscription on stone column from Laodicea. Permission granted by the photographer.

Marx, Karl, and Friedrich Engels. *The Manifesto of the Communists*. New York: International Publishers, 1886. Reproduced by permission of the British Library Board Shelfmark: 8282.de.24.(10).

Metropolitan Museum of Art. *The Death of Socrates*. Oil on canvas painting by Jacques-Louis David (1748–1825). This is a faithful photographic reproduction of a two-dimensional, public domain work of art.

New Living Translation. Scripture quotations marked (NLT) are taken from the Holy Bible, New Living Translation, second edition, copyright ©2008 by Tyndale House Foundation. Used by permission of Tyndale House Publishers. All rights reserved.

Palatine graffito of Alexamenos. Second-century pagan graffito depicting a man worshipping a crucified donkey. This is a faithful photographic reproduction of a two-dimensional, public domain work of art.

Schøyen, Martin. The Schøyen Collection is a museum-grade private collection owned and curated by Martin Schøyen. For the purposes of these terms and conditions 'The Schøyen Collection' refers to Martin Schøyen, and all staff and associates working to support activities relevant to schoyencollection.com ('this website') and other websites that may from time to time be used to provide research-related access to manuscripts and artefacts in the Schøyen Collection. We are the owner or the licensee of all intellectual property rights (including without limitation copyright, trade marks and design rights (whether registered or unregistered) database rights and rights in confidential information and know-how) in our Websites and in all information, articles and material published on our Websites (the "Material"). The Material is protected by copyright laws and treaties around the world and you are only permitted to use it as expressly authorised under these Terms. In consideration of you complying with these Terms, we grant to you for your personal and lawful use only a non-commercial, non-exclusive, non-transferable, royalty-free, revocable licence.

Stott, John R. W. Excerpts taken from *The Cross of Christ*. 20th anniversary ed. Downers Grove, IL: IVP, 2006. Reprinted with permission of the publisher.

Walton, John H. Excerpts taken from *The Lost World of Adam and Eve* by John H. Walton. Copyright (c) 2015 by John H. Walton. Used by permission of InterVarsity Press.

Wickramasinghe, Chandra. Poem "Tsunami: The Roiling Devastating Wall of Sea." *In Eyes, Winds, Seas, Skies*. Reprinted with permission of the author.

Foreword

THE BOOK YOU HAVE in your hands is the second in a project that Dr. Lyman Kulathungam put in motion in 2012. The first book was *The Quest: Christ Amidst the Quest.* In it he examined eight world religions. Putting his finger on human realities, he focused on the thirst for meaning and purpose that haunts us all—and he names it. We each, conscious of it or not, launch into a quest. I had heard the term applied religiously in aboriginal contexts, but Kulathungam's emphasis on the universality of the impulse carried me further into the human condition. *The Quest* has been well received. It is of interest to note two particularly affirming reviews. One of them came from a prominent Buddhist and the other from a leading Hindu. One of the features of Kulathungam's work is the depth of understanding he has for the religions he discusses.

The two religions Kulathungam does not deal with at length in *The Quest* are Judaism and Christianity. These are the focus of the current book. His decision to deal with these two in the same book is completely understandable. His subtitle captures the reality of their intimate commonality—*The DNA of the Judeo-Christian Community.* In spite of centuries of tension, which not infrequently have burst into flame, these two religions have a great deal in common. Second-century denier Marcion's opinions aside, Christianity cannot be understood without the Jewish story. Old Testament scholar Christopher Seitz makes comments supporting the intimacy Kulathungam sees between these two religions. For example, Seitz noted, "Efforts [by Christians] to leave the Old Testament as Jewish scripture, as someone else's mail, no longer properly comprehend who Jesus was, on his own terms and on the terms that the New Testament writers—is there a Gentile among them?—understand him."[1] Jewish influence pervades the New Testament: the Gospels, Acts, Romans, and James provide sufficient evidence. There

---

1. Seitz, *Word without End,* 68n17.

was also at least one Christian group that was clearly identifiable as Jewish well into the fourth century.

Ignoring postmodernity's signature rejection of metanarratives, Kulathungam convincingly points to one—a divine quest in which God, in love, reaches continually to all people. This is bold. In this book, Kulathungam inverts the flow of energy found in the first book. There, it was human beings searching after gods; here it is God reaching to people.

To develop the concept, Dr. Kulathungam navigates both Old and New Testaments plus the history of theology, identifying paradigms through which God's love for humans and his world moved, moves, and will move. He launches on a voyage that is not for the faint of heart. The material he grapples with is extraordinarily diverse and there is so much of it. But he carries it off successfully. He is a philosopher, and one who is deeply grounded in Scripture and in theology. However, he is not only a well-informed intellectual. In sections dealing with the Holy Spirit, and elsewhere, he is able to move profoundly into the relationship of the divine and the human.

This book and *The Quest* form a remarkably complementary pair. In the first, Kulathungam examines the roles that Christ can play in all the other quests. Here, he builds an account of what God has done in Jesus Christ.

—Reverend Dr. Ronald A. N. Kydd
 Emeritus Professor of Christian History
 Tyndale University College & Seminary

Preface

OCTOBER 27, 2018 WAS just another routine Saturday in the world's calendar, but at the Pittsburgh Tree of Life Synagogue, it was a day of death. Eleven Jews, while at worship, succumbed to death in a hail of bullets, while seven more were injured. Less than five months later, on March 14, 2019, fifty Muslims were killed and fifty more were injured while praying at two mosques in New Zealand. On April 21, 2019, while the Christian world celebrated Easter, more than 200 innocent Christian worshippers—including children—at three churches in Sri Lanka, were mercilessly bombed to death and many more injured. On April 27, 2019, the last day of Jewish Passover and six months to the day after the Pittsburgh synagogue tragedy, history repeated itself at the Chabad Synagogue in Poway, California, where one person was killed and many injured. Horrific slaughter of innocents at worship seems to be ever increasing!

In times of conflict, civilian deaths are bound to occur. These are often referred to euphemistically as inevitable collateral when they take place unintentionally. The United States has coined the somewhat oblique phrase "disposition matrix," which covers virtually all civilian casualties in its wide connotation. Civilian killings, particularly the deliberately targeted ones, are abominable at any time. Killing people while they are worshipping, whether they are Jews, Christians, Muslims, or of any religious community, is not only unjust and cruel but also carries a message: worshipping God is absurd, hypocritical, or even a menace to social well-being.

In the case of the massacre at the synagogue in Pittsburgh, political instigation, mental malfunction, anti-Semitism, and security lapses have all been cited as causing this tragedy. We need to remember that Jewish history has been interrupted with periods of harassment and persecution. At first, anti-Semitism was directed against the Jewish people, but after the Holocaust of World War II and the establishment of the Jewish state in 1948, the target became the state. Anti-Semitism has turned out to be a concerted effort to challenge the very existence of the State of Israel. Why is such a small sector of the human populace—less than 15 million in a world of over 7 billion people—so harassed but still able to survive? In 1891, Russian novelist Leo Tolstoy posed an interesting question about the nature of a Jew. He observed a

> creature that was insulated and oppressed, trampled on and pursued, burned and drowned by all the rulers and the nations, but is nevertheless living and thriving in spite of the whole world . . . The nation which neither slaughter nor torture could exterminate, which neither fire nor sword of civilizations were able to erase from the face of earth, the nation which first proclaimed the word of the Lord, the nation which preserved the prophecy for so long and passed it on to the rest of humanity, such a nation cannot vanish.[1]

The only way he could explain Jewish resilience and survival in such life-threatening challenges was to claim that: "A Jew is eternal; he is an embodiment of eternity."[2] What is it that makes the Jew an embodiment of eternity? Many people groups who have been harassed and victimized are now extinct. The Jews, however, have survived tortuous treatment by tyrannical powers through the years, like Pharaoh's Egypt, Nebuchadnezzar's Babylon, Pompey's Rome, and Hitler's Nazi Germany and Auschwitz atrocities.

What is it that gives the Jewish people the strength to survive? After all, they are also human. Of course, one could provide several reasons why the Jews have survived these life-threatening episodes. Dealing with such a question takes us to the core theme of this book: God's relentless quest. Let me suggest that it is this that provides the Jewish community the strength to survive amidst challenges. That does not mean God is concerned only with this community. His protective and redemptive interventions in the history of the Jewish community highlight his concern for all humanity. For instance, God brought the Jews miraculously across the Jordan River because he had promised them a new land, but that was not the only reason. "He did this so that all the peoples of the earth might know that the hand of the Lord is powerful and so that you might always fear the Lord your God" (Josh 4:24). That "you" includes you and me!

The concern for Israel does not mean that the Jews have been flawless in their dealings with other communities. In fact, the creation of the State of Israel resulted in the displacement of some people groups, particularly

---

1. Tolstoy, "What is a Jew?," 135–36.
2. Tolstoy, "What is a Jew?," 135–36.

the Palestinians, from their traditional habitat. These groups naturally feel that they have been treated unfairly by Israel's occupation of their territory.

Despite some significant differences between Judaism and Christianity, one cannot deny that Christianity came out of Judaism. Both Judaism and Christianity have an identity of their own, but at the grassroots level there is something the two communities seem to share: the awareness that God is trying to connect with them both at personal and communal levels. Let me suggest that the DNA that binds these two communities is God's relentless quest to relate with and free them, especially when they are in desperate situations. This interconnection between Judaism and Christianity has been there since ancient times. As we shall see in chapter 1, an image in stone located in ancient Laodicea depicts the menorah along with the cross. This trend to relate Christianity with Judaism continues. The photo below of the altar at a contemporary church (Miracle Family Temple, Toronto, Canada) shows how, even today, Christianity's connection to Judaism is recognized.

Cross and menorah at church altar (Photo credit: Kishore Kuventhirarajah)

For Jews, the menorah is a reminder of God's help, manifested as light in dark and desperate times. For Christians, the cross symbolizes God's sacrificial gift of salvation through Christ. Both these symbols effectively identify the DNA of the Judeo-Christian community: God's redemptive quest.

Discrimination, harassment, and persecution—all of which characterize the Jewish story—also figure prominently in the life of the Christian community from its origin. Even in this so-called accommodative world of ours, over 250 million Christians are persecuted for their faith each year.[3] Several organizations and churches call Christians to be proactive and pray earnestly for the persecuted Jews and Christians. *One Free World International Human Rights Organization,* founded by Majed El Shafie, advocates for the human rights of religious minorities and is well known for its decisive stand against the persecution of Jews as well as other groups who are persecuted for their faith.[4] The call to prayer of Reverend David Wells, the General Superintendent of the Pentecostal Assemblies of Canada, communicated in November 2018 in his monthly letter to the churches via email, is an appeal for the churches to join the Christian world to remember with gratitude the victims of war and also to pray earnestly for Christians persecuted for their faith. His appeal is founded on the conviction that God is the Lord of history and is not indifferent to the sufferings of people.

This book will look at the life of the Judeo-Christian community as presented in its narrative. The narrative is based mainly on the Scriptures of these religions and is woven around the theme of God's quest as enacted in the history of these communities. Despite some significant differences between the Jewish and Christian narratives, there is an underlying trend that gives structure to both versions and highlights the enactment of God's quest in the history of these communities. Certain significant revolutionary events play important roles. Some of them, like the blunder of Adam and Eve in the Garden of Eden that caused the rift between God and humans, and the anticipated final day of judgment, are featured in both narratives, though interpreted differently. Others, like the salvific revolution wrought by Christ on the cross and the spiritual revolution on the day of Pentecost, figure prominently in the Christian narrative, while remaining controversial from a Jewish perspective. God is involved in all these events, orchestrating

---

3. https://www.opendoorsusa.org/christian-persecution/world-watch-list/pressroom/.

4. Rev Majed El Shafie is a former Egyptian Muslim who converted to Christianity and was tortured and sentenced to death in Egypt for converting to Christianity and bringing awareness to human rights violations related to religious persecution. He escaped and claimed political asylum in Canada, where he is now a citizen. In 2012, he received the Queen Elizabeth II Diamond Jubilee Medal. More information available at: https://ofwi.org.

paradigmatic shifts in the history of these two communities, which is what makes them revolutionary. Such revolutions anticipate the grand finale that will exhibit the peak point of God's quest to relate to and redeem his creation.

It is my hope that this narrative will enable you to sense the depth and scope of God's relentless quest to relate with humans, which continues even to this day. It may also help you to appreciate that God has not given up on humanity despite several attempts to misrepresent, substitute, ridicule, exclude, and even kill him. He is not dead!

When doubt, disappointment, and desperation close in on those who trust in God, it is natural that doubt enters, challenging the faith of the faithful. The prophet Habakkuk expresses this sentiment in his complaint to God about the evil in Judah going unpunished, when "the wicked hem in the righteous so that justice is perverted" (Hab 1:1–2). The great Victorian poet Gerard Manley Hopkins expressed a similar sentiment. Just a few months before his untimely death in 1889, in his poem, "Thou art Indeed Just, Lord," he articulated his concern this way:

> Thou art indeed just, Lord, if I contend
> With thee; but, sir, so what I plead is just.
> Why do sinners' ways prosper? and why must
> Disappointment all I endeavour end?[5]

This frustration leads us to the perplexing question of why there is so much evil in this world. If God is almighty and all-loving, why does he allow evil? There are several explanations given. In theological circles, such explanations are called "theodicies." The narrative does not provide a theodicy for the existence of evil. On the other hand, it highlights God's intervention in the face of evil. The narrative also anticipates God's final act when evil will be annihilated. Although the narrative does not provide an explanation of evil, it highlights how God intervenes and redeems his creation from evil. Actions speak louder than words.

In such moments of doubt and desperation, it is essential to remember that God has not given up. His quest is relentless and does not dwindle, even during desperate situations. God's persistent quest to relate with people is motivated by unconditional love and is not dependent on circumstances or restricted by boundaries. Let me not start to preach but invite you to journey with me through the Judeo-Christian narrative, with the hope that it will provide you with the resilience to be on the mountaintop even when walking through the valley!

---

5. Hopkins, "Thou art Indeed Just, Lord," 67.

Acknowledgments

I THOUGHT I WAS finished with writing after my last book, *The Quest: Christ Amidst the Quest*, but it seems that I was not!

Many asked me why I did not include Judaism and Christianity in my earlier survey of religions. Due to the requests of my colleagues, mentors, pastors, and reviewers of *The Quest*, I launched into this strenuous but rewarding journey.

This book has a historical format and the most qualified person I could think of to help me articulate such a format is Reverend Dr. Ronald Kydd, Emeritus Professor of Christian History at Tyndale University College and Seminary. He patiently plowed through the manuscript and helped me stay on track, especially in the historical sections. He provided an excellent introduction to my former book, and I am once again honored that he has written a foreword that perfectly introduces my presentation of the Judeo-Christian narrative.

I am grateful to those who endorsed this book. Both Reverend Dr. David Wells and Reverend David Shepherd endorsed my previous book and have consented to endorse this one as well. I am pleased that they still have confidence in me! No doubt it is difficult for the General Superintendent of the Pentecostal Assemblies of Canada (PAOC) to find the time to read through a book like this. David Wells walked the second and even the third mile with me and encouraged me all the way, providing insightful suggestions in significant sections. David Shepherd, who has been my pastor and mentor since 1976, helped me in constructive ways in sections dealing with the ministry of the Holy Spirit, especially in the areas of healing and the deaf community. His wholehearted and prayerful support of my venture is indeed appreciated. From an academic perspective, Dr. Steven Studebaker's endorsement captures poignantly my strategy to relate the Jewish and Christian communities, while recognizing significant doctrinal differences between them. My ministry in Poland began in 1988, teaching at Warsaw Theological Seminary and preaching in local churches, and this brought me in contact with Reverend Włodzimierz (Wlodek) Rudnicki, then president of the seminary. His conviction that God was present amidst the challenges the Polish people faced through history widened my perspective of God's universal quest. The way Rudnicki and his wife, Renata, articulated their endorsement introduces a novel perspective to my work. I have enjoyed ministering over several years with Reverend Tom Quinn, Regional Director South East Region, Western Ontario District, PAOC, especially to the cultural churches in the Greater Toronto Area. He made time to read through and edit some of the chapters. His endorsement highlights God's quest both in the Jewish and gentile worlds.

David Kraemer, Professor of Talmud and Rabbinics and Joseph J. & Dora Abbell Librarian at the Jewish Theological Seminary of America in New York, is a prolific writer and scholar in Jewish studies. He helped to source the relevant scholarly literature on God's quest in Judaism. His research on the Judaic stance on suffering in rabbinic literature, the view of death in Judaism, and his appeal for Judaic action to deal with the ecological crisis, have been particularly relevant to my work. Several of his books are cited.

Remy Landau, a Jewish Harvard scholar from the Conservative tradition, has been a great help through the years to enable me to better understand Judaism. He hosted students from my World Religions class for several years during our visits to Adath Israel Congregation Synagogue in Toronto. He perused meticulously the sections dealing with Judaism and provided constructive suggestions.

Dr. Eli Lizorkin-Eyzenberg, president of the Israel Bible Center and an expert scholar in early and modern church history, helped me to articulate the relationship between Judaism and Christianity through his research and descriptions of his courses at the Center.

Chandra Wickramasinghe is a retired diplomat and civil servant who served in a senior advisory role to several Sri Lankan presidents and represented his country as the Sri Lankan ambassador to France. He provided insightful comments with a philosophical flavor. I appreciate his input, especially since it is from a scholar of a different religious background than my own.

Reverend Doug James, retired Professor of Theology and Biblical Studies at Master's College and Seminary, went through my manuscript in his typical patient and scholarly manner. He helped me to streamline my presentations to be biblically based and theologically sound. I needed some input from a pastoral perspective, and Reverends Scott Doggart, Bob

Wright, Kevin Begley, and Pam Begley met that need. Scott Doggart, Regional Director South West and Central Region of Western Ontario District, PAOC, and former Academic Dean of Thailand Pentecostal Bible College, has pastored at several churches in Canada. Bob Wright is the lead pastor at New Life Community Church in Brampton, Canada. Kevin and Pam Begley are founding pastors of Harvest Worship Centre in Brampton, Canada. All made time to read through a number of chapters of the book. Their observation that such a book is both timely and necessary motivated me.

My elder son, Niran, has an academic background in science and theology. This, combined with his involvement in real estate investing, ensured my presentation was both theological and down to earth. In his typically provocative manner, he helped me work through certain sections of the manuscript, especially the chapter on the salvific revolution, which needed to be articulated in a way that was amenable to a wider readership. He also steered me through several computer challenges including lost files and hard drive crashes.

His wife, Loria, who did a wonderful job copyediting and proofreading my first book, has edited this book too. Amidst her heavy work schedule, frequent World Vision travel assignments, and family duties, she spent long hours poring over every chapter and section of the book with meticulous attention to detail, and provided editorial suggestions that made this work more readable and cohesive. She went far beyond copyediting by researching long-lost sources and fact checking throughout.

My younger son, Jonathan, has an academic background in philosophy and law, which was a great help in articulating some important chapters of my work, especially where I handled philosophical and sociological issues. He helped me to make my presentation cogent and convincing.

His wife, Lilani, provided ideal conditions in her home for concentrated work. I treasure her support and encouragement of my venture.

Christina Thurairatnam, my niece and the librarian at Holmes County Public Library in Ohio, was the first person I thought of to compile the bibliography, and she has done an excellent job.

To my two eldest grandsons, a big thank you! Jaishan sketched the Egyptian Sun God Ra and Pharaoh's head, and Daniel sketched the bird hovering over stormy waters.

This venture would not have seen the light of day without my wife, Sarojini, who walked with me through this tedious journey. Her supportive and prayerful partnership enabled me to overcome many challenges and encouraged me to continue and finish the job. This journey was made lighter with the spirited support of my grandchildren: Jaishan, Daniel, Mikayla, and Micah. I dedicate this book to Sarojini and my grandchildren with the hope that both the present and upcoming generations will not lose hope in God.

1

God's Quest Amidst Paradigm Shifts

Two days before my seventeenth birthday, something significant happened in my life. I had a dream that is still vividly imprinted in my memory, even after the passing of several decades. In my dream, I saw a gray sky with dark, billowing clouds. The word "destruction" loomed large within the clouds. Behind and beyond that terrifying inscription poured out a blinding light, and from it came countless palm leaves and books. I saw a host of people from different cultures, each catching a book and a palm leaf and together joyfully raising their hands toward the light. I woke from my dream perplexed and confused. Two days later, I realized that God in his mercy had orchestrated his quest to enter my life through this dream. I believe I was one of those who caught a palm leaf and a book that fell from heaven! On that day, which happened to be my birthday, I accepted Christ as my Savior and received the baptism of the Holy Spirit. As the years went by, I began to realize the meaning and significance of the dream. I have seen through the years how that dream is materializing with the opening of countless doors to teach, preach, and pastor among people of various languages and cultures, commencing in Sri Lanka, the land of my birth, and then in Canada and abroad. I sense the dream goes far beyond the scope of my limited life. It helped me understand that God's quest supersedes everything.

Let me not build a theology based on my dream, but only note that certain facets of it seem to be in line with God's encounter with humanity:

he comes as light when the sky is dark, lavishly pours out heavenly blessings, and those who receive them thank him with exuberant praise.

A lingering question pertaining to my earlier book, *The Quest: Christ Amidst the Quest*,[1] is why Judaism and Christianity were not included in the study of the world's major religions. The reason for this is that these two religions need to be handled within a different conceptual framework.[2] Let me here attempt to present them within such a framework. At the outset, I must clarify that placing these religions in a special category does not imply that they are entirely different from all other religions, or that truth is found only in them, or that they are superior to other religions. We cannot dismiss other religions as totally false or demonic. Comparing religions may tempt us to consider some religions superior to others. When considering the doctrines, institutions, and rituals of religions, we observe certain core aspirations expressed by the people of religious communities. These aspirations generate from an underlying quest that seeks a way out of our perceived predicament: a salvific quest. This arises at the grassroots level, for underneath the superstructures of religions, there is the human factor. Regardless of whether we view ourselves as religious, prereligious, postreligious, or even nonreligious, we find ourselves gripped by a quest that seems to be an integral part of our human personhood.

My former book highlights humanity's salvific quest to be freed from the predicament of human existence as expressed in eight major religious communities. The book explores Christ's relevance to such a salvific quest and presents him as the one who could adequately satisfy it.[3]

The history of the Judeo-Christian community tells a different story. Today Judaism and Christianity figure as two separate religions, each with an identity of its own. Christianity started as a movement within Judaism; however, history shows the two began to diverge. Historians differ as to when and how it happened, and cannot agree on whether the parting was a result of several partings or of one catastrophic event.[4] History shows that even though both the religions have separated, they have not divorced. The close connection between them has been evident since very early times. Laodicea, one of the churches mentioned in Revelation, is believed to be the

---

1. Kulathungam, *Quest*.

2. Janes, "Review of *The Quest*," 72. Burton K. Janes, in reviewing *The Quest*, observes, "A chapter on Judaism would have been welcome but, as Kulathungam points out, it 'needs a different conceptual framework.' Perhaps he'll take up this task in a sequel" (72).

3. Kulathungam, *Quest*.

4. Shanks and Vermès, *Partings*.

location where early Jewish Christians lived. Recently, a stone column was discovered in Laodicea that shows the Jewish connection to Christianity.

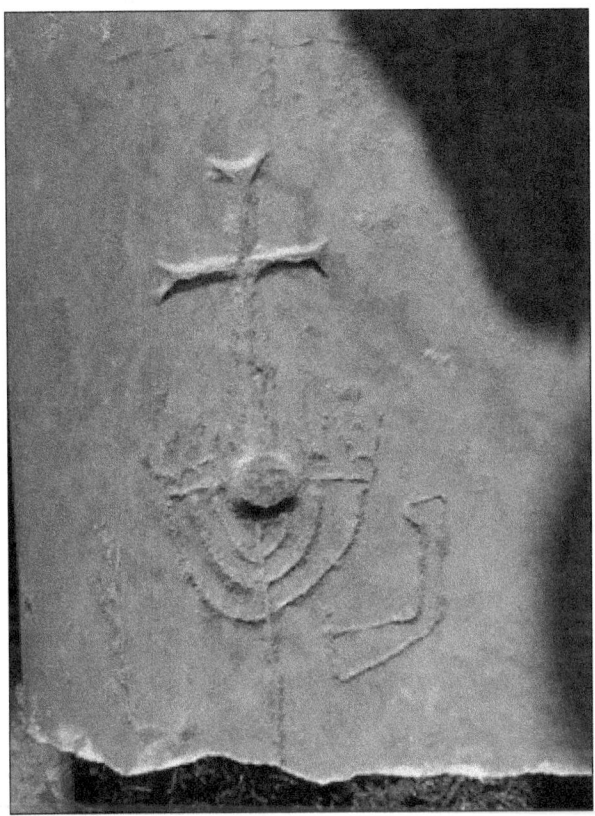

Cross and menorah inscription on stone column from Laodicea
(Photo credit: John W. Martens)

Historians are not sure about the date of the inscription or what it signifies. Archaeologist Steven Fine claims it was found in a pile of rubble from an earthquake dating to 494 CE. While he does not specify a date, he suggests that it may date from around the time of the Council of Laodicea (363–364 CE).[5] On the other hand, John Martens wonders whether the inscription could be dated to an even earlier time, portraying the emergence of Christianity from Judaism.[6] There is also controversy as to what the inscription signifies. Some see the inscription as a depiction of aggressive Christianization—the cross

---

5. Martens, "Menorah and the Cross," para. 6, in reference to Steven Fine's archaeological discovery.

6. Martens, "Menorah and the Cross," para. 8.

superimposed on the menorah. Fine does not see this carving as indicative of Judeo-Christianity or a sign of positive Jewish and Christian relationships in Laodicea, but rather of Christian domination over Judaism.[7] Scholars like John Martens suggest that the inscription may be indicative of a positive relationship between the two religions. The inscription does seem to signify a connection, whether in a positive or in a negative way, between the two religious traditions from earliest times.

Despite divergences between the two religions, can Christianity ever separate from its mother religion, Judaism? In response to such a query, James Charlesworth points out, "One can deny one's parentage, but that does not change the DNA."[8] Let me suggest that the DNA that binds these two religious communities is God's quest. This ideally illustrates his persistent pursuit to relate with humans, however desperate they may be.

In and through his study of Jewish history, the Jewish scholar Abraham Joshua Heschel concluded that all human history could be described as God in search of man,[9] and that the mysterious paradox of biblical faith is God pursuing man.[10] A recent work in Jewish scholarship that highlights God's quest is Martin Goodman's *A History of Judaism*. He points out that "[t]hroughout its history Judaism has claimed that its universal significance is encapsulated in the relationship of God to a divinely chosen group."[11] As Adam Kirsch points out, "for Goodman . . . the Jewish story has much more to do with shared ideas and beliefs. He is interested in what made Jews Jews, rather than in what made them simply human."[12] Goodman highlights God's commitment through covenants as that which binds him especially to his chosen people and lays special duties on them in return.[13] Both Heschel and Goodman indicate God's quest as characterizing the history of the Jewish community. In his meticulous research to find pieces of the puzzle of the Christian story, church historian and scholar Ronald Kydd makes an insightful comment that there is an even larger question that he has not yet addressed: What kind of puzzle is the story? He believes "the story of Christianity is the central part of God's working out His love for humanity and His will for the universe. It is God's story, but it is God's story as God

---

7. Martens, "Menorah and the Cross," para. 7.
8. Charlesworth, "Did They Ever Part?," 293.
9. Heschel, *God in Search of Man*, 136.
10. Heschel, *Man is not Alone*, 871.
11. Goodman, *History of Judaism*, xxviii.
12. Kirsch, "Why Jewish History," para. 18.
13. Goodman, *History of Judaism*.

relates to His world."[14] Daniel Fuller highlights that the unity of the Bible arises from God's redemptive quest, climaxing in his incarnation in Christ.[15] All these are indicative of Jewish and Christian scholars highlighting God's quest to relate with humans.

As humans, both Jews and Christians are also searching; however, in the Judeo-Christian narrative, God's quest stands apart as very different from that of humans. Other religious communities are also attempting to redeem themselves from the predicament in which they perceive themselves to be. On the other hand, the Judeo-Christian narrative highlights God's quest to redeem humans from their predicament. The quests of both humanity and God are salvific in intent. The human quest commences with humans and orchestrates ways and means to be freed from the predicament they perceive themselves to be in. God's quest commences with God and is orchestrated by God to free humans. Since God's quest and the human quest are different, we need a different conceptual framework to handle the story of the Jewish and Christian communities: one that highlights the character and direction of the divine quest amidst human aspirations.

If God's quest is so evident in the life of the Judeo-Christian community, does that mean that he favors one sector of society to the exclusion of others? Is he showing preference to Jews and Christians by his choice? Two questions are often asked: "Of all the nations, why did God choose the Jews?," and "Was God favoring a particular community by his choice?" God was neither choosing the Jews because they are superior to other communities, and nor was he favoring them. Heschel is careful to point out that God's choice of the Jews does not suggest preference for a people based upon discrimination among many peoples, nor on grounds of them being a superior race. For Heschel, "chosen people" means a people approached by God to initiate a relationship with him. They are chosen not on the grounds of an inherent goodness in them, but their willingness to relate to him.[16] For this type of relationship to work, those who are chosen should voluntarily respond to God's call.

A popular *Midrash* illustrates the Jewish response through a story that runs as follows:

> At first, God approaches the descendants of Yishmael and asks them if they want the Torah. "What does it contain?" they inquire. "Do not steal," God replies. "In that case," they respond, "it is not for us." The descendants of Esau similarly reject the Torah,

14. Kydd, *Finding Pieces of the Puzzle*, 8.
15. Fuller, *Unity of the Bible*, 21–22.
16. Heschel, *God in Search of Man*, 425–26.

in their case because it prohibits murder, while the descendants of Ammon and Moab, nations whose origins are rooted in an incestuous liaison between Lot and his two daughters, rebuff the Torah because it prohibits incest. The Midrash concludes with God offering the Torah to the Jews, who make no inquiries as to its content, simply declaring in unison: "We will do what it says, and we will listen to what it says."[17]

This story points out that God at first had offered his Torah to several groups of people. One by one they rejected it, finding its laws and prohibitions too burdensome, while only the Jews accepted it without question because it was God who made the offer. Whether historical or not, the story drives home a point. The fact that the Jews accepted God's call makes them "chosen." Abraham became the father of the "chosen nation" because he freely responded to God's call. God chose Abraham not because he was a Jew; in fact, he was a Mesopotamian. On the other hand, he became the patriarch of the Jews because he chose God over all Mesopotamian gods. It must have been a difficult decision. He may have realized that the Mesopotamian gods were just idols and in no way comparable to his God. Whatever made him decide, God did not force him.

In the Christian context, one may sometimes think that those who accept Jesus are predetermined by God. Since Jesus' salvation is a gift, it cannot be forced upon a person, but it has to be voluntarily received. God's foreknowledge does not entail restriction of human freedom of choice; foreordained does not imply predetermined without room for human choice.

We also need to remember that since God's quest is motivated by love, it cannot be forcefully imposed but must be voluntarily received. We find that when God relates to people, he gives them the option to respond to him in any way they like; they are given the freedom of choice. This is seen in the various ways people have responded and continue to respond to God's call. Their responses include wholehearted acceptance, hesitant acceptance, turning to other gods, ridicule, indifference, ignoring him, and even stubborn rejection. The story of God's interaction with these communities is a powerful pointer to his commitment to relate with people while giving them the option to accept, ignore, or even reject him.

God's choosing people indicates that he is willing to relate with anyone who responds to him. Even people outside the Judeo-Christian community have been sensitive to God's quest. For instance, Persian Sufi mystic Bayazef

---

17. Dunner, "Reason Why the Jews Accepted," para. 2. Midrash is a compilation of writings of rabbis during the first ten centuries CE. It contains mainly interpretations and commentaries on the Torah.

Al-Bastami (804–874 CE) made an insightful comment about his spiritual journey: "For thirty years I sought God until I recognized that God was the seeker and I the one sought."[18] History shows many who have sought God and have found him, for he is looking for those who are sincerely seeking him (Ps 105:4, 27:8; Zeph 2:3). God's call to relate with people is universal and not discriminatory. Whoever responds to that call qualifies to have a relationship with him and becomes his "chosen" in the Jewish context, and his "saved" in the Christian context. God's quest being manifested in these communities does not imply that he is favoring them, for the response to his quest ultimately depends on human choice.

The Judeo-Christian narrative is woven around God's quest. How best can we understand and appreciate the enactment of the quest in such a narrative? Despite some significant differences between the Jewish and Christian versions of the narrative, we could identify an underlying pattern that gives structure to both.

How best can we get at the character of this underlying pattern? It was Thomas Kuhn, the physicist, historian, and philosopher of science who introduced the term "paradigm shift" in his book, *The Structure of Scientific Revolutions*.[19] He proposed that scientific advancement is not evolutionary but rather punctuated with revolutions, which he termed paradigm shifts. One major scientific world view is replaced by another as in the Copernican, Newtonian, and Einsteinian revolutions. He describes the interludes between paradigm shifts as periods of "normal science."[20] These periods are not static but accommodate practices such as formulating and confirming hypotheses, structuring laws, and organizing them to construct theories. Such theorizing may generate world views, but they all fall within a paradigm and usually become questionable or even obsolete in another paradigm. A paradigm, though a kind of world view, is much wider in scope and provides the underlying presuppositions of world views that fall within it: a foundational world view. When a paradigm shift occurs, one paradigm is replaced by another and with it the world views also change. The shift is so drastic that those belonging to one paradigm find it difficult to even understand those in another paradigm.

Of course, there is no need for another book on the history of the Judeo-Christian community. Nevertheless, when we adopt Kuhn's pattern of the history of science, the revolutionary character of the Judeo-Christian history becomes more evident. We see it as one that is punctuated with

---

18. Schwartz, *Other Islam*, 44.
19. Kuhn, *Structure of Scientific Revolutions*, 962.
20. Kuhn, *Structure of Scientific Revolutions*, 6–7.

paradigm shifts with interludes between them that could be designated as periods of normal religion. During such periods, religious communities are preoccupied with doctrinal formulations and organizational structuring. Some Jewish and Christian scholars have identified the revolutionary character of the history of Judaism and Christianity. For instance, Abraham Heschel claims that "Judaism is a drama within history where certain extraordinary events occurred in which it originated."[21] The title of N. T. Wright's recent book, *The Day the Revolution Began*, highlights the paradigmatic character of what Christ accomplished on the cross.[22] When Roger Stronstad identifies certain "turning points in the history of redemption," he stresses the revolutionary character of the biblical narrative.[23] Calling these episodes "extraordinary events," "revolutions," or "turning points" shows the drastic nature of the changes that ensued from them. Since the term "revolution" has been associated with political revolutions like the French, American, and Russian Revolutions, it has acquired a sociopolitical flavor. When naming Judeo-Christian episodes "revolutions," we should be careful not take them as mere sociopolitical events, for factors beyond the human were involved in them. The above-mentioned scholars would agree that God was very much involved in the events under consideration. Characterizing them as "paradigm shifts" enables us to highlight how God's involvement so fundamentally provided the revolutionary character to Judeo-Christian history. Let us consider how these narratives tell the history of these communities and then reflect on the basis of these narratives: God's quest amidst human responses. First, let us look at the Jewish narrative

THE JEWISH NARRATIVE

Columnist and author Charles Krauthammer claims that "Israel is the very embodiment of Jewish continuity: It is the only nation on earth that inhabits the same land, bears the same name, speaks the same language, and worships the same God that it did 3,000 years ago. You dig the soil and you find pottery from Davidic times, coins from Bar Kokhba, and 2,000-year-old scrolls written in a script remarkably like the one that today advertises ice cream at the corner candy store."[24] Krauthammer notices several factors contributing to Jewish identity. It is significant that such an identity commenced with God's call coupled with human response. The Jews being called the chosen nation, speaking the same language, inhabiting the Promised

---

21. Heschel, *God in Search of Man*, 22.
22. Wright, *Day the Revolution Began*, 4.
23. Stronstad, *Pentecostal Biblical Theology*, 1.
24. Krauthammer, "At Last, Zion," 24.

Land, practicing their own religion, and sharing a common culture are all subsequent to and a result of Abraham's response to God's call.

Abraham Heschel's characterization of human history as God in search of man[25] is well reflected in the Jewish narrative, especially in several revolutionary events. Let us choose some of them that may be seen as significant paradigm shifts: the blunder in bounty, the call of Abraham, the Exodus, the messianic redemption, and the Final Revolution.

The Blunder in Bounty

Jews view what happened in the Garden of Eden as the blunder of Adam and Eve in that they disobeyed God's command, resulting in sin. In the Jewish context, sin includes crimes against God, against society, or against an individual member of society. There are three degrees of sin against God: *hattah* is breaking God's command in ignorance, *awon* is the breach of a commandment with full knowledge of it, and *pesha* or *mered* are rebellious acts against God.[26] Jews acknowledge the frailty of human nature that tends to lead people to sin and that there is no one who does not sin (1 Kgs 8:46; Eccl 7:20). However, they do not accept the doctrine of original sin, which claims that humans are sinful by nature and is inherited from the sin of the first humans. Jews believe that humans are born free from sin but tend to transgress God's laws and thereby commit sin. Since humans have free will, they can either obey God or disobey him and commit sin. Rejecting the doctrine of original sin does not mean that Jews belittle the action of the first humans in the Garden of Eden. We will investigate the seriousness of this action in chapter 2. Since this major blunder took place in bountiful conditions, it could be referred to as a blunder in bounty. Although this mistake resulted in disastrous consequences, God's relentless quest continued. This takes us to the next paradigm shift.

The Call of Abraham

The Bible (Gen 11) introduces Abram as the son of Terah, who journeyed with his family from Ur of the Chaldees (near Basra in modern Iraq) and settled in Haran (in Turkey, near the Syrian border). From here God called him (Gen 12:1–3). Throughout history, God has called a number of people, but why is the calling of Abram so paradigmatic?

God's call came with certain incredible promises. He would bless Abram, make his name great, make a great nation out of him, and all the

25. Herschel, *God in Search of Man*, 136.
26. Jacobs and Eisenstein, "Sin."

people would be blessed through him (Gen 12:1–3). With all these promises came a tall order. Abram had to leave his country, his people, and his father's household, forsake his gods, and go to a land that God would show him (Gen 12:1). We need to keep in mind the context in which such a call came. Those who came after Adam and Eve fell into more and more sin that ultimately led to the blunder at Babel (Gen 3–11), where they tried to reach God. As we shall see in chapter 3, even after God had shattered the Tower of Babel, making gods and striving to reach them was very popular, especially where Abram lived. It was a world of polytheistic idolatry and Abram was part of this culture.

Abram was old when he was called by God. There were no signs or miracles accompanying his call, no scriptures or even traditions he could draw on, no one to consult with or be coached by. He merely trusted the command of a God whose name he did not even know to go to a nameless land. Was it blind faith? No, it was a simple but strong faith. It was a faith in action that God rewarded. Seeing Abram's total obedience, God changed his name to Abraham, meaning "father of nations" (Gen 17:5) and his wife Sarai (princess) to Sarah, meaning "mother of nations and kings" (Gen 17:15–16).

Abraham's move from his homeland was not merely a change in location but a drastic change in his religion, from polytheism to monotheism. We need to note here that there were several worshippers in the land of Abraham who ardently worshipped a single idol. This, however, was worshipping a single god amidst many gods: monotheism in a henotheistic context. Moreover, idols served as the objects of worship. But Abraham's God was not chosen among these gods nor did he manifest himself as an idol. Abraham's father, Terah, was an idol worshipper, along with his family (Josh 24:2; Gen 31:9, 32–35). The Midrash provides some information about Abraham's leaning toward monotheism, even from his youth. One Midrash story on the book of Genesis tells that Terah was a manufacturer of idols and that young Abraham beheaded the idols using a hammer (Gen. Rab. 38).[27] This story appears also in the Quran (Surah 37:91–92). Although one is not sure of the historicity of this story, it highlights Abraham's distaste of idol worship. God's call of Abraham initiated the idol-devoid monotheism that has characterized the religion of the Jews through the ages.

The call commenced with a covenantal relationship between God and Abraham (Gen 12, 15:1–27), a relationship that runs through Jewish history. God relating with humans through covenants was unheard of in Abraham's

---

27. *Midrash* is a collection of interpretations of the Hebrew Bible by Rabbis. The story "Abraham and the Idol Shop" is found in *Genesis Rabbah* chapter 38 and contains a commentary on the early life of Abraham.

Mesopotamian world. There were contracts between kings, mostly based on mistrust between them, but never with the gods. Worshippers had to please these gods through offerings, fasts, and tortuous practices to receive blessings. No consistent relationship with such gods was possible. The God who called Abraham agreed to covenant with him with definitive promises. Abraham, fully trusting in God's dependability, covenanted with him. Abraham's decision to be sealed with the ritual of circumcision at the age of ninety-nine (Gen 15:11) shows his commitment.

The relationship with Abraham was not only consistent but intimate, for God called Abraham his friend (Isa 41:8; Jas 2:23). In his sermon, "The Friend of God," renowned preacher Charles Spurgeon convincingly presents the ways in which such friendship is evident in the life of Abraham. Just like friends, the Lord visited Abraham often, disclosed secrets to him, bestowed innumerable benefits, accepted his requests—such as his plea on behalf of Sodom—and favored his posterity.[28] These friends delighted in each other. Abraham rejoiced in the Lord as his shield and great reward. The Lord delighted to commune with Abraham. The Bible applauds Abraham for his faith. By faith he obeyed God and left Mesopotamia without knowing where he was going, lived with anticipation as a refugee in a strange land, and became a father in his old age (Heb 11:8–10). Such faith was not mere intellectual assent. He knew that his friend was dependable and would never harm him, even amidst hurtful situations. No doubt he would have been hurting when he took his son up the mountain on God's directions to be sacrificed, but his trust in his friend gave him that courage. God intervened and spared Isaac by providing a ram. The test of friendship was complete and God was delighted that his friend had been faithful. He reiterated his promises to Abraham of land and blessings to his descendants (Gen 22:12–18). Why was God pleased with Abraham's action? God said, "Now I know that you fear God" (Gen 22:12). One may wonder why Abraham, as God's friend, should fear him. The "fear" here does not mean being scared of an angry God, but rather an awesome respect of God and his directives, however hurtful they may sometimes appear to be. It is this fear that the psalmist calls the "beginning of wisdom" (Ps 111:10), fear that generates good understanding, following God's precepts (Prov 9:10).

The call of Abraham was paradigmatic in more than one way. It exhibited his complete obedience founded on trust in a faithful God, his move from worship of many idols to one God, and his intimate friendship, coupled with a consistent covenantal relationship, with God.

---

28. Spurgeon, "Friend of God." This sermon (No. 1962) was delivered at The Metropolitan Tabernacle, Newington, UK, on May 8, 1887.

Since the call of Abraham, Jewish history shows God's relationship with the chosen people through covenants, commandments, rules of conduct, miraculous interventions, prophetic warnings and directives, and administrative direction through kings. Such a relationship clearly shows that God did not give up on them even after the blunder in bounty (chapter 2) that ultimately led to the blunder at Babel (chapter 3). I do not need to go into this well-researched period of Jewish history, except to highlight that it ideally illustrates God's relentless quest despite human failures, deviations, rejections, and betrayals.[29]

The Exodus

The Exodus, another paradigmatic episode in the history of the Jews, deals with their move from bondage in Egypt, years of wanderings in the wilderness, and their final entry into the Promised Land, first under the leadership of Moses and then under Joshua. The books of Exodus, Leviticus, Numbers, Deuteronomy, and Joshua highlight the events that befell the Jews, and how God was very much part of their long and challenging journey. Exodus has been and continues to be a significant historical event and a crucial source of Jewish national identity. The recent book, *Exodus in the Jewish Experience: Echoes and Reverberations*, is an admirable attempt by eminent Jewish scholars to highlight how "the re-envisioning of Exodus throughout the unfolding of the Jewish experience has enabled it to function for thousands of years as the central motif for the Jewish people."[30] What is it that makes the Exodus so paradigmatic?

Just as Abraham figured as God's agent to free people from polytheistic idolatry, Moses acted as God's agent to deliver them from the bondage of Egypt. Moses grew up in the comfort of Pharaoh's palace while his people were groaning in slavery under Egypt. God heard their cry and promised to move them out of Egypt. Knowing the power of Pharaoh, this idea would have seemed impossible even to Moses, who was called to pilot the project. But God did it!

The first significant sector of the Exodus narrative deals with the Israelite people leaving Egypt and crossing the Red Sea (Exod 1–15). God orchestrated the Jews' escape by inflicting ten plagues upon Pharaoh's Egypt; the tenth plague resulted in the death of all Egyptian firstborn sons (Exod 11:5). The Israelites were instructed to mark the door posts of their homes with the blood of a slaughtered lamb. Upon seeing this, the Lord passed over the firstborn in these homes (Exod 12:23). This is where the term

---

29. Shanks, *Ancient Israel*, provides a comprehensive history of this period.
30. Barmash and Nelson, *Exodus in the Jewish Experience*, 5.

"Passover" originates. When the Israelites saw how God had accomplished an impossible task, they naturally believed in him and his servant, Moses (Exod 14:31). In their exuberance, they joined Moses in a chorus of praise and exaltation (Exod 15:1-18). This miraculous deliverance is still remembered and commemorated at one of the most important Jewish festivals, *Pesach*, or Passover, which takes place over seven days.

During Passover, Jews remember the story of their liberation from slavery. The *Seder* ceremony, which figures as part of the festival, involves eating symbolic foods, like bitter herbs that remind the Jews of their bitter experiences in Egypt. Eating unleavened bread is not to make the Passover feast tasteless, but carries a symbolic meaning since the Israelites left in such a hurry when they were freed by Pharaoh that they could not wait for their bread dough to rise, or leaven. Food historians claim that leavened bread originated in Egypt even before the pyramids were built. David Kramer points out that leavened bread was very much part of the Egyptian culture. In his view, the Israelites taking unleavened dough when leaving Egypt was a symbolic act indicating that they left not only Egypt behind, but also Egyptian culture (Exod 12:34).[31] This act was in accordance with the scriptural command concerning unleavened bread (Exod 12:15, 18:9). Commemorating this, unleavened bread is eaten at the festival and Passover is also called the Feast of Unleavened Bread. The *Seder* festival climaxes with the retelling of the story of liberation. The Bible readings include crossing the Red Sea, the Sinai episode (Exod 19—Lev 27), the crossing of the Jordan River (Josh 3:1-17), and the resurrection of the valley of dry bones symbolizing the spiritual rebirth of Israel (Ezek 37:1-14). These readings are in accordance with the biblical command: "You shall tell your child on that day, saying, 'It is because of what the Lord did for me when I came out of Egypt'" (Exod 12:26-27, 13:8). There is a point in this sort of reminder, since later, when the Jews experienced drought in the wilderness of Shur (Exod 15:22-23), their song of praise turned into a chorus of grumblings (Exod 16:2, 17:2-3). It is not only the Jews who tend to forget yesterday's blessings when overwhelmed by today's problems!

The Sinai episode follows the wilderness journey. The Ten Commandments given to Moses on Mount Sinai opened with the words, "I am the Lord your God who took you out of the land of Egypt, out of the house of bondage" (Exod 20:2). This preamble indicates that God brought the Israelites out of Egypt not merely for them to enjoy freedom in a new country.

---

31. Kraemer, "Leavened or Unleavened." See also Kraemer, *Jewish Eating and Identity*.

He wanted them to be equipped with a new ethic founded on worshipping him only.

After wandering in the desert for forty years, the Israelites finally were at the brink of entering the Promised Land when Moses died. At this critical juncture, God appointed Joshua to lead the final portion of the Exodus (Deut 31—Josh 1:1–5). He encouraged the Israelites to get ready to enter the Promised Land and even gave them details of its boundaries (Josh 1:1–4). First, they had to cross the flooded Jordan River. We should note that this happened (Josh 3:1–17) more than forty years after crossing the Red Sea. Most who had witnessed the earlier miracle would have died and even those who were still living would have lost all hope of the Promised Land, after such a long journey. But God did not forget his promise. To handle this difficult project, God endowed Joshua with divine wisdom (Deut 34:9) and guaranteed that he would be with him all the way (Josh 1–3). The miraculous parting of the flooded Jordan River reinforced God's commitment to the Israelites that their Exodus would climax with them entering the Promised Land.

Occupying the Promised Land signalled not only a break with Israel's past but also the start of Jewish identity as a nation. Since Israelite males born in the desert had not been circumcised, they were all circumcised at one time to give them Jewish identity (Josh 5:2–8). The provision of manna had stopped and so the Jews had to till the land and eat the produce of their labor (Josh 5:10–12). They were no longer pampered, manna-fed children, but began growing into mature adulthood. Their miraculous crossing affirmed God's presence and protection (Josh 3:10–13).

The Exodus from Egypt to Canaan serves as a pivotal paradigm shift in the Jewish narrative. It transformed the Jews from a nomadic community to one that took ownership of a land given by God. The Jews started to create their own identity as a community through living in a specific land, growing their own food, worshipping God in the tabernacle, following a God-given moral code of conduct, and organizing themselves through unique religious and political structures. They were asked to set up a memorial of twelve stones so they would not forget what God had done for them (Josh 4:4–7).

The Messianic Redemption

The Jewish Kabbalah scholar Gershom Scholem (1897–1981) views the messianic idea as a major force in Jewish history.[32] While Scholem dealt with messianism mainly with reference to the Jewish mysticism of Kabbalah, his

---

32. Scholem, *Messianic Idea in Judaism*; Scholem, *Major Trends in Jewish Mysticism*; also in Dan, "Scholem's View of Jewish Messianism," 117–28.

contemporaries Aaron Aescoly[33] and Rebekka Voss[34] put Jewish messianic movements into the broader historical context. Messianism anticipates a fundamental transformation of the world that will utterly change the character of human existence, one that will usher in universal peace. Jews are not all in agreement as to how such a transformation will occur. There are two main views regarding the transformation: it will be orchestrated either by a specific person or through the advent of a messianic age.

Orthodox Jews believe that the transformation will occur through the orchestration of a specific person, the Messiah. Basing their conviction on Maimonides's 12th Statement of Belief, they pray "I believe by complete faith in the coming of the Messiah, and even though he tarry in waiting, in spite of that, I will still wait expectantly for him each day that he will come."[35] Although "Messiah" is not explicitly mentioned in the Torah, traditional Judaism maintains that the idea of a Messiah has always been a part of Judaism. The Hebrew term *Meshach* means "the anointed one," and refers to the ancient practice of anointing kings with oil when they ascended the throne. Orthodox Jews cite the Talmud's reference to the coming of the Messiah. A Talmud tractate describes a person, the Son of David, who will usher in a period of peace and freedom (Sanh., 97–99). Even though no one knows when he will come, there will be war and suffering preceding his arrival (Ezek 38:16). He will bring spiritual redemption to the Jews, bring them back to Israel, and restore Jerusalem (Isa 11:11–12; Jer 23:8, 30:3; Hos 3:4–5). He will establish world government centered in Israel for both Jews and gentiles (Isa 2:2–4, 11:10, 42:1), rebuild the temple, and restore the religious court based on Jewish law (Jer 33:18, 15).[36]

On the other hand, many Jews are skeptical of a personal Messiah. Such skepticism is not surprising because Jewish history is replete with many false messiahs and many who were sincerely convinced of their role and honestly strived to fulfill their call, but miserably failed.[37] Instead of

33. Aescoly *Jewish Messianic Movements*.

34. Voss, "Messianic Thought and Movements."

35. This confession is included in the Jewish Prayer Book and is recited as a liturgical hymn: *Yigdal*.

36. Some scriptures cited for what the Messiah would accomplish: Isaiah 2, 11, 42, 59:20; Jeremiah 23, 30, 33, 48:47, 49:39; Ezekiel 38:16; Hosea 3:4–5; Micah 4; Zephaniah 3:9; Zechariah 14:9; Daniel 10:14.

37. Messiahs have figured in Jewish history in almost every century since Christ, including Simon bar Kokhba (or Bar Kosiba), hailed as Messiah after his revolt against Rome in 132 CE; in the fifth century, Moses of Crete promised to lead the Jews, like Moses, back to Palestine from Persia; Yudghan, in the eighth century, was called Al-Ra'i (the shepherd of the flock of his people); Moroccan Moses al-Dar'i (1127 CE); Shabbetai Zvi in 1666; and Menachem Mendel Schneerson (1902–1994)

anticipating a personal messiah, many Jews hope for the coming of an ideal messianic age.

Conservative Jews dream of an age when justice and compassion will be axioms of all as depicted in Isaiah 11. Affirming Isaiah's prophecy (2:3), they dream of the ingathering of all Jews in Zion, where they would be masters of their own destiny. They claim that "through the doctrine of a messianic figure, Judaism teaches us that every individual human being must live as if he or she, individually, has the responsibility to bring about the messianic age."[38]

Reform and Reconstructionist Jews generally do not accept the idea of a Messiah, but rather hope for a messianic age. Reform Jews reject the concept of an individual Messiah in favor of the idea found in the Bible of an age of peace and justice (Isa 2:1–5; Mic 4:1–5) that is achieved through human efforts.[39] Their prayer book contains prayer hoping for a *geulah* (a messianic era) rather than one hoping for a *goel* (a personal redeemer).

Hasidic Jews passionately believe in the immediacy of the Messiah's coming and in the ability of their spiritual masters to hasten his arrival. Some believe that in every generation there is a person born to be the potential Messiah, but they hesitate to name them. Rabbi Menachem Mendel Schneerson (1902–1994), popularly known as "The Rebbe," led the Chabad-Lubavitch Hasidic movement from 1950 until his death in 1994. He motivated Jews to actively participate in spiritual and social activities and thereby prepare for the coming of the Messiah.[40] After Rebbe Schneerson died, his followers believed that he was the Messiah and that he would return soon.[41] Since then, the Chabad-Lubavitch Hasidic movement has debated whether Rabbi Schneerson should be recognized as Messiah. Some agree and some disagree, but all of them believe that the coming of the Messiah can be hastened through the performance of *mitzvoth* (divine ordinances).[42]

David Levenson notes that although intense interest in messianism has not been consistent in Jewish history, it has been very much there, especially during times of suffering.[43] Hope of a Messiah or a messianic age is intertwined in the Jewish psyche. The Talmud was compiled over some 600 years. After the Roman destruction of the State of Israel following the Bar

---

38. Gordis and Commission on the Philosophy of Conservative Judaism, *Emet Ve-Emunah*, 28–32.

39. Levenson, "Messianic Movements," 628.

40. Loewenthal, "Schneerson, Menachem M."

41. Levenson, "Messianic Movements," 628.

42. Telephone, e-mail and in-person conversations with Remy Landau, Jewish scholar of the Conservative tradition.

43. Levenson, "Messianic Movements," 621–28.

Kochba revolt in 130 CE, the Jews in exile were not worried so much about messianism, but were far more worried about whether God had abandoned them. In response to this query, the authors of the Talmud gave a resounding "No" and categorically stated that miracles would continue to occur even outside of Israel wherever there were Jewish people.[44] Perhaps it is such hope that enables the Jews to overcome so many challenges. Alex Ryvchin points out that it was the hope that better days would come that compelled many Jews not to flee from Europe before they were consumed by the Holocaust.[45] It is noteworthy that just three years after the Holocaust, the reborn State of Israel titled its national anthem *HaTikvah*, or "The Hope." Such a hope is very much tied up with the Jewish anticipation of the end times. This takes us to the next paradigm shift: the Final Revolution

The Final Revolution

Like the stance on Messiah, Judaism accommodates several views on end times and the day of the Lord, or the day of judgment. Traditionalists hold that there will be such a day following the resurrection of the dead. But some believe the day of judgment happens every year at *Rosh Hashanah*, the Jewish New Year. Some believe that judgment happens when one dies, while some others hold that the last judgment applies only to the gentiles and not to the Jews.

According to the popular view, the coming of the Messiah or the messianic age would eventually usher in the day of the Lord, which is the Jewish version of the Final Revolution. The Jews anticipate the day of the Lord on the grounds of several prophecies that refer to it in different ways: day of divine judgment, punishment, and blessing.[46] The declaration of the last prophet Malachi provides definitive grounds to anticipate the final day of the Lord: "Look, I will send to you Eliyahu the prophet before the coming of the great and terrible Day of Adonai" (Lord).[47]

"The day of the Lord" is a scriptural term that refers to the final day. On that day, "The sun shall be turned into darkness, and the moon into

---

44. Babylonian Talmud Tractate Arachin, as cited in conversation with Remy Landau.

45. Ryvchin, "Not Yet." Alex Ryvchin is co-CEO of the Executive Council of Australian Jewry and a member of the Jewish Diplomatic Corps.

46. "The day of the Lord" is described in the Bible as: "That day" (Isa 17:7, 30:23, 38:5; Hos 2:18; Mic 2:4, 4:6–7, 5:10; Zech 9:16, 14:4, 6, 9), "those days" (Joel 3:1; Jer 50:4, 20), "that time" (Jer 31:1; Zeph 3:19–20), or simply "the day" (Ezek 7:10) or "the time."

47. Rubin, *Complete Jewish Study Bible* places this verse as Malachi 3:23, while NIV places it as Malachi 4:4.

blood, before the great and the terrible day of the Lord comes" (Joel 2:31). The New Testament also refers to it (Acts 2:20). This day is described both as a terribly sad as well as a happy day. It will be a sad day for God's enemies who will be punished (Joel 2:1–2; Amos 5:18–20; Zech 1:14–15), but it will be a happy day for those who were faithful to God, when they will be showered with divine blessings (Isa 4:2–6, 30:26; Hos 2:18–23; Joel 3:9–21; Amos 9:11–15; Mic 4:6–8; Zeph 2:7; Zech 14:6–9). It will be a day when the world will finally see that God is sovereign and is both just and compassionate. Ultimately, all nations will recognize Yahweh as the one and only true God (Joel 3:17). By that time, it will be too late for others (Zeph 2:12–14).

Jewish scholars like Shimon Bakon note that the prophets presented two interconnected eras: the "day of the Lord" and the "End of Days." The day of the Lord will usher in a new and idyllic era in history as proclaimed by prophets (Isa 2:2; Mic 4:1). The day of the Lord will move into the End of Days when there is universal peace under God. Despite the differences among scholars concerning the Final Revolution, they seem to agree on three points: it is the Lord's power that will move all nations toward this ideal era, the whole world will acknowledge the one and only true God as Lord, and the faithful remnant of Israel will live in peace and harmony in the land of Israel.[48] All this will occur not by human power and might but by the Lord's Spirit (Zech 4:6).

The spirituality that the day of Pentecost introduced as seen in the Jewish narrative highlights how God's quest to relate with the Jewish community is evident in the various pivotal paradigm shifts. The Christian narrative, which is similar in some ways to the Jewish narrative, is also woven around the core theme of God's relentless quest.

THE CHRISTIAN NARRATIVE

Five paradigm shifts may be observed in the Christian story: the blunder in bounty, the silent revolution, the salvific revolution, the spiritual revolution, and the anticipated Final Revolution. The narrative commences with God creating "the heavens and the earth" in the beginning (Gen 1:1) and climaxes in his creation of "a new heaven and a new earth" as presented in the book of Revelation (Rev 21:1). The narrative highlighting God's involvement with his creation stretches from the beginning until the very end.[49]

---

48. Bakon, "Day of the Lord."

49. "Heavens and the earth" (Gen 1:1) refers to everything or all things (Isa 45:18; Eccl 11:5; Jer 1:16; John 1:3; Col 1:16; Heb 1:2). These references indicate the universal scope of God's creation. God's involvement from the beginning of time to the creation of the new heaven and new Earth indicates God's involvement throughout time.

The Blunder in Bounty

As in the Jewish narrative, the first paradigm shift occurred in the Garden of Eden. Adam and Eve enjoyed fellowship with God, had dominion over the earth, and a healthy marital relationship. Due to their blunder amidst such ideal conditions, they had to forego perfection and were turned out into a world of death and destruction. The change of location led to the replacement of an ideal world where they had dominion, with a world where they became overwhelmed by the vicissitudes of nature. They lost their vocation as well their identity as God's image bearers. Such a default may be traced to the fact that they sinned. In the Christian context, sin came to be characterized as "original sin."[50] This means that the sin the first humans committed resulted in making all humans sinful by nature (Rom 5:12). Humanity continued to commit the blunder of Adam and Eve, and even worse, because they inherited a sinful nature. In the next chapter, we will study the depth and scope of this catastrophic blunder and observe that humans continued to fall into more and more sin. God did not give up on them, however. As already noted, God's call of Abraham and his continued covenantal relation with the Jewish nation shows his persistent quest. The Old Testament provides the history of God's relationship with his chosen people. The Christian narrative accommodates this historical period, but it seems to end rather abruptly with the last prophet of the Old Testament, Malachi. This takes us to a period that experienced a significant paradigm shift in the way God relates to people.

The Silent Revolution

Both the Jewish and Christian narratives go beyond the Old Testament. The Christian narrative goes beyond the Old Testament in accommodating the New Testament and refers to the 400-year gap between the two testaments as the Intertestamental Period. The Jewish narrative, though it does not accept the New Testament, refers to this period as the Second Temple Period. Did God become silent after his communication through the prophet Malachi?

As already noted, the Jewish narrative traces God's relationship with the Jewish nation as one orchestrated through covenants. God covenanted that he would not only bless his chosen but also preserve them (Isa 41:10–11, 49:14–16; Ps 89) and make them a blessing to the nations by being a light to them (Isa 42:6).[51] It would not have been in God's character to forget

---

50. Saint Augustine was one of the first to articulate the concept of original sin.
51. Netanyahu, "Full Text," paras. 50, 51. In his speech to the United Nations General Assembly on September 19, 2017, Benjamin Netanyahu quoted Isaiah: "As the

about his commitment to his chosen with the end of the Old Testament era. Moreover, for the Jewish messianic anticipation to be fulfilled, whether enacted through a personal Messiah or through the messianic age, the Jewish nation had to be preserved. From the Jewish perspective, God could not be silent during this period. He had to preserve the nation amidst many challenges.

From the Christian perspective, the Messiah had already arrived in the person of Jesus. For him to fulfill his mission as savior of all people, the world had to be prepared to receive him. This period saw God's orchestration of history beyond the Jewish world to prepare for the advent of Jesus. The Old Testament anticipates the coming of the Messiah, while the silent years show us how the world at large was prepared to receive him. It is clear that the silent years were not at all silent!

Let me suggest that this period saw a significant paradigm shift that could be aptly described as the silent revolution. It was a significant shift in God's ways of relating with people. He did not relate to them through traditional channels, as recorded in the Old Testament, such as guidance through prophets and covenants, but rather through the orchestration of history. We also notice that several of the Old Testament prophecies came to be fulfilled during this period. God's activity is exhibited not only through prophetic proclamation but also through the historical enactment of prophecy. In chapter 4, we will see the paradigmatic significance of the silent years.

The Salvific Revolution

This takes us to a paradigm shift that, from the Christian perspective, changed the destiny of humanity: the salvific revolution. It centers on Christ and what he accomplished, which revolutionized the history of redemption. Who Christ was, why he came, why he died, and how one appropriates what he provided were all revolutionary, especially in the world to which he arrived. He drastically changed the salvific paradigm in vogue at the time. The Bible presents Christ not as a mere teacher or prophet but as God's one and only Son. For the monotheistic Jews worshipping only Jehovah, Christ as God the Son was idolatry. For them, God is not only one but is transcendent and relates with the world through his presence, prophetic communications, and miraculous interventions, but never in person and not as a human. It is the central tenet of Judaism that God is not corporeal. Maimonides claims that God has no body and is not affected by physical

---

prophet Isaiah said, 'I have made you a light unto the nations, bringing salvation to the ends of the earth.'"

occurrences.[52] God incarnating jeopardizes his transcendence, while God becoming human flouts his incorporeal makeup. Moreover, God becoming entangled with the sin of humanity and dying on a cursed cross undermines the very foundations of the Jewish view of God as being holy and eternal. God cannot become sin and cannot die.

The world where Christ came was not only Jewish but also gentile, predominantly Greek. In such a context, the way of redemption was through self-effort, such as good deeds, proper moral conduct, modes of knowledge, and ritualistic practices. Proclaiming that the redemption through Christ's vicarious death is a gift to be appropriated through God's grace rather than human effort appeared to be utter foolishness. Paul noticed that in a world where Jews demanded miraculous signs and Greeks looked for wisdom, redemption through "Christ crucified" was "a stumbling block to Jews and foolishness to Gentiles" (1 Cor 1:22–24). This alternative went against the popular ways of salvation and so revolutionized the salvific paradigm of the Judeo-Gentile world. But if Jesus redeemed humanity from sin, why does the problem still linger?

The Christian narrative acknowledges that what Christ accomplished on the cross, though complete, is yet not fully realized. The narrative anticipates the Final Revolution for the realization of all that was accomplished by Christ. However, that does not mean that humanity is left helpless until that final redemption. The narrative introduces another paradigmatic shift. Just before he died, Jesus assured his disciples that after he had gone, he would send a person just like him, the Holy Spirit, to guide them into all truth and empower them (John 16:5–11; Luke 24:49). This person revolutionized the history of human spirituality. This takes us to the paradigmatic shift that occurred in the history of spirituality.

The Spiritual Revolution

The salvation that Christ provided revolutionized the lives of those who received it, but they had to live their newfound faith in a world where Christ was extremely controversial. They needed help. Divine enablement became a necessity, and this is what happened on the day of Pentecost. That eventful day saw the display of a spirituality that ran counter to the spiritualities in the Judeo-Greek world and was so revolutionary that it brought about a paradigm shift.

The point of reference of the spirituality of the day of Pentecost was the Holy Spirit, the third person of the triune God. One becomes spiritually alive with the entrance of the Spirit at salvation, for one is spiritually dead

---

52. ben Maimon, "Thirteen Principles of Jewish Faith," Principle 3.

before that (Eph 2:1; Col 2:13). Spiritual growth occurs when one fellowships with the Spirit through yielding to him. The baptism in the Spirit that occurred on the day of Pentecost exhibited a highpoint in yielding to Spirit. The spirituality of Pentecost was essentially involvement of the Holy Spirit in the lives of yielded believers. For the Jews, this was controversial. First, the Holy Spirit as the third person of the triune God tampers with the Jewish concept of God as one. Second, the Holy Spirit in residence in humans shatters the Jewish dictum that the transcendently holy God can never dwell in human vessels. There are some verses in the Old Testament suggesting the indwelling of the Spirit. For instance, "Take Joshua son of Nun, who has the Spirit in him, and lay your hands on him" (Num 27:18 NLT); "Then the Spirit of the Lord came on Jephthah. He crossed Gilead and Manasseh, passed through Mizpah of Gilead, and from there he advanced against the Ammonites" (Judg 11:29); "Then the Spirit of the Lord came on Gideon, and he blew a trumpet, summoning the Abiezrites to follow him" (Judg 6:34); "When he [Saul] and his servant arrived at Gibeah, a procession of prophets met him; the Spirit of God came powerfully upon him, and he joined in their prophesying" (1 Sam 10:10). The Jews took these verses as suggesting the presence of God's Spirit and not as an indwelling of the Holy Spirit as the third person of the triune God. They also believed that the presence of the Spirit was not for all, but only for those chosen by God.

As we shall see in chapter 8, spiritualities of the time outside the Jewish world commenced with the human spirit. Spiritual growth occurs with the enhancement of the spiritual in the human through modes such as divination, meditation, prayer, and devotional practices. Such spiritual enhancement provided spiritual fulfillment but did not accommodate relationship with the divine on a personal basis.

The spirituality that the day of Pentecost introduced ran counter to both Judaic and gentile spiritualities and so brought about a pivotal paradigm shift in the Judeo-Greek spiritual world.

The early Christians viewed baptism in the Holy Spirit as an indicator of the last days before the second coming of Jesus. Such an eschatological perspective takes us to the next paradigm shift.

The Final Revolution

The Christian depiction of the Final Revolution is very much aligned with the Jewish depiction. Accommodating the Old Testament references concerning this revolution, the Christian depiction is based on the New Testament. Peter emphasizes that what was told by the prophets as well as by Jesus through the apostles should be taken as a valid depiction of the day of the Lord (2 Pet 3:1–2). The day of the Lord is used in both the Old and New Testaments, as, for example, this verse: "The sun will be turned to darkness and the moon to blood before the coming of the great and dreadful day of the Lord" (Joel 2:31, cited in Acts 2:20). The main difference between the Jewish and Christian depiction of the Final Revolution is Christ, who figures prominently in the Christian narrative. In fact, certain New Testament passages seem to name the day of the Lord as the day of Jesus Christ (1 Cor 1:8; 2 Cor 1:14; Phil 1:6, 10; 2 Pet 3:10, 12; 2 Thess 2:2). The Christian narrative highlights that the Final Revolution will usher in not only a redeemed humanity but also a fully transformed world, when the redeemed of all nations would be citizens of the new heaven and new earth, free from death and destruction (Rev 21:1–4).[53] This would bring to fruition all that Christ accomplished through the cross: redemption of both humanity and the world. In both the Jewish and Christian depiction of the day of the Lord, it is God who has the final say. It is his relentless quest that ultimately brings about this paradigmatic shift that transforms, once and for all, his fallen and dilapidated handiwork into what he initially intended it to be; it could be described as the final paradigmatic shift. The anticipation that underlies the Judeo-Christian narrative renders in history a sense of hope and destiny that was novel in the Greco-Roman world. People of this world did not consider history to have purpose, but as a process orchestrated by human decisions and natural occurrences.

To capture the full scope and impact of God's quest, it is best to take both the Jewish and Christian narratives as facets of one metanarrative. To capture the revolutionary character of the Judeo-Christian narrative, we need to accommodate both the facets. Even though they differ in some significant ways, they are in fact complementary. The underlying theme of the narrative is God's quest enacted in and through certain significant paradigm shifts. The Judeo-Christian narrative is not a mere fictional masterpiece or even literary exposition of exuberant religiosity, but has God-inspired scriptural basis.

THE SCRIPTURAL BASIS OF THE JUDEO-CHRISTIAN NARRATIVE

The Bible provides the main scriptural source of the narrative. The Christian Bible includes both the Old and New Testaments, while the Jewish Bible, *Tanakh*, is the Old Testament organized into three main sections. The *Torah*

---

53. Lewis, *Last Battle*. This is the seventh and last book in The Chronicles of Narnia. It is an allegory that depicts the end times and the experience of death and new life in heaven.

contains the first five books of the Bible. The *Nevi'im* accommodates the prophets, ending with Malachi, and the *Ketuvim* contains poetry, theology, moral directives, apocalyptical material, and drama in Psalms, Proverbs, Job, Song of Solomon, Ruth, Lamentations, Ecclesiastes, Esther, Daniel, Ezra, Nehemiah, and Chronicles. Post-biblical rabbinic Judaism takes the *Talmud* (includes *Mishnah* and *Gemara*) as the authentic supplementary to the Tanakh. It is necessary to take both the Tanakh and Talmud to get a comprehensive picture of the Jewish narrative.

The Bible, both Jewish and Christian, is a work articulated through the perspective of authors hailing from different walks of life, and belonging to different time periods and linguistic-cultural backgrounds. Despite multiple literary genres, one senses an underlying theme in their presentations that gives a cohesive character to the narrative. They highlight God's involvement in history. In this sense, the Bible may be taken as a narrative with a historical basis, articulating the theme of God's involvement in the history especially, but not exclusively, of the Judeo-Christian community. First let us look at its narrative character.

The Bible as Narrative

The Bible contains divine commandments, doctrinal statements, moral codes, pungent proverbs, poetic expressions, prophetic exhortations, parables, sermons, letters, and expositions. All these fall within the ambit of the narrative and are in line with the underlying theme of the narrative. Narrative is a distinct genre of language and there are certain specific ways to understand and appreciate it. It is essentially a story. A story is not a mere jumble but an ordered sequence of events that is executed through the interaction of characters. It is not static but has movement and plot that orchestrates such movement. When understanding a story, one needs to adopt a diachronic approach. A synchronic approach analyzes an event, an exposition, or a condition at a specific moment in time, rather than taking into account how it came about. On the other hand, a diachronic approach considers how it came to be. A story often provides a diachronic account of how some event or condition came to be.[54] The Bible as narrative is essentially a diachronic presentation of how God relates to the Judeo-Christian community through history. Synchronic methods like semantic and syntactic modes of analysis may be used when we are trying to understand certain sections that deal with expositions of doctrine, arguments, and counter-arguments. Rabbi Yishmael proposed thirteen rules that exemplify this usage to understand and assess parts of the Torah that pertain to concepts

---

54. Taylor, *Language Animal*, 291.

and arguments.[55] The synchronic method may be used, but it should not impede our understanding the Bible as a diachronic presentation. The plot in a narrative relates events or conditions in a sequence and often resorts to causal connections. But what type of connection? The most popular theory of causal explanation was articulated by the empirical British philosopher David Hume. According to this theory, one can claim that "X" causes "Y" only if one can subsume such a connection under a covering law, where events like "Y" invariably follow events like "X." In such a context, there is no such thing as a singular causal event. Such a theory works well in empirical sciences, but in a narrative, as Charles Taylor points out, there are several "singular causal attributions."[56] Here we trace the cause of an event to the singular action or motive of a person or a singular event that cannot be subsumed under a covering law. Laws are about relationships between types of events but what we explain through a narrative is often a singular event, with unique features.[57] Narrative is not a network of impersonal conditions or states but interaction between characters, usually people. Such interactions involve intentions and motives which are personal and restricted to a specific context. In the biblical narrative, such interactions also involve God. How can we subsume God's actions like his creating the universe (Gen 1:1), or giving his one and only Son (John 3:16) under a covering law? We find several instances of singular attributions in the biblical narrative, like Peter denying Jesus (John 18:15–27).

A narrative needs to be a continuous story, but there is a noticeable gap in the narrative when we examine both the Old and New Testament: the Intertestamental Period. Though there is a time span between the Old and New Testaments, as we will see in chapter 4, there is really no gap in the narrative of God's quest. The Intertestamental Period depicts God orchestrating history beyond what the Scripture covers. However, the major part of the narrative is based on the Old and New Testaments and they both highlight God's involvement in history. The Bible is not mere fiction, but a historical narrative.

The Bible as Historical Narrative

Even a casual reading of the Bible indicates that it is not merely a set of doctrines, a book of devotions, or a moral code, but essentially a history book. It is not a mere account of events arranged in a timeline, but a chronicle. It goes beyond a chronicle in that it reveals a meticulous selection of material

55. ben Elisha, "13 Rules of Rabbi Yishmael."
56. Taylor, *Language Animal*, 292.
57. Taylor, *Language Animal*, 293.

articulating a story, or rather a compendium of stories, within a metastory. We should be careful not to categorize it as historical fiction just because of its story format. Historical fiction is the genre of literature comprising narratives that are believed to have taken place but characterized by the imaginative reconstruction of events and personages. Edward Rutherfurd's book, *New York: The Novel*, is an ideal example of historical fiction.[58] Even though his book comes out of his meticulous research on 400 years of New York's history, he places the addendum, *The Novel*, to the title, thereby highlighting the fictional character of the book. The Bible is not such a novel, for none of its authors ever admit that they are involved in creating interesting historical stories to capture the market. In fact, they claim that what they are communicating is not their literary creation, but inspired by God. It does not do justice to the biblical authors to label their work as mere historical fiction. When we read the Bible, we cannot but sense the utter conviction of the authors that what they are writing is historical. This raises a question: Is the Bible a reliable historical document?

On the grounds of the discovery of historical records from various countries, some scholars challenge the historicity of the Bible. Thomas Thompson, Professor of Old Testament at the University of Copenhagen, points out: "Today we no longer have a history of Israel. Not only have Adam and Eve and the flood story passed over to mythology, but we can no longer talk about a time of the patriarchs. There never was a 'United Monarchy' in history and it is meaningless to speak of pre-exilic prophets and their writings; the Bible is not a history of anyone's past."[59]

We cannot ignore how considerable archeological research indicates significant sections of the Bible have historical validity.[60] Despite challenges, there are reasonable grounds to accept the Bible as a historical document. As a historical work, it is more than a mere chronicle in the sense that it attempts to articulate a theme and convey a message. Columbia University historian Joseph Yerushalmi points out: "If Herodotus was the father of history, the father of meaning in history was the Jews."[61] The Judeo-Christian narrative tells us that history has meaning since it exhibits God's involvement.

---

58. Rutherfurd, *New York*.

59. Thompson, *Mythic Past*, xv. Thompson is best known for his three previous books: *The Historicity of the Patriarchal Narratives: The Quest for the Historical Abraham* (1974); *The Origin Tradition of Ancient Israel* (1987); and *Early History of the Israelite People* (1992).

60. Tabor, "Who Wrote the Dead Sea Scrolls?"; Dever, "Overview of Biblical Archaeology."

61. Yerushalmi, *Zakhor*, 7.

The Bible may best be described as a historical narrative despite the following issues.

Beyond Historical Assessment

If the Bible is taken as a historical narrative, traditional methods of historical assessment become useful. However, there is a problem. A historian can handle an event provided it occurred or at least is assumed to have occurred in time and space. History's subject matter covers persons, events, and episodes that fall within the realm of time and space. But a significant event in the biblical narrative did not occur in a specific time and so cannot be assessed for its historicity using traditional modes of assessment. The narrative commences with the definitive assertion, "In the beginning God created the heavens and the earth" (Gen 1:1). First, it is God who created. Isaiah declares in definitive terms what Genesis 1:1 states, that it is God and no one else that was involved in the creative act:

> For this is what the Lord says—
> he who created the heavens, he is God;
> he who fashioned and made the earth, he founded it;
> he did not create it to be empty,
> but formed it to be inhabited—
> he says: "I am the Lord and there is no other." (Isa 45:18)

Introducing God into the biblical narrative poses a challenge pertaining to its historicity. How could God, who is beyond space and time, be accommodated as part of history's subject matter? Moreover, how could we comprehend God's reasons, intentions, and modes of action, especially when he is taken to be transcendent and beyond human comprehension? It is such a God who created. The Hebrew term "create," in the Old Testament, is used only of divine and never of human activity.[62] What did he create? The phrase "heavens and the earth" may be taken to refer to "everything."[63] The uniqueness of God's creative act is that he created everything. If everything was the result of such an act, the implication is that there was nothing before that, not even space and time. His creation was *ex-nihilo* (out of nothing). How can we respond to the questions, "Where did God create?" and "When did God create?" "Where" and "When" assume the existence of space and

---

62. NIV Study Bible, footnote on Gen 1:1, 6NTn.

63. In the Bible, "heavens and the earth" could mean "everything," as seen in Isaiah 44:24, Ecclesiastes 11:5, Jeremiah 10:16, John 1:3, Colossians 1:16, and Hebrews 1:2.

time, but neither existed before God's creative act. Such an act assumes that space and time are not infinite but had a beginning.

Three prominent astrophysicists—Stephen Hawking, George Ellis, and Roger Penrose—investigated the theory of relativity and its implications regarding notions of time. They extended Einstein's theory of relativity to include measurements of time and space.[64] Based on their calculations, time and space had a finite beginning that fell in line with the origin of matter.[65] They concluded that this beginning point had a singularity of its own in that it did not occur in space or time. On the other hand, both space and time came as a result of it. The question is where did this singularity come from? Being true scientists, they acknowledged they did not know. All that they could conclude was that we are all within its dimension and at one time it did not exist, and neither did we!

The biblical narrative provides a response to such puzzlement. It commences with God's creative act that happened "in the beginning." It refers to an occurrence when God, who lives in the dimension of eternity, initiated a world structured within the dimension of time and space, but the occurrence itself was not part of such a dimension. What happened "in the beginning" initiated both time and space and so was part of neither.

Historical assessment is applicable to events that occur in time and space, so there is no way to assess the historicity of God's initial act, even though the legitimacy of the occurrence in the narrative cannot be denied. Such an occurrence cannot be dated. God created everything including the conditions for their existence, namely time and space, in the beginning and this made history possible. God's creative act is indispensable to the commencement of the biblical narrative even though not amenable to historical assessment. The Bible, though historical, goes beyond the scope of traditional historical assessment.

Beyond Historical Legitimacy

The legitimacy of a historical event depends on whether there is at least some evidence that it occurred. Historians resort to various sources, including archaeology, to provide evidence for the authenticity of an event. The biblical narrative relies on faith to authenticate certain sections. For instance, "By faith we understand that the universe was formed at God's command, so that what is seen was not made out of what was visible" (Heb 11:3). Both the "Who?" and "How?" of this act need to be authenticated on the grounds of faith. It is God who created the universe, but we need to accept him by

---

64. Hawking and Ellis, "Cosmic Black-Body Radiation," 25–36.
65. Hawking and Penrose, "Singularities of Gravitational Collapse," 529–48.

faith. How did he create? He commanded "what is seen" out of "what was not visible." If we take "what is seen" as what exists, then "what was not visible" would refer to what did not exist. A historian cannot authenticate what originated from what did not exist. Here we need to resort to faith that provides "evidence of things not seen" (Heb 11:1). Accommodating faith as a mode of authenticating certain sections of the Bible naturally poses a challenge to its legitimacy as a historical work.

Beyond Historical Prediction

History being a study of the past, a historical narrative is essentially a story about the past. The biblical narrative does not stop with the past but moves into the future. A significant section of the Bible is apocalyptic. The biblical narrative ends with the book of Revelation, which deals with what is going to happen in the future. Anticipated future events are very much part of the biblical narrative. They are indispensable to the development of the plot of the narrative, but on what grounds are they accommodated in the narrative? Whether history can predict is controversial among historicists. Scholars like John Stuart Mill and Oswald Spengler claim that any attempt to predict events belonging to a future period on the grounds of laws of the present period is futile. They argue that historical laws are applicable to specific periods and not transferable to other periods. On the other hand, historians like Auguste Comte and Karl Marx claim that through studying historical trends, predictions could be made, like in astronomy.[66]

Even if we concede that historical predication is possible, are the anticipations of future happenings in the biblical narrative based on this type of predication? Most biblical anticipations are orchestrated through prophecy. Prophecies in the Bible, though communicated through humans, are God-authored and are expected not to be tampered with by humans. A prophet, unlike a historian, does not predict based on historical trends but rather on divine injunction. The biblical narrative is founded on the conviction that history has a destiny that is orchestrated by God through human partnership. Prediction is possible in the biblical narrative but based on modes that go beyond historical prediction, like divine directives and prophecies.

---

66. Auguste Comte (1798–1857) claimed that just like in natural sciences, there are laws in social sciences, and on the grounds of such laws, we can predict social developments. Karl Marx's theory of historical materialism sees human society as fundamentally determined at any given time by the *material conditions*—in other words, the relationships that people have with each other in order to fulfill basic needs such as feeding, clothing, and housing themselves and their families. Based on this presupposition he claimed that we could predict future historical developments.

Although certain popular modes of traditional historical assessment and methodology may not be applicable to the Bible, it could still be categorized as a legitimate historical narrative. Provan, Long, and Longman conclude their study of historical narrative by pointing out that it "is essentially an ideological narrative about the past that involves, among other things, the selection of material and its interpretation by authors who are intent on persuading themselves or their readership of certain truths about the past."[67] The biblical authors, though belonging to different cultures and time periods and adopting a variety of modes of communication, all seem to be working under the conviction that God's quest relates to them and their readership.

The ways in which God's quest works out in the history of the Judeo-Christian community are so varied. God uses different modes of orchestration to articulate his quest while the people of the community react in different ways to his quest, impacted by their preferences and ultimately their world views. Amidst such varied human responses, God's quest shows itself as being persistently protective, redemptive, and restorative. The Judeo-Christian narrative, as we shall see, reflects God's quest amidst human responses.

WHAT LIES AHEAD?

This book will journey through the Judeo-Christian narrative, highlighting some of the pivotal paradigm shifts. The journey will start with "the blunder in bounty," when the default of Adam and Eve disrupted the relationship between humans and God. Such a catastrophic blunder initiated a slippery slope of falling further and further into sin that ultimately led to "the blunder of Babel." Chapter 3 deals with this blunder that shows the folly of humans trying to reach God through self-effort. Such folly ushers in another significant paradigm shift that figures prominently, especially in the Jewish narrative. God reaches frustrated humans in and through his call of Abram, initiating his covenantal relationship with the "chosen nation." The Jewish narrative shows God's relentless quest enacted through paradigm shifts like the call of Abram and the Exodus and various other modes to keep the chosen people on track. Did God stop his quest with Malachi, the last prophet of the Old Testament? Chapter 4, "The Silent Revolution," attempts to show that God was not silent during the silent years, but was orchestrating history to preserve the Jewish nation amidst the challenges it faced and to prepare the world at large for the advent of Christ. Chapter 5, "The Salvific Revolution," highlights Christ and his accomplishment on the cross. Chapter 6,

---

67. Provan, et al., *Biblical History of Israel*, 49.

"The Spiritual Revolution," deals with the spirituality that climaxed on the day of Pentecost. Even though many received what the salvific and spiritual revolutions offered, the newfound faith was a "stumbling block and foolishness" to many. Chapter 7 is entitled "The Cross: Stumbling Block or Folly?" and considers that what Christ accomplished on the cross was a stumbling block or a scandal to the Jews and foolishness to the Greco-Roman gentile world. Chapter 8, "Pentecost: Blasphemy or Off Track?," investigates how the spirituality that Pentecost ushered in was blasphemy to the Jews and off track in the context of the spirituality in vogue at that time in the gentile world. Nevertheless, the Judeo-Christian narrative does not end on such a negative note. Both narratives have a grand finale: the Final Revolution. Since that revolution has not yet come, not surprisingly there are a host of interpretations given as to how it will come, when will it come, and what it be like when it comes. Becoming entangled with such a medley of hyper-theological controversies would distract us from what this book is trying to highlight: God's relentless quest. No doubt the anticipated revolution is God's final quest, but it has not yet come. Nevertheless, there is the period preceding this peak point of the Judeo-Christian narrative. This period may be called "The Now." Whether we like it or not, we are caught up in The Now. What should we do in this almost never-ending period, when God seems tired of his quest or could even be dead? The concluding chapter 9, "Until Then," attempts to handle this with the conviction that "Faith is the substance of things hoped for" (Heb 11:1).

2

The Blunder in Bounty

THE FIRST PIVOTAL PARADIGM shift in both the Jewish and Christian narratives may be titled the blunder in bounty. There are some differences between the Jewish and Christian interpretation of certain facets of the story. Nevertheless, there is agreement on the core themes: God was involved in the process that brought about the world and humans. He provided ideal conditions for Adam and Eve to live an abundant life. Due to some serious default on their part, drastic consequences followed that affected not only them, but also the world in which they lived. Since God was involved, let us start with him.

GOD IN THE BEGINNING

The biblical narrative commences with: "In the beginning God . . ." (Gen 1:1). This is not surprising; if God's quest is the core theme of the narrative, it needs to start with him. In some ancient cosmologies, gods evolve as the story progresses. For instance, in the Babylonian myth, *Enuma Elish*, gods did not even exist at the beginning. The story depicts the beginning this way:

> When on high no name was given to heaven
> Nor below was the netherworld called by name . . .
> When no gods at all had been brought forth,
> None called by names, none destinies ordained.[1]

---

1. Hallo and Younger, *Context of Scripture*, 111.

The Hindu *Rgveda* creation hymn, *Nasadiya Sukta*, concludes this way:

> But, after all, who knows, and who can say
> Whence it all came, and how creation happened?
> The gods themselves are later than creation,
> So who knows truly whence it has arisen?
> Whence all creation had its origin,
> He, whether he fashioned it or whether he did not,
> He, who surveys it all from the highest heaven,
> He knows—or maybe even he does not know. [2]

The hymn states that gods did not exist in the beginning, and even if there was one who fashioned the world, he did not know how it all began.

The biblical creation story does not commence with God as a mere onlooker, speculating as to how the world began, but actively involved in creating the heavens and the earth (Gen 1:1). "The heavens and the earth" may be taken as encompassing everything,[3] so the narrative commences with God as the creator of all.

One may wonder why God's creation was empty and formless, for Genesis 1:2 describes God's Spirit hovering over a dark, empty, and formless earth. There is a literary format that serves as a preamble to a descriptive account, and this format is used in the book of Genesis (5:1 and 6:9, for example). Charles Halton sees Genesis 1:1 as a preamble to the creation account in the first chapter of Genesis.[4] Verses 1 and 2, however, could be taken as one unit referring to God's activity in the beginning. Verse 1 highlights his creative act, while verse 2 tells us how his Spirit protected what was dark and chaotic. The description contained in these two verses may be interpreted as a preamble to God's involvement as creator, protector, and ultimately redeemer of the universe from the very beginning.

God's Creative Act

Following this preamble, the story traces the stages by which God created the universe, climaxing with humans. In a world where the theory of evolution has become canonized in the literature of science, the creation story is viewed as myth.

---

2. Basham, *Wonder that was India*, 247–48.

3. The phrase "The heavens and the earth" is taken to refer to "all things," as in Isaiah 44:24, and mentioned in Ecclesiastes 11:5, Jeremiah 10:16, John 1:3, Colossians 1:16, and Hebrews 1:2.

4. Halton, *Genesis*, 27.

How did the universe come into existence? Both the creation story and the theory of evolution respond to this question in their own way. In our naturalistic-oriented world, the tendency to reduce the mental to the physical, human actions to bodily behavior, and supernatural to the natural is not surprising. The naturalistic explanatory model traces every event or condition in the world to causes usually subsumed under natural laws. The theory of evolution falls under such a model. The various states in the evolutionary process are traced to natural causes and incorporated under laws like the law of natural selection. We would then attempt to assess the creation story using the naturalistic criterion: whatever could be traced to natural causes is accommodated while whatever cannot be so explained is discarded. However, the creation story cannot be explained through natural causes; since God, who created the world, is not a natural cause. Just because the creation story does not meet the criterion of naturalistic explanation, should we discard it? Does the story provide an alternative explanatory model?

To accommodate such a possibility, making a distinction between causes and reasons seems helpful. Wittgenstein proposed that causes and reasons belong to different categories and that reasons cannot be reduced to causes.[5] Here, "reason" is viewed as an expression of intent or an act of will. On the other hand, "cause" is understood as the necessary and sufficient condition for an effect to occur. When providing a cause for something, say "X," the condition that brought about "X" is identified. When providing a reason for "X," the intent of the person(s) that brought about "X" is highlighted; conditions pertain to causes, while actions pertain to reasons. In this context, one could differentiate explanation through reasons from causal explanations. Donald Davidson acknowledges the possibility of explanation through reasons, which he calls rationalization. Nevertheless, he goes on to claim that rationalization is also a kind of causal explanation.[6] Causal explanation attempts to show the event that is explained as an instance of some lawlike regularity. For instance, we could explain the whistling of a kettle by reference to laws involving the behavior of gases. Davidson claims that the reason for an action also falls under some lawlike regularity, even though it is sometimes not even known to the agent. There is an explicit or implicit lawlike regularity under which the reason of an action could be subsumed. He concludes that rationalizations are also a type of causal explanation.[7]

Can we do justice to the creation story by adopting Davidson's strategy? It may be applicable in explaining the reasons of some human actions,

---

5. Ambrose, *Wittgenstein's Lectures*.
6. Davidson, "Actions, Reasons and Causes," 79.
7. Davidson, "Actions, Reasons and Causes," 79.

but is it applicable to God's initial act of creating the universe out of nothing? To formulate a law, we need a condition that precedes another condition; an antecedent and a consequence. When we have an antecedent—consequence occurrence on a regular basis—then there could be a law or lawlike regularity. When God created the world out of nothing, there was no antecedent. We also cannot subsume God's creative act under a lawlike regularity that tells us how God has acted in the past. This was his initial act and we do not know how he acted in the past. Therefore, Davidson's explanatory strategy to understand God's initial creative act is not applicable. We can conclude that the creation story and the theory of evolution belong to two different modes of explanation; one through reasons, and the other through causes.

On days one to six, everything that was created was the result of God's intentional act. Most of the acts of his creation commenced with the phrase, "Let there be," and some with the phrase, "And God said." This is indicative that creation was intentional. When God created Adam and Eve, he said, "Let us make mankind in our image" (Gen 1:26). Jewish and Christian theologians interpret the term "us" in this statement differently. Committed to the view that God is one and indivisible, Jewish scholars take the term "us" as an honorific description of God's majesty. In the Christian context, the use of "Let us" expresses God's intention as a triune being. The rationale for such a stance is the construction of the statement "God created" (Gen 1:1). For in it, the noun "God" in Hebrew is *Elohim*, which is plural, while the verb "created" is singular.[8] Such a construction seems to indicate a triune God who is plural yet singular. No matter how we interpret the term, "Let us," the statement "Let us create" shows that God intended to create Adam and Eve; it was an intentional act. After creating the world and humans, he commended them as being "very good" (Gen 1:31). Both God's intentional expressions and commendations indicate that creation as described in Genesis 1 was the result of God's intentional act and could best be described in terms of reasons rather than causes. The creation story provides an alternative explanation of the origin of the world; alternative to causal explanation. These two models explain the origin at two different levels, and reducing one mode to another leads to what I call the reductionist fallacy.[9]

In addition, these explanations come from different perspectives about the world. Benjamin Warfield describes these perspectives this way:

> A glass window stands before us. We raise our eyes and see the glass; we note its quality, and observe its defects; we speculate on its composition. Or we look straight through it on the great

---

8. NIV Study Bible, footnote on Gen 1:1, 6OTn
9. Kulathungam, "Scientific Understanding and Christian Faith."

prospect of land and sea and sky beyond. So there are two ways of looking at the world. We may see the world and absorb ourselves in the wonders of nature. That is the scientific way. Or we may look right through the world and see God behind it. That is the religious way.[10]

Warfield considers that both these perspectives are useful in their own way. The problem arises when we try to adopt the scientific perspective to understand a religious account. To really appreciate that God created the world, we need to look through the glass to see God behind the world. To be able to do this, as Paul points out, we need faith: "By faith we understand that the universe was formed at God's command, so that what is seen was not made out of what was visible" (Heb 11:3). The naturalistic way of looking at the world, acclaimed as scientific, concentrates on what can be seen, often using hyper-technocratic digital tools to go beyond what the naked eye can see. The perspective adopted to understand the origin of the world as God's creation requires faith in God. Such faith is not microscopic sight, for God cannot be seen. The perspective, methods, and vocabulary of the theory of evolution and the creation account are different; the modes of explanation are of different categories. We can appreciate the creation account without getting bogged down by the challenges of evolutionism. The creation story does not end with God's creative acts, but continues to the seventh day when he rested.

God's Rest

God rested on the seventh day, but not because he was so tired that he had to take a break. His rest may be viewed as an enactment of his accomplishment during the previous six days. After creating the world and bringing order to it, he did not forget about it. His rest beautifully portrays how he intended to relate with it and fellowship with Adam and Eve. His rest indicates not an impersonal rule over creation, but that which involved an intimate relationship with humans. The idea of a "sacred space" was familiar in the ancient Near East, especially in the context of temple building. At that time, the inauguration ceremony marked the transition of a building to a temple, when it becomes a sacred space, when the house becomes a home.[11] When and how does a temple become sacred space? The Middle Eastern temples became sacred when they were inaugurated through the supplications, prayers, sacrifices, and offerings of priests and people. Like

---

10. Warfield and Meeter, *Selected Shorter Writings*, 108.
11. Walton, *Lost World of Adam and Eve*, 52.

the builders of Babel, they hoped that their untiring efforts would enable deities to take residence in their temples. The temple of Jerusalem became sacred when God consecrated it and graced it with his presence. Solomon invoked God through prayer (1 Kgs 8:15–61), but the temple became sacred only when God consecrated it (1 Kgs 9:3).

The Israelites living in the Middle East would have appreciated the significance of God's rest on the seventh day. They would have felt comforted that God had not given up on his creation but continued to relate to it through his presence. God's rest showed that the world he had fashioned was not just a house but a home.

The creation story is not just about the origin of the world, but reflects God's quest through his creative act. Such an act cannot be assigned a date. All we know is it happened "in the beginning." Moreover, the period of six days does not pertain to how long it took to build the house; it pertains to the process by which the house became a home, fellowshipping with Adam and Eve.[12] During these seven days, God created the world and made it his home. After the seventh day, something catastrophic happened!

THEN THE BLUNDER

Adam and Eve were born fully made, not half evolved. They lived in ideal conditions. The world was in perfect order. The ground was fertile and provided nutritious food. The animal kingdom was cooperative with Adam, who named the animals and cared for them. He effectively performed his stewardship role of looking after the world under the guidance of the creator with whom he fellowshipped daily. Adam and Eve lacked nothing and, in short, they were living in bounty.

Then, on one of God's evening visits, they hid from him. If Adam and Eve had such a close relationship with God, why did they hide from him (Gen 3:10)? Their relationship became disrupted, which eventually caused all of creation to fall into disequilibrium. What caused such a catastrophe? Not God, but human blunder.

God did not give up. He looked for Adam and Eve and found them hiding among the trees. He expressed his concern in a one-word question to Adam. In Hebrew, that word is *ayeka*, which could be translated as "Where are you" (Gen 3:9)? In fact, it was a rhetorical question, redemptive rather than interrogative in intent. Of course God knew where he was, but the question was to make Adam realize the plight he was in. Adam's response—"I was afraid!"—was not surprising. The fear came from the feeling of guilt

---

12. Walton, *Lost World of Adam and Eve*, 51.

in facing a holy God. The first separation of Adam and Eve from God resulted in this blunder.

The Blunder's Aftermath

Though the biblical narrative does not name the blunder as sin, their actions reflected what sin does: it alienates one from God.[13] First, Eve listened to the serpent and believed what it said. Adam listened to Eve and both ate the forbidden fruit. It was not the eating of the fruit, per se, but that in eating the fruit they accepted the serpent's word (Gen 3:1) over God's word, and believed the lie that they would become like God and not die. Such a blunder caused them to hide among the trees when they heard God coming. They separated themselves from God.

Even though it was their decision that brought about their plight, there was something beyond them that influenced their decision: the serpent's articulation. The mention of sin does not occur until Genesis 4, which describes what sin does. It is in the context of Cain's bitterness towards his brother, Abel, whose sacrifice was accepted while Cain's was not. The Lord warns Cain, "Sin is crouching at your door; it desires to have you, but you must rule over it" (Gen 4:7b). The Hebrew word for "crouching" is the same as an ancient Babylonian word referring to an evil demon crouching at the door of a building to threaten the people inside.[14] The serpent sowed seeds of doubt as to whether God had indeed said not to eat the fruit (Gen 3:1), and caused Eve to doubt God's directive. She succumbed to the serpent's deception. The Lord's directive to Cain that sin "desires to have you but you must rule over it" (Gen 4:7b) assumes that Cain had the freedom to either give in to sin or overcome it. Both Adam and Eve also had the freedom to choose between God's command and the serpent's countersuggestion. Eve could have told the serpent to return later, when God was available, so that she could decide who was lying: God or the serpent. Adam could have said "No" to Eve's request. Both gave in to the serpent's deception and this was more than a mere mistake. It was a blunder that occurred in bountiful conditions. They had absolutely no excuse for such an error.

This blunder undermined the role that God had assigned to Adam and Eve. They were called to have dominion over the earth and take good care of it (Gen 1:28–30). They were not hired to do an agricultural job on contract but were offered a vocation. Their vocation was founded on their identity as humans created in God's image (Gen 1:28). As N. T. Wright points out: "The main task of this vocation is 'image-bearing,' reflecting the Creator's

---

13. Col 1:21; Isa 59:1–2; Ezek 39:23–24.
14. NIV Study Bible, footnote to Gen 4:7, 12OTn.

wise stewardship into the world and reflecting the praises of all creation back to its maker."[15]

As image bearers, the first couple were to take care of the earth in a manner that would fulfill God's purposes. This was a sacred service and they were called to be priests. Citing ancient sources like the Hittite document, John H. Walton characterizes Adam's vocation in light of the role of priests in the ancient world. We often think of priests as leading people to observe God's laws and follow the rituals of worship. That is true, but they were also called upon to keep the temple clean and sacred.[16] In caring for the earth, Adam and Eve were to perform the role of priests in caring for God's creation and not exploiting it.

Jewish writings, like the *Talmud*, stressed the great expectations God had in creating humans in his image. A *Talmud* legend tells that when God gave the *Torah* to Moses, he called not only the Jews of Moses' day, but all Jews, to live up to the high ideals of God's law. Not living up to those standards constitutes failure to be "image bearers"[17]: missing one's vocation. The disobedience of Adam and Eve also caused them to miss their vocation.

Sin also makes us miss the mark.[18] Missing the mark led Adam and Eve to entirely different destinations. They had to leave the idyllic garden and become exposed to the world outside. The world once deemed "good" by God had now become cursed, disjointed, and hostile to them (Gen 3:17–19). They had to sweat and toil for survival in a land that produced thorns and thistles. Missing the mark also changed their destination. They were destined to have eternal life, but now were destined to die (Gen 3:19).

In banishing Adam and Eve from the Garden of Eden, God appears harsh and unjust. However, it was all for their good. How could sinners fellowship with a holy God? How could sin dwell in the sacred place? God knew what would happen to them if they stayed in the garden. Knowing good and evil in a perverted way, they would also have tried to eat the fruit from the tree of life. This would have resulted in eternal death, for sin results in death (Rom 6:23; Jas 1:14–15).[19] It would have been impossible for them to have eternal life separated from God. To prevent such a catastrophe, God placed cherubim and a flaming sword to guard the way to the tree of life (Gen 3:23, 24). Although

15. Wright, *Day the Revolution Began*, 76.
16. Walton, *Lost World of Adam and Eve*, 108, 225n10.
17. Kertzer, *What is a Jew?*, 33.
18. Biddle, *Missing the Mark*, vii–viii.
19. Here "death" must be understood as eternal death, not mere physical death. In Romans 6:23, death is contrasted with the eternal life that Jesus provides. Such death is spiritual and causes separation from God. The theological view that sin leads to spiritual death was first articulated by Origen of Alexandria (184–253 CE).

God's act of taking them out of the garden appears cruel, it was to prevent them from eating the fruit from the tree and thereby living eternally in a sinful state; it was a preventive act that was redemptive in intent.

From both the Jewish and Christian perspective, Adam and Eve sinned through their blunder. From the Christian perspective, their legacy affected all future generations. In theological terms, their blunder is described as "original sin." This sin had the lasting effect of placing all humans in a sinful state and causing separation from God, the author of life. While acknowledging that Adam and Eve had committed sin, Jews reject the doctrine of "original sin." Referring to Adam and Eve's blunder, Rabbi Federow points out, "We human beings do not die because of their sin, we die because G-D made Death a part of life from the moment of creation. There may be such a thing as the "original mistake," but Jews do not believe that there is "original sin."[20]

Whether it was an "original mistake" or "original sin" that Adam and Eve committed, both Jews and Christians agree that God did not give up on them. He sought and found them. When they tried to clothe themselves with leaves, he provided them with protective attire. He prevented them from eating from the tree of life by taking them away from the garden and placing a guard.

A very enigmatic figure in the story is the serpent. It caused Eve to eat the forbidden fruit. The Bible describes the serpent as cunning and able to converse with Eve. But how and why did God punish it?

The serpent symbolism of the ancient Middle East helps us understand how the Israelites would have understood the full impact of God's punishment of the serpent, one that resulted in its metamorphosis. God cursed the serpent in three ways.

First, the serpent would crawl on its belly (Gen 3:14). Snakes have been honored and worshipped in the ancient near East and Asia. In serpent symbolism, an upright snake is in attack position and therefore dangerous, while a slithering snake is not threatening. For instance, the headdress of the Egyptian sun god, Ra, has an upright snake, symbolizing divine power and authority.

---

20. Federow, "Essay #5," para. 9.

The Egyptian sun god, Ra. Above his head is the Eye of Ra, a sun disk encircled by a cobra (Digital drawing by Jaishan Kulathungam)

The death mask of King Tutankhamun, featuring a rearing cobra or *uraeus* (Digital drawing by Jaishan Kulathungam)

The pharaohs of Egypt wore crowns featuring a rearing cobra or *uraeus*, which was the symbol of Wadjet, the Egyptian serpent goddess, and represented sovereignty, royalty, and divine authority.

The Egyptian pyramid texts contain several spells designed to aid pharaohs in this life and in the afterlife. These texts help in understanding the biblical narrative and in determining how biblical phrases and terms were understood in the Middle East. For instance, in parallel to the biblical statement, "crawl on your belly," there were certain spells to make a snake lie down and crawl away with its face on the ground.[21] These spells were meant to make the snake docile and thereby nonthreatening. When God ordered the serpent to crawl, it may be that he intended to make it docile.

Second, the serpent was cursed to eat dust for the rest of its life (Gen 3:14). In the Middle Eastern context, this would refer to the snake's desert habitat, which would in turn affect its diet. Some pyramid text spells were used to banish snakes to the desert where they would eat dust.[22]

Finally, God cursed the serpent by declaring: "I will put enmity between you and the woman, and between your offspring and hers; he will crush your head, and you will strike his heel" (Gen 3:15). Here also the pyramid texts help us to understand how a spell crushing a serpent's head

---

21. Egyptian Pyramid Texts 226, 233, 298, 386, and 288, as numbered in Faulkner, *Ancient Egyptian Pyramid Texts*, 35–36, and cited by Walton, *Lost World of Adam and Eve*, 129–30.

22. Egyptian Pyramid Texts 230 and 237 in Faulkner, *Ancient Egyptian Pyramid Texts*, 35–36, as cited by Walton, *Lost World of Adam and Eve*, 130, 232.

would have been viewed as a deadly blow.[23] Since a snake's poison is in its head, when the head is crushed it loses its venom and it cannot harm. Genesis 3:15 could be interpreted to mean that when the serpent was crushed and lost its venom, any strike it made would hurt, but would not kill.

One hermeneutical question lingers when we try to read the creation story in light of later biblical texts, especially from the New Testament. There is no mention of Satan in the story. Can we associate the serpent with Satan? Can we claim that the "offspring of the woman" is Christ and the crushing of the serpent's head and the serpent bruising the offspring's heel were enacted on the cross? To respond to this, we again need to look at how certain key terms in the creation story were understood in the biblical context.

The serpent's role in the story was to deceive and thereby disrupt the relationship that Adam and Eve had with God. The word "Satan" does not appear here, so can we view the serpent as an agent of Satan? Even though Satan may not figure as a specific person expressed through a proper name in the Old Testament, it describes what he does. He acts as an adversary, thwarting God's plans or those of his people.[24] This is very similar to the role the serpent played in the garden when he tempted Eve.

Nevertheless, the New Testament uses "Satan" as a proper noun, referring to a spiritual being with a personality of his own. He figures as an opponent and deceiver of Jesus (Mark 1:13) and a prince of the devils opposing God (Luke 11:15–19; Matt 12:24–27; Mark 3:22–23, 26). Jesus temporarily terminates Satan's reign (Luke 10:18) and his head is crushed at the cross. Finally, in the book of Revelation, Satan is described as "the ancient serpent" (Rev 12:9, 20:2). Does this refer to the serpent in Eden? When Isaiah described Leviathan, he may have referred to near-Eastern Canaanite myths that describe snakes as coiling and gliding serpents (Isa 27:1–2). We need to note the reference here is to wicked nations like Egypt and not to Satan.[25] In the book of Revelation, on the other hand, "that ancient serpent" explicitly refers to "the devil, or Satan, who leads the whole world astray" (Rev 12:9). This is exactly what the serpent in the garden did; it led the first humans away from God. The serpent's main function was to deceive and thereby disrupt the relationship that Adam and Eve had with God.

We can conclude that both the traditional Judaic and Christian interpretations agree that the serpent in the narrative refers to Satan, the adversary. Jews turn to the Old Testament (1 Chr 21:1), which shows Satan as an

---

23. Egyptian Pyramid Texts 378 and 388 in Faulkner, *Ancient Egyptian Pyramid Texts*, 35–36.

24. Dolansky, "How the Serpent Became Satan."

25. NIV Study Bible, footnote on Isa 27:1, 1046OTn.

adversary. Most Jewish kabbalistic commentators equate the serpent with the *Yetzer Hara*, the inner self-destructive tendency to do evil and move away from God.[26] Christians cite both the Old and New Testament (Isa 53:5, 10; Heb 2:14–15; Rom 16:20; Rev 12:9, 20:2) to support their stance on Satan. We could conclude that Satan commenced his work in human history in the Garden of Eden. This view has been traditionally accepted in theological circles[27] and highlighted in English literature in Milton's *Paradise Lost*. However, as Paul points out, the blame for the first blunder must be placed on Adam and Eve and not on the serpent, even though it aided and abetted in the act (Rom 5:18; 1 Cor 15:21–22).

Concerning the woman's offspring crushing the serpent's head (Gen 3:15), Jews identify the "offspring" as referring to the coming Messiah. The rabbinic commentary known as the *Midrash* points out that the offspring or "seed" is the anticipated Messiah (Gen. Rab. 23:5). As Katy Jon Went observes, twelfth-century rabbi David Kimchi, also known as RaDaK,[28] seems to refer to this passage: "As you went forth for the salvation of Your people by the hands of *Meshiha*, the Son of David, who shall wound Satan, who is the head, the king and prince of the house of the wicked."[29] Christians claim that the Messiah is Christ and he crushed the serpent's head on the cross (John 12:31), bound him for 1,000 years at his second coming (Rev 20:1–4), and eventually threw him in the lake of fire (Rev 20:7–10). Both Jews and Christians interpret "the offspring of the woman" to refer to the Messiah, who will "crush the head of the serpent" or Satan. The controversy is about the identity of the Messiah and whether the events predicted in Genesis 3:15 have already taken place or are to occur in the future.

Returning to the hermeneutical question as to whether we can interpret a Bible passage in the light of later texts, we need to note that the Bible is essentially a narrative. In any narrative, the significance of a specific statement or event that occurs in an earlier section of the narrative becomes clearer as the plot progresses. The people who read an earlier section of the narrative may not fully understand its meaning, but as the narrative progresses, its meaning becomes clearer. The serpent's role as Satan's agent and the prophetic significance of Genesis 3:15 both become clearer as the narrative progresses.

---

26. Rudman, "Chumash Themes #3."
27. Justin Martyr, Tertullian, Cyprian, Irenaeus, and Augustine.
28. French Bible commentator and grammarian Rabbi David Kimchi (1160–1235 CE), popularly known by the acronym RaDaK.
29. Went, "Difficult Sayings," para. 15, quoting Rabbi David Kimchi.

We can conclude that, from both the Jewish and Christian perspectives, the blunder of Adam and Eve signifies the first pivotal paradigm shift in human history. This shift transported them from the hallowed place of fellowship with God in the Garden of Eden to banishment to a disjointed outside world. Such a move not only affected humans, but the world of nature. Despite such a move, God did not forget or forsake them. He searched for them among the trees, clothed them, and transported them out of the garden for their protection. Nevertheless, the blunder of the first humans did not end with them.

THE SLIPPERY SLOPE AFTER THE BLUNDER

After Adam's fall, the history of humanity reveals a slippery slope into various degrees of sin, leading humans away from God. Let me introduce you to a mountain known as Adam's Peak.

Adam's Peak in Sri Lanka (Photo credit: Palitha Ekanyake)

Adam's Peak is acclaimed as the holy mountain of Sri Lanka by the Sri Lankan indigenous Veddahs, as well as Buddhists, Hindus, Christians, and Muslims. It is 7,359 feet tall with a footprint-shaped imprint in a rock formation on its summit. The Veddahs called the mountain *Samanala Kanda* (the peak of the god *Saman*). According to *Mahavamsa*, an early Sri Lankan chronicle, *Saman* is one of the guardian deities of the island. In the Buddhist tradition, it is known as *Sri Pada* (sacred or illustrious footprint). Buddhists identify the footprint as that of the enlightened Buddha who visited Sri Lanka three times. Hindus believe that the footprint is that of Lord Shiva. Some Muslims and Christians believe it marks the place where Adam stepped when he was exiled from the Garden of Eden. The pilgrims who climb this mountain consider the journey as reaching a pinnacle of spiritual experience. When one reaches the summit, one is at the feet of Lord Shiva, or with the enlightened Buddha, or with Adam.[30] Coming down the mountain is especially tricky, since it has several slippery slopes, causing many pilgrims injury and even death over the years. It typifies what happened to Adam and his descendants after the fall.

This type of slippery slope is evident in three significant events that followed Adam's blunder. They show how people drifted away from God through their actions, attitudes, and ambitions. We may refer to these events as the brother's blunder, when Cain killed Abel; the flood blunder; and the Babel blunder. Despite human failure, God was present; his quest was persistent and redemptive. Even though Eve was punished with pain in childbirth, God helped her to deliver Cain and then Abel (Gen 4:1, 2). Though Cain killed his own brother, God put a mark on Cain so that no one would kill him (Gen 4:15). Polygamy was introduced through one of Cain's descendants, Lamech (Gen 4:19–24), and the morality of the time continued to degrade to the point that God regretted creating humans (Gen 6:6). This led to the devastating flood, from which Noah and his family were spared: "God remembered Noah and all the wild animals and the livestock that were with him in the ark, and he sent a wind over the earth, and the waters receded" (Gen 8:1). The other events described in the story are also important, but not nearly as important as the message of Genesis 8:1, that God remembered Noah. This event marks the triumph of mercy over judgment. God remembered Noah, just as he would later remember Abraham (Gen 19:29) and other great figures of Israel's redemptive history—and, perhaps most importantly, the people of Israel during the yet-to-come Passover deliverance from Egypt. At that time, God remembered his covenant with Abraham, Isaac, and Jacob (Exod 2:23–25).

30. "Adam's Peak," and "Adam's Peak: Myth, Legend and Geography."

Although the flood killed people, it did not destroy humanity's sinful nature. Even after God spared Noah and his family, his descendants soon forgot what God had done and deviated from God. They even went to the extent of trying to reach God through pious religiosity. This takes us to the blunder of Babel, which will be our next chapter.

3

The Blunder of Babel

Building of the Tower of Babel (Detail of a miniature from the "Bedford Hours," illumination on parchment, c. 1410–1430)

THE TOWER OF BABEL narrative highlights another episode of fallen humanity caught in the slippery slope of sin that began with the catastrophic blunder of Adam and Eve. Their son, Cain, killed his own brother for a petty reason. Cain's descendant, Lamech, married two women and initiated polygamy. Along with later population growth came a degradation of moral conduct that caused God to grieve over his creation. This resulted in a devastating flood, from which God rescued Noah and his family. After this miraculous rescue, we would expect the survivors to live a life pleasing to God, but that was not the case. Noah's overindulgence of wine led to disgraceful conduct (Gen 9:21–24). Genesis records a genealogy of Noah, or table of nations, which concludes that after the flood all nations descended from the sons of Noah: Shem, Ham, and Japheth (Gen 10:32). The Bible goes on to trace the family history of the descendants of Shem starting from Arphazad (Gen 11:10–26) through Terah, leading up to Abraham (Gen 11:27—12:3). The Babel narrative (Gen 11:1–9) figures in the middle of this long and winding story. To capture the meaning and message of the narrative, we need to place it in its proper literary and historical context. Let us first look at its literary context.

THE BABEL NARRATIVE: ITS LITERARY CONTEXT

It should be noted that chapter and verse divisions of the Bible were not part of the original script, but were added later to render the Bible more reader friendly. The chapter-verse structure sometimes prevents us from understanding the flow of a narrative. For instance, if we pick out the Babel narrative (Gen 11:1–9) and abstract it from the context in which it appears, we would miss the point of the story. It figures in a broader narrative that really commences with the table of nations in chapter 10 and ends with God calling Abram from the post-Babel land of Mesopotamia (Gen 12:1, 2).

The broader narrative provides a detailed account of the family histories of the descendants of Noah. The narrative falls into two sections. The first section introduces us to the table of nations that arose from the descendants of Noah's sons and concludes: "These are the clans of Noah's sons according to their lines of descent, within their nations. From these the nations spread out over the earth after the flood" (Gen 10:32).

The second section of the story starts: "This is the account of Shem's family line. Two years after the flood, when Shem was 100 years old, he became the father of Arphaxad" (Gen 11:10).

The second section commences where the first ends, with the mention of the flood connecting the two genealogical accounts. The Babel narrative is placed in the middle, separating the two sections of the narrative. What is the purpose of placing such a story between these two genealogical accounts? We noted in chapter 1 that the Bible is a historical narrative rather than a chronicle, which is an account of events arranged in a timeline. A narrative goes beyond a chronicle in that it exhibits the meticulous selection and organization of material articulating a story, or rather a set of stories within a metastory. Introducing the Babel narrative seems to interrupt the chronological sequence of the broader narrative but, on the other hand, illustrates a careful organization of material intended to drive home a point. The placement of the Babel narrative in the middle of the broader narrative seems to be intentional. If we want to really understand the meaning and appreciate the message of the Babel narrative, we need to place it in its proper literary context within the broader narrative.

Is the placement of the Babel story within a broader narrative just to provide relief to the reader caught up in the monotony of ploughing through tedious genealogies? Is it simply an entertaining legend? We should concede that the story does have some historical roots. It records the historical reality of the origin of ever-increasing, multiple languages. Even though it does not indicate the time when this multiplicity of languages occurred, it identifies the location of the event: the plain of Shinar in Babylon (Gen 11:20). This allows us to consider the Babel narrative as telling a story about a historical event, and not a fictional interruption. As a piece of history, this event turns out to be controversial, and this brings us to its historical context.

THE BABEL NARRATIVE: ITS HISTORICAL CONTEXT

As an account of a significant historical event about the multiplication of languages and the separation of nations, is there a serious chronological discrepancy? Genesis 10 records the table of nations that arose from the sons of Noah; each ethnic group having its own language (Gen 10:5, 20, 31). This record of the dispersion of ethnic groups along with multiplication of languages comes before the Babel narrative (Gen 11:1–9), which tells about God multiplying languages from one language. Such an ordering of chapters 10 and 11 is intriguing, if not "dischronologized."[1] Based on such a perceived chronological discrepancy, one could question the historical validity of the Babel story and dismiss it as a mere legend. On the other hand, some biblical scholars attempt to explain away the discrepancy by claiming that the biblical text came from different sources. The documentary hypothesis provides an alternative solution to the apparent contradiction between

---

1. Strawn, "Holes in the Tower," para. 11. See also: Hamilton, *New International Commentary*; and Hiebert, "Tower of Babel," 29–58.

chapters 10 and 11, suggesting different sources for these chapters.[2] Many scholars agree that the five books of the Torah have four sources: J (Jahwist), E (Elohist), D (Deuteronomistic), and P (Priestly). These scholars regard Genesis 10:5 as coming from the Priestly (P) source while the Babel narrative (11:1–9) arises from Jahwist (J) source. Does such a strategy really solve the problem? If we take the text as it is found in the Bible, the Babel story follows chapter 10, even if they come from different sources. Suggesting these biblical passages come from different sources may tell us why there is a contradiction, but do not resolve the contradiction; it is still there. The documentary hypothesis must acknowledge that there is a contradiction for it also presupposes that chapter 10 and the Babel story belong to the same time period. If one presupposes that there is a rigid chronological sequence between Genesis 10:5 and Genesis 11:1, and take them as belonging to the same time period, one has to acknowledge a chronological discrepancy in the narrative. Can it be that the Babel narrative belongs to a different time from that of the broader narrative in which it is set? In describing the Babel narrative as a piece of proto-history or a portrait of the past, Gordon Wenham places the narrative in the distant past and belonging to a different time.[3] When we place the Babel narrative and the broader narrative in different time periods, then there is no chronological discrepancy between the narrative of the multiplicity of languages as found in chapter 10 and the Babel story that appears in chapter 11. This placement enables us to get at the vital role the Babel narrative plays in the broader narrative. The following diagram will help us to understand the literary format of the broader biblical narrative (Gen 10:1—12:3) and the placement of the Babel narrative in it.

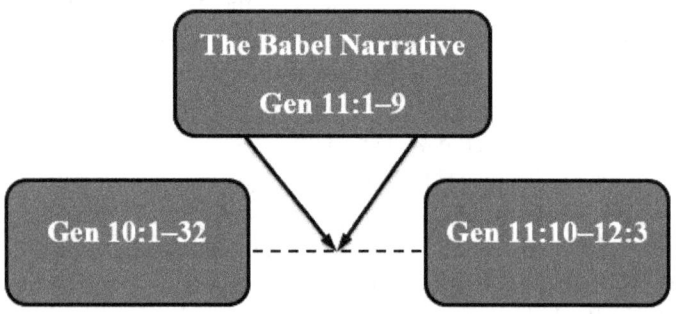

The Babel Story in the Broader Narrative

---

2. Wellhausen, *Prolegomena to the History*. The documentary hypothesis came into prominence mainly through the writings of theologian Julius Wellhausen (1844–1918) on Jewish history.

3. Wenham, "Genesis 1–11 as Proto-History," 94.

The narrative begins: "At one time all the people of the world spoke the same language and used the same words" (Gen 11:1 NLT) or "Now the whole world had one language and a common speech" (NIV). The transliteration of the beginning of the sentence in Hebrew (וַיְהִי) would be "It came to pass." Such translations of the opening sentence do not indicate that people spoke one language after there were multiple languages. If the opening sentence had started with the word "then," it would mean that the whole world spoke one language after the multiplicity of languages, which would indicate a chronological discrepancy. We also need to be careful not to take the phrase, "It came to pass," or "At one time," to mean "Once upon a time" which would lead us to think that we are being introduced to a fairy tale. The introductory statement claims that there was a time when all people spoke the same language. After making such a historical claim, the story continues to narrate how multiple languages came out of one language as people were scattered throughout the world. This story seems to be set in the past, sometime before the dispersal of the nations and the multiplication of languages that the table of nations describes in Genesis 10. We could conclude that the Babel narrative, while acknowledging the multiplicity of languages that the broader narrative describes, tells why it happened. It is trying to relay this from a time previous to that of the broader narrative. Such a placement seems to solve the problem of chronological discrepancy.

Even if there is no chronological discrepancy, the Babel narrative is still challenged on the grounds of the historicity of its core claims. First, the story commences with the claim that the world initially had one language. The question is whether the world had one language at any one time. While some claim that languages evolved sporadically in different parts of the world at different times, there are some extrabiblical sources supporting the biblical claim that people once spoke one language. There is a popular belief, supported by linguistic and historical research, that there was probably a time when humans were confined to a specific place and everyone spoke one language. Some scholars point out that Sumerians recall a golden age when the world had one language.[4] Some anthropologists suggest that all humans came from a small group of African primates because evidence indicates that at some time in Africa there was a common language that could be taken as the "mother language."[5] There is no substantive evidence as to what that language was or where it was spoken. Linguist Noam Chomsky claims language to be an integral part of human nature that enters every aspect of

---

4. Hoffmeier, "Genesis 1–11 as History," 57; Kramer, "Babel of Tongues," 154–56; Sparks, "Genesis 1–11 as Ancient Historiography," 135.

5. Atkinson, "Phonemic Diversity," 346–49; Fitch, "Unity and Diversity," 376–88.

human life, thought, and interaction: "a species property."[6] He proposes that all human languages arose from a deep invariant structure. Despite their very different "surface" grammars, they all share a deep set of syntactic rules and organizing principles.[7] For him, language at the foundational level exhibits "a generative grammar and each language is what is called in technical terms an I-language—I standing for internal, individual and intentional."[8] Chomsky claims that all languages arose from and are based on an underlying syntactical structure that was lost with the multiplication of languages.

Even if we acknowledge that the world had one language at one time, the question is whether the multiplication of languages took place in the way the Bible records it. Can we consider the Babel narrative as a valid etiology? Etiology is a narrative that explains the origin of a custom, ritual, geographical feature, name, or any other phenomenon. Though the Babel account qualifies as a narrative about the origin of languages, is it historically valid?

Kenton Sparks points out that as an etiology, the Babel narrative does not align with the history of linguistic evolution. According to him, languages developed gradually from primitive languages through a process of linguistic evolution. His opinion is that "the Babel episode, while culturally fascinating and sociologically illuminating, does not offer dependable linguistic history."[9] He dismisses the Babel narrative on two counts. First, he thinks that since, according to the Israelite etiology, humans spoke only Hebrew until God intervened to create other languages, Hebrew was the original language in the Babel narrative.[10] Just because the biblical narrative is written in Hebrew, it does not mean that the original language was Hebrew. The Bible merely states that "at one time all people of the world spoke the same language" (Gen 11:1) and does not identify it as Hebrew. Second, Sparks claims that, according to the Bible, "the languages listed in Genesis 10 (such as Egyptian) appear suddenly as through a miracle."[11] According to the Babel story, the multiplication of languages was orchestrated by God and may be seen as miraculous. That does not mean that all God's miracles need to be instantaneous. The Bible merely states that the Lord scattered the tower builders and confused them with different languages (Gen 11:8, 9), but does not indicate how long this took. The narrative could

---

6. Chomsky, *New Horizons*, 3; Chomsky, *Language and Problems of Knowledge*, 1–2.
7. Chomsky, *What Kind of Creatures?*, 4–10.
8. Chomsky, *What Kind of Creatures?*, 4.
9. Sparks, "Genesis 1–11 as Ancient Historiography," 69.
10. Sparks, "Genesis 1–11 as Ancient Historiography," 71.
11. Sparks, "Genesis 1–11 as Ancient Historiography," 71.

be historical even though the story time does not align with real time. The narrative in this context highlights a historical event of the multiplication of languages, but does not indicate the time it took for such multiplication to occur. Even if we accept Sparks's view of the evolution of languages, it does not deconstruct the historicity of the Babel narrative. We can consider it not as a mere legend or myth, but as presenting in story format a significant and perhaps ongoing trend in the history of human languages. Languages are still multiplying, gods are increasing as religions birth multiple cults, and new nations are still being formed![12] In this context, it is helpful to identify the pivotal event in the Babel narrative, which changed the linguistic and demographic map of the world.

THE PIVOTAL BABEL EVENT

The phrase "Tower of Babel" does not appear in the Bible; it is always "the city and the tower" (אֶת־הָעִיר וְאֶת־הַמִּגְדָּל) or just "the city" (הָעִיר). The derivation of the term "Babel" may be from the Akkadian word, *bab-ili*, meaning "gate of god."[13] According to the Bible, the city got its name from the Hebrew word, *balal*, which means "to confuse or babble" (Gen 11:7, 9). Both these meanings are applicable to the Babel event, which tells how people trying to build a gateway to God ended up being confused and scattered.

The event occurred as the people migrated east and settled in the plain of Shinar (Babylon); it was there they decided on an ambitious building project.

"Come, let *us* build a great city for *ourselves* with a tower that reaches into the sky. This will make *us* famous and keep *us* from being scattered all over the world" (Gen 11:4 NLT, italics added).

The builders were enthusiastic about their project, but God was not. He found something so wrong with the Babel venture (Gen 1:6, 8) that he stopped the building project and scattered the people. What was so wrong with Babel? The tower's height was not an issue for him since it was not high enough to reach him; he had to come down to see it. When and where did he come? Though the time of his coming down is not mentioned, the location is given as somewhere in Babylon. The tower builders migrated to central Mesopotamia, specifically Shinar. If the event took place after the flood (Gen 9), then the migration described in Gen 11:2 was probably

---

12. "World's Youngest Countries." Five nations have been formed since 2000: South Sudan in 2011, Kosovo in 2008, both Montenegro and Serbia in 2006, and East Timor in 2002.

13. Day, *From Creation to Babel*, 179–80.

in the Ararat (Urartu) region.[14] After settling in the plain of Shinar, they feared being scattered. Perhaps they found the antediluvian location good for agriculture or the memory of the flood made them hesitant to go further. God was not really concerned about the location, but rather about the goal and motivation. They were all motivated to make a name for themselves. Look at the number of times the personal pronouns "us" and "ourselves" are used in the declaration of intent to build Babel. Such a declaration showed human egotism was at play. The builders were motivated to become famous through their joint venture. What was such a venture? They wanted to reach God! This venture could not have succeeded, for if it did it would have been fatal. It was this folly that bothered God. In tearing down the tower, he toppled their target for their own good. It is helpful to investigate the sociohistorical world of the tower builders to understand what they really wanted to achieve through their effort.

The meaning of Babel, as derived from the Akkadian name, *bab-ili* ("gate of god"), sheds some light on Mesopotamian temple-tower building. Building temple-towers was a popular religious practice in most major cities in Mesopotamia. These were called ziggurats and were usually adjacent to temples. A ziggurat was part of a temple complex that included a courtyard, storage rooms, bathrooms, and living rooms, around which a city was built.[15] More than thirty ziggurats have been discovered. Though the main function of ziggurats was religious, they also served as places of escape and security for both priests and people. Being built high, they served as a place of escape from the floods that inundated this area almost annually. The ziggurats were constructed with levels of steps that made it difficult to reach the shrine at the top and served as a place of security for priests to perform their rituals. These ziggurats were dedicated to various gods. Mesopotamians worshipped a pantheon of gods and many of them were believed to reside in the skies. Mesopotamian gods living in the heavens included *Ahad*, the Babylonian god of storms; *An*, the Sumerian god of heaven; *Anshar*, the Babylonian god of the sky; and *Nammu*, the Sumerian goddess of the watery abyss, primeval sea, and the primordial mother. The structural format of these towers as well as the names given to them shows the purpose for which they were built: to reach the gods living in the heavens. The ziggurat structure was square at the base, having sloping, stepped sides leading upward to a small shrine at the top. The names given to these ziggurats indicate that they were meant as stairways from earth to the heavens. Some popular names of ziggurats were: "The house of the link between heaven and earth" in Larsa; "The house of

---

14. Sarna, *Genesis*, 81.
15. Oppenheim, *Ancient Mesopotamia*, 326–28.

the mountain of the universe" in Ashur; "The house of the seven guides of heaven and earth" in Borsippa; "*Esagila*: House of the raised head," a Sumerian name signifying a temple whose top is lofty; and "*Etemenanki*: The house of the foundation-platform of heaven and earth," dedicated to *Marduk*, the protector god of Babylon.[16] The names of these ziggurats and their structural patterns indicate that these temple towers were built to reach the gods who resided in the heavens. People of other religions, like Buddhists and Hindus, shared the belief that gods appeared to humans at the highest point in the land.[17] Since Mesopotamia is mostly a flat country, Mesopotamians had to build their own mountains.

How did the ziggurats serve as a way to reach the gods? They were constructed to facilitate the descent of the deities from their residence in the heavens and provided a convenient means by which deities could descend and receive the worship of the people.[18] Herodotus, one of the earliest Greek historians, noted that at the top of each ziggurat there was a shrine dedicated to one of the pantheon of gods.[19] Worshippers in each temple-tower incanted, fasted, prayed, and waited earnestly for the day when their deity would descend to their shrine on the top. Orchestrating their deity to descend to their shrine would make their temple popular and enable them to make a name for themselves. In this context, one could expect rivalry among the worshippers to become the most famous: a type of holy egotism. Does this not sound familiar?

Were the builders of the Babel tower influenced by Mesopotamian ziggurat architects, or did these architects follow the practice of the Babel builders? Scholars like Stephen Harris think that the Tower of Babel in the biblical story was likely an imitation of the famous Babylonian ziggurat, *Etemenanki*.[20] There are noteworthy similarities between this ziggurat and the Tower of Babel. As we have noted, the Babel story does not belong to the same period as the broader narrative, but to an undated earlier period.

---

16. Schøyen, "Tower of Babel Stele," paras. 3–5. In 2011, scholars discovered the oldest representation of *Etemenanki* carved on a black stone known as the Tower of Babel Stele in the private collection of Martin Schøyen. King Nebuchadnezzar II is shown standing beside the ziggurat. See also George, "Stele of Nebuchadnezzar II," 153–69.

17. One example is the Buddhist Hanging Temple on Mount Hengshan in China. Also, the Indian Himalayas have been home to intensive religious life since times immemorial. Sages, rishis, and yogis came to hidden places to meditate. Indian sacred texts and epics tell stories about miracles and revelations that happened here. The most important Himalayan *mandirs* (temples) lie along the ancient pilgrimage route of Chota Char Dham in India.

18. Walton, *Lost World of Adam and Eve*, 183.

19. Crawford, *Sumer and the Sumerians*, 73.

20. Harris, *Understanding the Bible*, 50–51.

Genesis 10 speaks of a time when different nations spoke different languages and worshipped several gods, especially in the Mesopotamian region. The building of ziggurats was part of the religious practice in this region during this period and the *Etemenanki* ziggurat belonged to this period. It is believed to have been originally built by Hammurabi (1810–1750 BCE), the sixth king of the first Babylonian dynasty. King Nebuchadnezzar is supposed to have restored it (604–562 BCE).[21] Since many ziggurats were built in the region where the Tower of Babel was initially constructed, most probably the Mesopotamian architects emulated the Babel builders, adopting their target and being motivated in a similar manner. Perhaps that is why the *Etemenanki* ziggurat was named "the Tower of Babel." We could conclude that *Etemenanki* belonged to the later period, when Mesopotamians built such temple-towers to reach their gods and make a name for themselves, emulating the practice of the Babel builders.

Nimrod (Oil on canvas painting by David Scott, 1832)

21. Horvat, "Nebuchadnezzar's Etemenanki Ziggurat," para. 3.

Both Jewish and Christian traditions feature a biblical character named Nimrod in the building of the Tower of Babel,[22] even though the Bible does not make such a claim. The Bible mentions him first in the table of nations (Gen 10), where he is identified as the son of Cush, grandson of Ham, and great-grandson of Noah. He is described as "a mighty hunter before the Lord" (Gen 10:9) and "a mighty warrior on earth" (1 Chr 1:10). The "land of Nimrod" was a synonym for Assyria or Mesopotamia, and is mentioned in Micah 5:5. The first centers of his kingdom were Babylon, Erech, Akkad, and Calneh in Shinar (Gen 10:10). Since the Babel event occurred in the Shinar region of Mesopotamia, part of Nimrod's kingdom, it may be that he had built many temple-towers (ziggurats). The question is whether he built the original Babel tower. The Jewish historian Flavius Josephus mentions the Tower of Babel and surmises that Nimrod may have been the king who had the tower built,[23] but he does not give any definitive evidence. The Jewish Talmud (Chullin 89a, Pesahim 94b, Erubim 53b) and the Midrash speak of Nimrod's involvement in the building of the tower. On the other hand, some scholars debate whether Nimrod even existed. The Bible does not state that Nimrod built the tower. Regardless of whether there was a king called Nimrod or whether he built the Babel tower, he is an ideal representative of the mindset of both the original Babel builders and the later ziggurat architects of Mesopotamia.

In the middle-Eastern world, names help us to form an idea of what kind of a person that name signifies. "Nimrod" comes from the Hebrew verb *marad*, which means "rebel." Citing certain linguists,[24] archaeologist David Livingston claims that adding an "N" before the "M" causes it to become an infinitive construct, "Nimrod," which renders its meaning as "The Rebel." This meaning causes Livingston to conclude that "Nimrod" is more a derisive term describing a people or a system that is in rebellion against God.[25]

The Bible describes Nimrod in Genesis thusly: "Since he was the greatest hunter in the world, his name became proverbial. People would say, 'This man is like Nimrod, the greatest hunter in the world'" (Gen 10:9 NLT). How can we understand the Bible's depiction of Nimrod as "mighty hunter"? He may have been good at hunting animals, but when we consider the aggressive way that he extended his kingdom, "mighty hunter" could be taken in a

---

22. Menner, "Nimrod and the Wolf," 332–84.

23. Josephus, *Antiquities of the Jews, Book I*.

24. Kautzsch, *Genesius' Hebrew Grammar*, 137b; Brown et al., *Hebrew and English Lexicon*, 597.

25. Livingston, "Who Was Nimrod?" paras. 6–7.

figurative sense to mean a "hunter of men" (a trapper of men by stratagem and force): a tyrant king.²⁶ One cannot expect a person like this to be submissive to anyone, not even God. As the meaning of his name indicates, he was the epitome of rebelliousness. If we understand the depiction of him as "mighty hunter" to be one who hunted and exploited people, then, in keeping with such a depiction, the phrase "before the Lord" cannot be taken as one who ruled his kingdom in full submission to God. Instead, the Bible seems to say that Nimrod was a tyrannical hunter of people, and ruled his kingdom in defiance of God.²⁷ Josephus's description of Nimrod as a tyrant who tried to turn people away from God tallies with this rendering of the biblical description.²⁸ His name became used to indicate the type of person who exploited people in defiance of God. In the Babel story, Nimrod epitomizes the mindset of the Babel builders as well the ziggurat architects who followed them. They had a defiant mindset and attempted to manipulate God by causing him to descend to their own shrines to make a name for themselves. This helps us appreciate why the Babel story is placed in the middle of the broader narrative, since it conveys a message.

BABEL'S MESSAGE

When God saw what the Babel builders were striving to do, he said: "Look! The people are united, and they all speak the same language. After this, nothing they set out to do will be impossible for them" (Gen 11:6 NLT). God was not threatened, but he saw the disastrous consequences that would occur when people united through one language became united to do the wrong thing, especially that which would be fatal to them. Trying to reach God or facilitate God's descent to them on their own terms was not only futile, but also fatal. They wanted to see God at the top of their temple towers. When Moses pleaded with God to show his glory, God said, "You cannot see my face, for no one may see me and live" (Exod 33:20). This is precisely why God toppled the Tower of Babel and confused the people by multiplying their languages. Since language was the bond that united these people, God had to confuse them by multiplying the languages. God's action to shatter

---

26. Keil and Delitzsch, *Commentary on the Old Testament*, 165.

27. Keil and Delitzsch, *Commentary on the Old Testament*, 166.

28. Josephus, *Antiquities of the Jews, Book I*. In this work, Josephus recounted history as found in the Hebrew Bible and mentioned the Tower of Babel. He wrote that it was Nimrod who had the tower built and that Nimrod was a tyrant who tried to turn the people away from God. Judaic interpreters as early as Philo and Yochanan ben Zakai (first century CE) interpreted "a mighty hunter *before* the Lord" (Heb.: לפני יהוה, lit. "*in the face of the Lord*") as signifying "*in opposition to* the Lord"; a similar interpretation is found in Pseudo-Philo, as well as later in Symmachus.

their project, destroy their tower, confuse them through a multiplicity of languages, and separate them to different parts of the world was a redemptive act and not the vengeful act of a threatened God. Babel exhibits the error of the tower builders in their aim to reach God and become famous. God had to shatter their plans.

After all this occurred, did the people understand the message of Babel? In post-Babel Mesopotamia, as presented in the broader narrative, people were separated into several ethnic clans and spoke different languages but continued to commit the same mistakes. The message of Babel had to be told once again to the various nations of Mesopotamia. In this sense, the Babel story becomes relevant to post-Babel Mesopotamia, which is why the Bible interjects this story in the middle of the broader narrative (Gen 10–11). The post-Babel, Nimrod-minded ziggurat builders had to be warned that they would face the same fate as the Babel builders if they followed their plan. The Babel story had a message to the nations mentioned in Genesis 10 and its message it still relevant today. The Bible highlights that those who seek God will find him (Deut 4:29; Jer 29:13; Prov 8:17; 1 Chr 28:9). In fact, God is looking for those who seek him (Ps 14:2; Isa 55:6–7; Matt 7:7–8). When we try to reach God through our own efforts to make a name for ourselves, we will end up in Babel!

The Babel message also highlights the vital role that language plays. When God placed Adam and Eve in the garden, they could converse with him in a language. The Bible does not state what that language was, but they were able to speak to God directly in that language; it bonded them to God. The language also bonded Adam and Eve as a married couple. It is of interest to note that God gave Adam the task of naming the animals (Gen 2:19–20). Adam could perform such a difficult task with absolutely no scientific knowledge. If God had created these creatures haphazardly, then naming them would not have been a problem; any name would be in order. God created them each according to their kind (Gen 1:24). Categorizing them according to their kind and naming each kind required Adam to know God's categorization of the living creatures and to also have the linguistic expertise to name them in accordance with God's taxonomy. Surely the first human was not a primitive ape to articulate such a complicated assignment! We should also note that such a language was not programmed by God to be used by Adam and Eve only as he directed. They were not robots but were given the freedom to speak to anyone, even to the serpent! In fact, the conversation between Eve and the serpent was the occasion for the first deception. The fall of Adam and Eve into sin disastrously affected every area of their personalities and lives. Language is an essential part of human nature and when it is warped by sin, language is also damaged. The language that

Adam and Eve spoke in the garden was affected by their default through sin. We could claim that after their fall, the language they spoke was not the same as the one they spoke in the garden. Though their descendants still spoke one language, they started using it for the wrong purposes. Cain used language to persuade Abel to come to a field so he could kill him. Language facilitated perverse relationships between "sons of God" (fallen angels) and "daughters of humans" (human women) during the days of Noah (Gen 6:2–5). Language reached its lowest level when it became a means to act in defiance of God; if this had been successful, it would have been fatal to humanity.

This expression of the corrosive impact of language indicates that it is much more than a skill employed by humans to communicate, but is intimately connected with human nature. The term "tongue" in the Bible, though sometimes used in a literal sense to refer to the physical organ (Mark 7:33; Jas 3:5), is often used figuratively of human language. When used this way, the Bible takes language to be vitally connected with and descriptive of the inner makeup of a person, whether it be one's emotional, cognitive, moral, relational, or spiritual facet.[29] We will have occasion to find out how language functions in such areas when we examine the role of "tongues" in the baptism of the Holy Spirit in chapter 6, "The Spiritual Revolution." Philosophers of language like Noam Chomsky and Charles Taylor are critical of the popular view that language is merely a skill that humans use to encode and communicate information. As we have noted, Noam Chomsky claims language to be an integral part of human nature—a unique species property[30] and not "a more complex instance of something to be found in the animal world."[31]

In Charles Taylor's recent book, *The Language Animal*, he proposes a theory of "linguistic holism," highlighting the crucial role language plays in shaping the very thought it purports to express; language does not merely communicate but constitutes meaning and fundamentally shapes human experience. In illuminating the full capacity of the "language animal," he sheds light on the very question of what it is be a human being.[32]

Babel shows how language and human nature are closely connected. God recognized how sinful humans, united through a universal language, could err so blatantly. He saw their vain attempt to reach the impossible, strengthened by unity that was facilitated through a universal language. In

---

29. Kulathungam, "Why Tongues?" 24–25.
30. Chomsky, *New Horizons*, 3.
31. Chomsky, *Language and Mind*, 60.
32. Taylor, *Language Animal*.

fact, God's dispersing the people through multiplying languages prevented this catastrophic blunder.

The multiplication of languages not only degraded language's communicative quality but also diminished its effectiveness as a unifying agent. The Bible states that "the Lord confused the language of the whole world" and scattered the people (Gen 11:9). A multiplicity of languages entails confusion in communication and disrupts human relationships. How many confusing misinterpretations occur when translating from one language to another or even among people speaking the same language? How many feuds and religious controversies occur due to misunderstandings? Noam Chomsky's depiction of the character and history of language is relevant to the biblical perspective on language. He believes that all languages originated from a single language that subsequently led to the multiplication of languages. Such a multiplication carried with it a degrading of the character of language, rendering it more divisive than unifying and therefore deprived of its communicative efficacy. He finds that: "If we could investigate in sufficient detail, we find that no two individuals share exactly the same language in this sense, even identical twins who grow up in the same social environment. Two individuals can communicate to the extent that their languages are sufficiently similar."[33] Chomsky's depiction of what happened to language as a result of being multiplied metaphorically describes the aftermath of the Babel event.

Following Chomsky's diagnosis of the problem, there has been a concerted effort among linguists to search for a generative grammar or a syntactical structure that underlies all languages. With the hope that a common language would unify humanity, the search for the "unknown tongue" features in the world of linguistics. Since language is integrally connected with human nature, a fundamental change in human nature is required to unify humanity, which goes further than articulating in a common language. What happened on the day of Pentecost is precisely that: a fundamental change in human nature enhanced the quality and function of language. Those who were filled with the Holy Spirit did not speak in one language, but in many. Despite the diversity of languages, a unity among the people who spoke them was evident; they were united in exalting God and in their witness of Jesus as the risen Lord and Savior. As we shall see later in the chapter on spiritual revolution, Pentecost was God's remedial response to Babel's blunder; what was lost at Babel was in a way regained at Pentecost.

Speaking the same language unified the Babel builders, but how did they execute their building project? The construction was enabled by the

---

33. Chomsky, *Language and Problems of Knowledge*, 36.

science and technology of their time. In our technocratic world today, where skyscrapers clutter our architectural landscape and humans are planning to reach the planets beyond the moon, the Babel tower project appears to be mere child's play. During Babel times, building such a tower-city was an impressive architectural achievement, and would have been praiseworthy. The problem was the purpose for which the tower was built. As we have noted, the tower was designed with a shrine at the top to facilitate the gods to descend and bless the devotees. In other words, the builders were trying to use their scientific knowledge and technological expertise to manipulate God and to make him act in and through artifacts of human engineering. The Tower of Babel was the first of this kind, followed by the ziggurats of Mesopotamia. The Bible interjects the Babel story to remind and warn the Mesopotamian ziggurat builders that they were making the same mistake that the Babel builders had made. The Babel message points out the blunder of this brand of hyper-religious human egotism that aims to reach the divine with the aid of science and technology. The Bible calls atheism foolish (Ps 41:1, 53:1), but trying to manipulate God through human ingenuity is more deviant and detrimental than atheism. Perhaps that is why God had to intervene and topple the tower. Babel's message has not become out of date. It is especially relevant today. In a world where people worship science and are so technology driven, God becomes accommodated in the shrines of science and channelled through our ever-present devices. Science-biased theological stances mold concepts of God, his miraculous actions, and his teachings. Principles of moral conduct and ethical norms are assessed through so-called scientific criteria offered by disciplines like evolutionary biology, behavioral psychology, pragmatic ethics, and naturalistic physics. God has endowed humans with science and technology, but he is too awesome to be domesticated by any human artifact, whether it is a shrine at the top of a temple tower or the edifices of contemporary science. God and his ways go beyond human orchestration.

GOD'S RESPONSE TO BABEL

This becomes evident when God reverses Babel's strategy by reaching down to humanity in his own way and not through strategies engineered by humans. After multiplying the languages and scattering the nations (Gen 11:9), God went on to articulate an alternative to the Babel endeavor by calling Abram out of Mesopotamia. These events are covered in the second section of the broader narrative (Gen 11:10—12:1). This section continues the genealogy of Noah's descendants, starting from Shem and leading up to God's call of Abram. It is God's call of Abram that provides the finale to the broader narrative. First, the call was God-initiated; God came down to where Abram was. The Babel and ziggurat builders tried to reach their gods, while God on his own accord came to Abram. The directions between Babel's way and God's way are entirely opposite: not from the human to the divine but from the divine to the human. Second, where was God's call to Abram given? A casual reading of Genesis 12 may give us the impression that the call came in Haran, since Abram's father had moved there (Gen 11:31). Stephen, standing before his skeptical Jewish brethren while tracing the history of the chosen people, pointed out that: "The God of glory appeared to our father Abraham while he was still in Mesopotamia, before he lived in Haran. 'Leave your country and your people,' God said, 'and go to the land I will show you'" (Acts 7:2–5). Both Haran and Ur were in Mesopotamia, which was reputed to be the land of many gods. Sin, the moon god, was the main deity of these cities. God did not descend at a ziggurat built for a Mesopotamian god but came to Abram where he was. Such an act of God would have shocked the Mesopotamians, who believed that their gods would only descend to the shrines at the top of their ziggurats. God called Abram not only out of polytheistic Mesopotamia, but also out of his own household. Haran was well known for moon worship and Abram's father, Terah, and his family were ardent devotees of the moon god. Perhaps that is the reason they settled in Haran (Gen 11:29, 31).[34] In Joshua's farewell speech before his death, he stated that Terah worshipped other gods (Josh 24:2). Terah was an idolater like those of his days. It was no wonder that God commanded Abram to leave his father's house (Gen 12:1). God had to pull Abram out this polytheistic world and household. God promised Abram that he would make his name great if he trusted God and obeyed him (Gen 12:1, 2). Those who built Babel, as well as the Mesopotamian ziggurat builders, tried to make a name for themselves through their temple-tower projects, but God himself gave Abram a new name: Abraham. God promised that he would be the father of many nations, that he would be fruitful, and that his descendants would be kings (Gen 17:3–8).[35] God also assured Abraham that he would be a blessing, not only to his family and his nation, but also to people all over the world (Gen 12:2–3). The universal scope of such a blessing stands in complete contrast with what the Babel and ziggurat builders looked forward to: a parochial sense of security centered on their temple-towers. In a way, the Babel story highlights the difference between Babel's venture and God's response through his calling of Abram

34. Holy Bible, New Living Translation, Second Edition, footnote on Gen 11:29, 450Tn.

35. It is God who made David's name great (2 Sam 7:9), as well as Solomon's (1 Kgs 1:47).

(Gen 12:1). Abram's call may be the highpoint of the broader narrative, highlighting God's relentless quest amidst Babel's blunder of trying to reach God. We can conclude that the Bible does not commit a chronological discrepancy in placing the Babel story after Genesis 10. The Bible's interjection of the Babel story in the middle of the broader narrative enables us to understand the message of Babel. God's call of Abram following Babel's blunder falls in line with a divine-human relationship pattern we have already noted; whenever humans fail, God does not give up but responds in a redemptive manner. To capture the core of Babel's message, we must view the Babel narrative in the light of God's redemptive response. His relentless quest amidst human failure does not end with God's call of Abram. God's continuous relationship with humanity in and through the Jewish nation as recorded in the Old Testament bears testimony to his persistent redemptive quest. His quest reaches its pinnacle when God himself in Christ incarnates to save humanity. We will have occasion to deal with this later in chapter 5, "The Salvific Revolution."

4

The Silent Revolution

THE PREVIOUS CHAPTER HIGHLIGHTED God calling Abraham during the blunder at Babel, illustrating God's redemptive quest amidst human failure. Even after Babel, he continued to relate with humanity, especially through the Jewish nation, called to be the "Light to the Nations" (Isa 49:6). Despite the recurrent failure of the Jews, God pursued them by providing them with moral directives such as commandments, miraculous interventions, prophetic guidance, and covenants. The Old Testament tells the story of such a relationship, but, as N. T. Wright observes, the story seems to stop abruptly:

> But this story is strangely inconclusive. It seems to be pointing toward, but not finding, an appropriate ending. The Hebrew Bible is arranged so that the books of the Chronicles come last. In the traditions that shaped most modern translations, including the English Bibles, Chronicles comes after Kings, and the collection ends with the prophets, the last of which is Malachi. But whether it's Chronicles or Malachi, a quick read through leaves us straining forward, wondering what's going to happen next."[1]

The anticipation increases since, after such an abrupt ending, there is a long gap. Christians who accommodate both the Old and New Testaments call this gap the Intertestamental Period. Jews, who do not acknowledge the New Testament, identify these years as the Second Temple Period. This period has been popularly described as the silent years, suggesting that God was silent during these years; was he actually silent?

1. Wright, *Day the Revolution Began*, 90.

The underlying theme of the biblical narrative is God's relentless quest that commenced with creation. When the first humans sinned by disobeying God, and when their descendants became entangled with murder, polygamy, and despicable moral conduct, he did not give up on them. Amidst their blunder at Babel, God chose Abraham. When they deviated from him, he rebuked them but did not forsake them. If this God, who persistently related with his people, suddenly became silent after Malachi, the last prophet of the Old Testament, then it would jeopardize the theme of the narrative and demean the very character of God. Although he may not have related with people during these years through the modes he had used in the past, does that mean that he stopped relating with them altogether, especially with his chosen ones with whom he had a covenantal commitment? This period may not be part of Scripture, but is very much part of the Judeo-Christian narrative.

This period shows how God used modes of relating with humanity that went beyond the traditional. One example was his orchestration of history to accomplish his plans. The grounds for such orchestration are founded on his lordship over history. He initiated creation but did not stop with that. He is Lord over the whole historical process: past, present, and future.

The prophet Isaiah's depiction of a dramatic scene highlights the lordship of God over history. Here, Jehovah calls the gods of the nations to a debate while the people of the world listen. Isaiah describes it this way:

> "Present your case," says the Lord. "Set forth your arguments," says Jacob's King. "Tell us, you idols, what is going to happen. Tell us what the former things were, so that we may consider them and know their final outcome. Or declare to us the things to come, tell us what the future holds, so we may know that you are gods. Do something, whether good or bad, so that we will be dismayed and filled with fear. But you are less than nothing and your works are utterly worthless; whoever chooses you is detestable. I have stirred up one from the north, and he comes—one from the rising sun who calls on my name. He treads on rulers as if they were mortar, as if he were a potter treading the clay. Who told of this from the beginning, so we could know, or beforehand, so we could say, 'He was right'? No one told of this, no one foretold it; no one heard any words from you. I was the first to tell Zion, 'Look, here they are!' I gave to Jerusalem a messenger of good news. I look but there is no one—no one among the gods to give counsel, no one to give answer when I ask them. See, they are all false! Their deeds amount to nothing; their images are but wind and confusion." (Isa 41:21–29)

The point at issue is over which god is the true God and the decision will be based on which god is the Lord of history. Jehovah stands out, since it is he who had raised up Cyrus, the destroyer of world powers and the liberator of the remnants of the Jewish nation. The gods of that nation did not expect such a development. They did not even know about it and were dumbfounded. The dispute ends with the verdict that, unlike these gods, Jehovah alone is the Lord of history, for he has shown that he knows the past and the future and thus he makes history.[2]

Jehovah is the Lord of all history, whether revealed through biblical or extrabiblical, Judaic or gentile, religious or secular avenues. He reveals his plans through history as presented in Scripture, but also through various avenues enacted in history. Eusebius, an early church historian (260–340 CE), identified an intelligible pattern in historical trends that he attributed to God. In his view, history with all its haphazardness moves toward a God-chosen goal.[3] In recent times, Ephraim Radner highlights how Scripture is related to history. In his book, *Chasing the Shadow*, which is a follow-up from his earlier book, *The World in the Shadow of God*, he notices that Scripture orders history rather than being ordered by it, and that ultimately God is in charge.[4] Through poetic description, Radner shows how history proceeds according to the biblical pattern.[5]

The silent years depict God as Lord of history, orchestrating the history of the Jewish nation as well as the world surrounding it. This orchestration prepared the way for some significant future events. From the Christian perspective, this period was preparatory for the advent of Jesus Christ, as the Messiah. Though not acknowledging Jesus as Messiah, Jews take this period as God preserving the Jewish nation through formidable challenges, preparing the world for the coming of the Messiah or the messianic age. The silent years are an integral part of both the Jewish and Christian narratives, highlighting God's involvement in history. When one accommodates both the Testaments, there is clearly a scriptural gap, but there is really no gap in the narrative. God was involved in orchestrating history outside the parameters of Scripture. In fact, God's way of relating with people using nontraditional methods ushers in another significant paradigm shift, which provides the rationale for us to call this period the silent revolution. Let us see how such a revolution figures in each narrative.

2. Tillich, "God of History."

3. Eusebius, *Ecclesiastical History*. This is the first surviving history of the Christian church as a chronologically ordered account, based on earlier sources, covering the period from the apostles to his own time (fourth century CE).

4. Radner, *World in the Shadow of God*.

5. Radner, *World in the Shadow of God*.

THE JEWISH NARRATIVE

The prophet Malachi's message (Mal 1-4) provides a preamble to the Jewish story. He communicated God's concerns for the Jews when they were returning to Judea from their seventy years of Babylonian captivity. They began restoring Jerusalem and rebuilding the temple. After its completion, they returned to the practice of worshipping in the temple. They started well but over time their worship turned into empty ritualism. They began to doubt God's love (Mal 1:1, 2), became discouraged that the glorious future proclaimed by their prophets had not been fulfilled, and began to lose hope (Mal 2:17, 3:14-15).

It was during this low point in Jewish history that Malachi appeared. Though his message was mainly to the Jews, "the sons of Jacob" (Mal 3:3), he goes on to address a wider audience when he introduces the "day of the Lord" (Mal 4). His message to the Jews reveals the situation at that time. There was a failure in Jewish leadership. The priests, mandated to keep the Jews on track, did not follow God's directives and instead caused many to stumble (Mal 2:8-9). The covenant of life and peace (Num 25:10-13) with the Levitical priesthood during Moses' time would have brought great blessings had the priests remained faithful. Instead, they lost their place of leadership and became despised and humiliated (Mal 2:9). Led by such depraved priests, laity lived as they wished; tithing dwindled and divorces increased (Mal 2:10-16). This moral and spiritual laxity in Jewish society resulted in poverty, famine, drought, and oppression (Mal 1:6-10, 12-14, 2:1-9). However, God did not give up on them. He called them to repent and return to him (Mal 1:9). Although they had become unfaithful and had forgotten God's covenant with their forefathers (Mal 2:10-11), he appealed to them, "Return to me, and I will return to you" (Mal 3:7). It is in God's character that, even though people deviate, he does not give up; his quest is relentless.

Malachi ended his message by warning the Jews about the day of the Lord and did not mince words in describing how terrible that day would be. He pointed out that the day would not only affect the Jews, but all people, and all should be prepared for it (Mal 4:1). He warned that a day of judgment was coming and God would punish anyone who transgressed his law. The distinction was not between Jew and gentile, but rather between the righteous and the wicked, between those who served the Lord and those who did not (Mal 3:14-18, 4:1-3). Amidst such a warning, there was a promise. When referring to that fearful day of the Lord, Malachi proclaimed that God would send two messengers: "my messenger" and the "messenger of the covenant." "My messenger" would prepare the way for the "messenger of the covenant" (Mal 3:1). Malachi proclaimed that amidst the calamities of the day of the Lord, there was an assurance for those who revered God's name: "The sun of righteousness will rise with healing in its rays" (Mal 4:2) and would send Elijah to prepare people to be reconciled both with God and one another (Mal 4:5). Jews and Christians do not agree about the identity of these messengers. Christians identify "my messenger" as John the Baptist, who exhibited the spirit of Elijah in calling people to repentance, and preparing the way for Christ, the "messenger of the covenant." The Jews claim that the Messiah has not yet come since Elijah has not yet appeared. Despite this controversy, Malachi's warning was relevant to both Jews and gentiles.

Knowing his chosen people well, God gave them certain definitive reminders through Malachi, especially since they were leaping from the frying pan into the fire! Malachi made it clear that God was just and hated sin and so, if they deviated, they would have to face the consequences. Nevertheless, he would not break his covenant with them. He reminded them that they could get back on track if they repented and returned to him (Mal 3:7). They would be able to face the day of judgment with confidence provided they did not ignore his two messengers.

The Jews experienced God's protection amidst many formidable challenges they faced that spanned six eras: the Persian (397–336 BCE), the Greek (336–323 BCE), the Egyptian (323–198 BCE), the Syrian (198–167 BCE), the Maccabean and Hasmonean (167–63 BCE), and the Roman (63 BCE–70 CE) eras. During this period, God did not relate with the Jews through any of the modes to which they were accustomed. They thought that God had forgotten them. But had he? The preservation of the Jewish nation was part of God's plan. Not only did he have a covenantal commitment with the Jews, but also the Messiah had to be a Jew.[6] For this to happen, the Jewish nation had to survive. The Old Testament anticipates the coming of the Messiah, while the silent years enable us to understand how the Jews and the world beyond were prepared to receive him. Here we see how God orchestrated history to accomplish his plan. Powerful, self-centered emperors acted without realizing that they were fulfilling God's purposes. For instance, Daniel's prophetic vision was fulfilled during this period through political giants who did not know about the God of the Jews. God's activity was exhibited not only in prophetic proclamation, but also in its fulfillment in history. This period shows that amidst several threats to the

---

6. Some Bible verses indicate that the Messiah would be a descendant of Abraham (Gen 12:1–3, 28:10–15), of the tribe of Judah (Gen 49:10), and from David's family (2 Sam 7:17; Jer 23:5–6).

Jewish nation, God was preserving this nation by orchestrating history from behind the scenes.

Under the Persians (397–336 BCE)

Pan-Mesopotamian empire building commenced with the Assyrians. Assyria was the first nation to rule over the kingdoms of Israel and Judah in eighth century BCE. At the beginning of this period, the Jewish nation came under the Persian Empire. Under Cyrus II of Persia, also referred to as Cyrus the Great (558–529 BCE), Persia replaced the Median dominance[7] and later Darius I (522–486 BCE) extended and consolidated the Persian Empire. This occurred almost two centuries after Isaiah proclaimed that a man named Cyrus would permit the exiled Jews to rebuild Jerusalem and the temple (Isa 45:28). Cyrus issued a decree that permitted the Jews to return to Jerusalem and rebuild the temple (2 Chr 36:22–23; Ezra 1:1–4). This enabled Jews to create a community in their ancestral homeland. For about 100 years, Judea was a Persian territory under the governor of Syria, assisted by the Jewish high priest. This was an ideal time for Jews to come under the Persian Empire; they needed relief after being so cruelly treated by the despotic Assyrian and Babylonian Empires. The Persian Empire facilitated such a relief. Paul Wright points out that Judea functioned "as a semi-autonomous province of the Persian Empire, with a lively Jewish identity centered on a temple rebuilt on holy ground in Jerusalem and cultural life shaped by the authority of priests and Levites."[8]

This may be seen as an enactment of God's plan as predicted in Daniel's vision that Darius would take over as ruler on the night the Babylonian king, Belshazzar, was killed (Dan 5:30–31). The book of Chronicles states that Cyrus II and Darius I were God's special agents sent to protect the Jews in their ancestral homeland. The book records that God moved Cyrus's heart to allow the Jews to rebuild the temple and return to their homeland (2 Chr 36:22–23), which was in accordance with Jeremiah's prophecy (Jer 25:1–4; Dan 9). Isaiah referred to Cyrus as God's "shepherd" ordained to fulfill God's desires for the Jewish nation (Isa 44:28), and his "right hand" to enable the Jews to overcome the onslaughts of powerful nations (Isa 45:1). Here we see how God orchestrated history to protect the Jewish nation. Although the Jews were not politically independent during this era, Persia gave them an identity as a nation and this in turn equipped them to handle

---

7. The Medes were related to the Persians and both wanted to supplant the Assyrian Empire. The Medes occupied the region northeast of Assyria and reached their height under Cyaxares (625–586 BCE), but their dominance was short-lived.

8. Wright, *Understanding Biblical Kingdoms & Empires*, 27.

the challenges they were to face under the rule of subsequent powerful empires, commencing with the Greeks.

Under Greek Rule (336–323 BCE)

The Greek era started with Alexander the Great taking control of the Persian Empire (334–331 BCE). Although he is not mentioned in the Bible, he may be taken as fulfilling prophecy. Daniel's vision refers to a series of rams that represented great empires, and when mentioning these rams (Dan 8), he identifies them: "The two-horned ram that you saw represents the kings of Media and Persia. The shaggy goat is the king of Greece, and the large horn between its eyes is the first king" (Dan 8:20–21).

Daniel's vision predicts not only the rise of the Greek Empire, but also mentions "the great horn" as signifying its first king. Was this Alexander?

Josephus cites an incident that highlights the relevance of Greece and Alexander to Daniel's vision.[9] Josephus mentions that Alexander came to Jerusalem around 332 BCE. The high priest, knowing how Alexander had destroyed Tyre and Gaza, cried out to God for divine protection. Through a dream, God asked the high priest to meet Alexander. Adorned in his traditional white garments, and confident that he would be divinely protected, the high priest along with other priests met Alexander outside the walls of the city. Surprisingly, Alexander did not kill any of them. When a Greek soldier asked Alexander why he acted this way, he replied that he had seen the man in a dream he had while in Macedonia. When the passage from Daniel referring to the first king destroying the Persian Empire (Dan 8:20–21) was shown to Alexander, he was convinced that he was that king. The exuberant Alexander told the high priest that he would grant whatever the priest wanted. The high priest asked that the Jews be permitted to live according to their religious laws and be exempt from paying taxes on the seventh year. Alexander allowed the Jews to govern themselves if they paid taxes and swore loyalty to him. The temple remained the center of worship and the leadership of the priests was intact. A council of scribes and elders (*gerousia*) were permitted to share in local administration.[10]

---

9. Josephus, *Antiquities of the Jews,* Book XI, ch. 8, paras. 4–5.
10. Lupovitch, "Challenge of Hellenism," 27.

Mosaic of Alexander the Great meeting the Jewish priests

This 1,500-year-old mosaic was unearthed during archaeological excavations in 2014 and 2015 by a team of specialists and students led by archaeologist Dr. Jodi Magness, from the University of North Carolina-Chapel Hill. The mosaic decorated the floor of a fifth-century CE synagogue at Huqoq, a site in Israel's Lower Galilee region.[11] The image apparently depicts the first nonbiblical story ever discovered decorating an ancient synagogue, perhaps the legendary meeting between Alexander the Great and the Jewish high priest. There is controversy concerning the historicity of this event. Although Paul Wright questions Josephus's account of Alexander's encounter with the priests, he acknowledges that the Jewish leaders must have had some interaction with Alexander or his subordinates.[12] Whether such an incident happened and whether it was an enactment of Daniel's prophetic

---

11. Magness et al., "Huqoq Excavation Project," 95. Archaeologist Dr. Jodi Magness is President of the Archaeological Institute of America and holds a senior endowed chair in the Department of Religious Studies at the University of North Carolina at Chapel Hill.

12. Wright, *Understanding Biblical Kingdoms & Empires*, 30.

vision, it is evident that the Greek Empire under Alexander's leadership played a significant role in Jewish history.

During this era, the Greeks made a lasting impact on the life of the Jewish nation. Alexander did not merely conquer territories, but strove to unify the world through Greek culture. Aristotle, Alexander's teacher, had a consuming passion to integrate all facets of knowledge into a single system. Influenced by the strategy of his guru, Alexander passionately pursued the unification of the world he conquered through Greek language and culture, popularly referred to as Hellenization. Hellenism comes from the Greek verb *hellenizien*, literally meaning "to speak Greek," and implied "to imitate or become Greek." It exhibits an all-encompassing way of life that includes political, social, economic, cultural, and religious aspects.[13]

Hellenization became so popular and widespread that it persisted even after the demise of the Greek Empire and found its way into the Roman era. The Hellenistic culture, coupled with Alexander's policy of allowing the Jews to live in peace as a religious community, were both a blessing and a disadvantage to the Jewish nation. Although Jews did not adopt Greek polytheism, Hellenization impacted Jewish society in other facets of Jewish culture.[14] Hellenization made Greek the language of the empire and Jews eventually became bilingual. This enabled them to spread their stance on religion and morality to non-Jews. The Greek translation of the Hebrew Bible (the Old Testament), the *Septuagint*, became an effective channel to communicate Judaism to the Greek world.

On the other hand, Hellenization turned out to be a type of cultural imperialism. To be a privileged citizen of the empire and enjoy fully its socioeconomic opportunities, one had to be a good Hellenist. Hellenism was more widespread among affluent Jews: the Jewish aristocracy and upper echelon of the priesthood.[15] This was also the educated sector. Those proficient in Greek had significant influence on the political and economic activities of the world of Alexander the Great. Moreover, the spread of the Greek language facilitated the dissemination of Greek secular philosophy, polytheistic religion, customs, and culture. Hellenization became a threat to Judaism because the Greek way of life was so sophisticated, intellectually appetizing, and culturally cool that many Jews were attracted to give up their rigorous religious convictions. Though Jews were careful to not worship the Greek and Roman idols, they were drawn to Greek conceptual idols like reason, pleasure, relativism, skepticism, and ego-centric humanism.

13. Wright, *Understanding Biblical Kingdoms & Empires*, 31.
14. Lupovitch, "Challenge of Hellenism," 26; also in Efron et al., *Jews*, 56–64.
15. Lupovitch, "Challenge of Hellenism," 26.

The Greek era was both an asset and a liability to the identity and survival of the chosen people.

Under Egyptians (323–198 BCE)

When Alexander suddenly died in 323 BCE, the Greek Empire was left without a successor. Four of his generals took over four segments of the empire. Ptolemy I Soter, probably a half-brother of Alexander, took control of Egypt as well as Palestine. It is sometimes called the Egyptian era because it was centered in Egypt, and sometimes called the Ptolemaic Period since twelve kings, all named Ptolemy, were in power in Egypt for almost 300 years. This period was one of relative peace for Jews in Egypt. Alexandria was a major cultural and commercial center under the Ptolemies,[16] and became a hub of Jewish activity. The Hebrew Bible was translated into Greek in Alexandria. Institutions that would eventually develop into synagogues first appeared in Egypt during the third century BCE.[17]

Even in the Egyptian era, Hellenization continued to infiltrate the Jewish community, causing a rift in the community. Some Jews were enamored by the Greek way of life and were pro-Hellenization, while some, especially Orthodox Jews, resisted it.

Under Syrians (198–167 BCE)

In 312 BCE, one of Alexander's generals, Seleucus I, took control of Syria, leading to the Syrian or Seleucid period. Jews came under Syrian control during the rule of Antiochus III (223–187 BCE) and his son and successor, Seleucus Philopater (187–175 BCE). Seleucids actively promoted Hellenism. Jews were given limited autonomy to maintain local rule under their high priest. A short time later, Seleucus Philopater was assassinated and his brother, Antiochus IV, began his reign in 174 BCE. To resist the rising Roman power, he aggressively promoted Hellenism and advocated the emperor cult. His supporters hailed him as *Antiochus Epiphanes,* meaning "the illustrious one." He appointed Jewish priests and bribed them to support him. Mustering support, he moved twice against Egypt but failed both times. Humiliated, he took out his frustration on the Jews. He outlawed circumcision, cancelled Sabbath observance, disallowed celebration of festivals, and mutilated copies of the Hebrew Bible. Jews were forced to eat pork and make sacrifices to idols. Then, in December 167 BCE, Antiochus

---

16. Brisco, *Holman Bible Atlas,* 179.
17. Wright, *Understanding Biblical Kingdoms & Empires,* 32.

desecrated the Jewish temple by sacrificing a pig at an altar to the god Zeus.[18] Not surprisingly, the Jews reacted against such an atrocity, resulting in the Maccabean revolt. We can sense how God allowed conditions to become so desperate for his people that they had to wake up. Sometimes God uses waking up techniques!

The Maccabean Revolt (167–143 BCE) and the Hasmonean Jewish State (143–63 BCE)

While some Jews acceded to Antiochus's atrocious acts (1 Macc 1:43), many revolted against this tyrant. Jewish opposition commenced with the emergence of two groups: the Hassideans and Hasmoneans. Reacting against forced Hellenization and the desecration of the temple, Hassideans fled to the hills and conducted a series of guerilla attacks. Many Hassideans were killed and they were the first Jewish martyrs.[19] Hasmoneans continued the revolt that started in 167 BCE in the small village of Modiin, ten miles north of Jerusalem, with the shocking act of an elderly priest, Mattathias ben Johanan (also known as "the Hasmonean" after his ancestor, Hasmoneus).[20] Antiochus IV sent his henchmen into the countryside to enforce his law that only pagan worship and sacrifices were permissible. One of his men built an altar in the marketplace in Modiin and ordered the Jews to offer sacrifices. When Mattathias saw a Jew obeying the order, he killed both the Jew and the Syrian agent. The priest and his five sons, along with many Jews, fled to hide in the hills of Judea. The Seleucid army tried to subdue the brewing rebellion led by three of Mattathias's sons—Judas Maccabeus, Jonathan, and Simon—but failed. The family of Mattathias became known as the Maccabees. Seleucids were routed by Judas and his hill-country warriors, and this led to the Maccabean revolt. After winning a series of battles against the Seleucids, Judas and his followers captured Jerusalem in 165 BCE; they entered the temple and cleansed it, clearing all the idols.

After this battle and the clearing of the temple, the Jews wanted to rededicate the temple. To do this, they had to rebuild the altar and light the traditional Jewish candle stand, the menorah. The Talmud describes the events that followed:

---

18. 1 Macc 141–46, as cited by Wright, *Understanding Biblical Kingdoms & Empires*, 33. The Book of Maccabees is not part of the Jewish canon but is part of Jewish literature.

19. Lupovitch, "Challenge of Hellenism," 28–29.

20. Lea and Black, *New Testament*, 18. Also in Lupovitch, "Challenge of Hellenism," 29.

> When the royal Hasmonean family overpowered and was victorious over [the Greeks], they searched and found only a single cruse of pure oil, enough to light the menorah for only a single day. A miracle occurred, and they lit the menorah with this oil for eight days. On the following year, they established these [eight days] as days of festivity and praise and thanksgiving to G-d. (*Talmud*, Shabbat 21b)

Jews celebrate this miracle with the eight-day festival of Hanukkah, known as the festival of dedication or lights, and light menorah candles each night in commemoration. The festival commemorates the miraculous victory of the Maccabees over a strong imperial army.

Do Jews celebrate Hanukkah just to commemorate a military victory? As with all commemorative festivals, some celebrate Hanukkah with devotion while others ignore it and even challenge its historicity. Those who celebrate see it as a miracle, confirming that God has never given up on his people; just like then, he is present even today. Hanukkah is still celebrated as a feast of dedication. Rabbi Yosef Jacobson stresses the purpose for which Hanukkah was instituted: "To commemorate the display of Divine graciousness in a world usually enslaved to nature, the leaders of Israel instituted the eight-day holiday of Chanukah, in which we would kindle a menorah each night."[21] For him, oil "embodies the essence of Chanukah and serves as the focus of the festival of lights."[22] Perhaps that is why Zechariah's prophecy, "'Not by might nor by power, but by my Spirit,' says the Lord Almighty" (Zech 4:6) is read during Hanukkah festivities. Among the traditional blessings and hymns of this season, *Maoz Tzur*, or "Rock of Ages" (not to be confused with the Christian hymn), is most popular and widespread. Though the hymn acknowledges the military victory, it attributes the victory to God. The hymn begins:

> Rock of Ages, let our song,
> Praise Thy saving power;
> Thou, amidst the raging foes,
> Wast our sheltering tower.
> Furious they assailed us,
> But Thine arm availed us,
> And Thy Word broke their sword,
> When our own strength failed us.[23]

---

21. Jacobson, "Paradoxes of Oil," subsection "Why Celebrate Oil?", paras. 7–8.
22. Jacobson, "Paradoxes of Oil," subsection "Four Qualities of Oil," paras. 10–11.
23. "Rock of Ages, Let Our Song." Words in Hebrew by Mordecai (possibly

The symbolism of the feast highlights that the military victory was ultimately due to God and not human strength. The sixteenth-century Maharal of Prague, Rabbi Judah Loew, clarifies the rabbinic emphasis on the miracle of the oil: "The main reason that the days of Hanukkah were instituted was to celebrate the victory over the Greeks. However, so that it would not seem that the victory was due only to might and heroism, rather than to Divine Providence, the miracle was denoted by the lighting of the Menorah, to show that it was *all* by a miracle, the war as well."[24] Over the years, the festival came to be commemorated as the miracle that happened in the temple, rather than focusing on what occurred in the war zone. The faith of the community continues even though the memories of military victories have faded.

After capturing Jerusalem, Judas led further Jewish revolts until he was killed in battle in 160 BCE; the Maccabean revolt continued under the leadership of his brothers, Jonathan and Simon.[25] Jonathan served as high priest and later governor of Judea until he was killed in 143 BCE, and he was succeeded in these roles by Simon. In 142 BCE, Syrian king Demetrius II finally recognized Judea as an independent state under the leadership of Simon.[26] The emergent Hasmonean kingdom (143–63 BCE), though much smaller in population, territory, and resources, was an independent Jewish state. Simon—brother of Judas Maccabee and son of Mattathias—was the first Hasmonean ruler of the autonomous Jewish state.

The significance of the Maccabean episode in the Jewish narrative goes beyond the Jewish nation gaining independence. It is a poignant reminder that God had not forsaken his people. The Maccabean era may be viewed as confirming God's preservation of the Jewish nation after decades of being subject to despotic imperial powers. How did the Jews lose their hard-earned freedom so soon? This takes us to the Roman era.

Under Roman Rule (63 BCE—70 CE)

The Roman era commenced in 63 BCE, when the Roman general Pompey shattered the Jewish Hasmonean state.

Mordecai ben Isaac ha-Levi), in the fourteenth century CE, later translated into German, and then into English.

24. Alperin, "Hanukkah," para. 7.
25. Wright, *Understanding Biblical Kingdoms*, 33, citing 1 Macc 5:1—13:33.
26. Wright, *Understanding Biblical Kingdoms*, citing 1 Macc 12:33–41.

A rare Roman silver denarius depicting Pompey the Great and the sailing ship, Q. Nasidius

The Roman general Pompey was called in to settle an ongoing conflict for the throne of Judea between two Hasmonean brothers, Hyrcanus II and Aristobulus II, also known as the Hasmonean Civil War. This led to the Roman capture of Jerusalem in 63 BCE. The Jews were devastated, not merely because they lost their freedom so soon, but also because of Pompey's desecration of the temple. Josephus points out that, "there was nothing that affected the nation so much, in the calamities they were then under, as that their holy place, which had been hitherto seen by none, should be laid open to strangers; for Pompey, and those that were about him, went into the temple itself whither it was not lawful for any to enter but the high priest, and saw what was reposited therein."[27] Why did such a catastrophe occur? Had God forsaken his chosen people? The popular response is that Jewish collapse was inevitable due to Roman military strength. Should Rome get all the credit? Goodman's citation of Josephus as the first eyewitness to the catastrophe provides fresh insight. Josephus started as a general of the Jewish rebels and participated in the revolt, but was captured by Roman forces in 67 BCE, and eventually became a Roman citizen supporting the Roman regime. What made him change his stance? Based on Josephus's testimony, Goodman claims that the rebel, who contemplated suicide to avoid falling into Roman hands, was persuaded by divine guidance through dreams revealing that God, the creator of the Jewish nation, had decided to break what he had made. Josephus came to believe that the Roman victory was in God's plan, resulting in his surrender to the Romans.[28] Josephus's narrative is permeated with the "ambivalence which arose from his complex political career, first as a defender of Jerusalem, then as an apologist for the Roman regime."[29] This ambivalence is reflected in his writings, *The Jewish War* and *The Antiquities*. He was convinced that it was God's plan that Judea should come under Rome. This conviction falls in line with the view of the Roman era as a fulfillment of Daniel's prophetic interpretation of Nebuchadnezzar's dream of a giant

---

27. Josephus, *Wars of the Jews*, Book I, ch. 7, para. 6. Also cited in "Overview."
28. Goodman, *History of Judaism*, 4.
29. Goodman, *History of Judaism*, 5.

statue (Dan 2:31–40). The "legs and feet of iron" of the statue are typically identified as referring to the Roman Empire.

Though Rome had "legs of iron," should it get full credit for the Jewish collapse? The Jewish community was already divided when it came under Roman rule. Though Romans replaced the Greeks as rulers of Judea, Hellenism continued during the Roman era. Roman gods became part of the Greek pantheon. Greek philosophy complemented the legalistic military culture of Rome. The Jews were united in rejecting the Greco-Roman gods, but they were divided in their response to the Romanized Hellenism.

The rift between two religious groups, the Pharisees and the Sadducees, continued into the Roman era. Pharisees gave prominence to Jewish written and oral tradition and were meticulous in their ritualistic practices. They were hesitant to accommodate Hellenistic ideas and practices. Jewish literature of this period advocating the return to the days of biblical prophets (such as Esdras, Tobit, Judith, Enoch, and Jubilees) reflected the pharisaic stance.[30] Sadducees were the temple-based, aristocratic, urban sector of the community. They wanted to remain Torah based, but were willing to participate in various opportunities offered by Hellenism.[31] The Pharisaic-Sadducee rift was also over religiopolitical issues; who should be the high priest and who should be the king of Judea? The Sadducees recognized the Hasmonean leader, John Hyrcanus, as high priest and king of the Jews. The Pharisees could not accept Hyrcanus as high priest since he was not a descendent of Aaron, or as the legitimate Jewish king since he was not of the lineage of King David. The Essenes (sect of the Dead Sea scrolls community) advocated a life of withdrawal from the traditional temple-based Jewish lifestyle. Together with these three groups, Goodman identifies the Zealots as the fourth factor of the Jewish community.[32] The Zealots were keen to regain political independence, by force if necessary. Some groups were pro-Roman, some were anti-Roman, and some were indifferent. The multiple reactions to Roman domination within the Jewish community that ranged from exclusive confrontation to inclusive accommodation caused rifts within the community. It was not only Roman power, but also conflicts within the Jewish community that cost the Jews their independence.

When Pompey ascended to power, Judea was still wrought with conflicts. Aristobulus II revolted against Rome and Antipater I was sent to quell the revolt. As a reward for his successful efforts, he was made Rome's puppet

30. Wright, *Understanding Biblical Kingdoms & Empires*, 34. Also in Dimant, *From Enoch to Tobit*.

31. Lupovitch, "Challenge of Hellenism," 28.

32. Goodman, *History of Judaism*; and Goodman, "Jews, Greeks and Romans," 110–39.

ruler of Judea. In the meantime, Julius Caesar killed Pompey and became the emperor in 48 BCE. During Caesar's reign (48–43 BCE), Jews were treated leniently and granted religious freedom. A year after Caesar came to power, Antipater died and his son Herod became the procurator of Judea around 40 BCE. Herod the Great, as he was called, rebuilt the Jerusalem temple, and prided himself as the king of the Jews. He was a devoted Hellenist and hated the Hasmonean family. Ultimately, he killed descendants of the Hasmoneans, including his own wife and his two sons. Though despotic, he was very insecure in his position as king of the Jews. When the wise men from the east asked him about another king of the Jews, he was disturbed (Matt 2:2–3). It is not surprising that he ordered the killing of innocent children. Under his rule, Jews remained relatively independent if they caused no disturbances and paid their taxes.

The alliance between Roman rulers and Jewish subjects was cordial but strained. After suffering under Syrian atrocities, Jews were free to practice their religion, follow their moral codes, and adhere to their dietary rules. The government policy of *Pax Romana* (Roman peace) enabled the Jewish community to live in peace. Although Romans were puzzled as to why Jews refused to eat pork, which the Romans loved, circumcised young boys, worshipped without idols, and seemingly became lazy on Sabbath days, they were not hostile to the Jews. Even when the empire expanded, Jews retained a distinctive identity. Romans accepted them and exempted them from certain obligations imposed on other communities.

Nevertheless, there was a clash between these two civilizations.[33] Rome's centrality in the empire was founded on its political power and military strength, while for the Jews, Jerusalem was the capital city of God. Rome had several temples with many gods, while Jerusalem had one temple with one God. For Romans, history flowed indifferently through the passage of time like a river. For Jews, history had purpose since God was very much involved in history. Romans and Jews had different concepts of the purpose of the state. For Romans, even though the state was the arena for public business (*res publica*), where people made decisions for the common good, state policy was ultimately determined by the emperor. Jews operated under a theocratic political system where God was the ultimate authority; laws were based on God's standards. Although the relationship between Jews and Romans was precarious, the Jewish nation survived for some 133 years under Rome's imperial power. Daniel's visions portray Rome as the terrifying and frightening beast with legs of iron. Their survival was possible only because God was behind the scenes.

---

33. Goodman, *Rome and Jerusalem*.

WHAT DOES THE JEWISH NARRATIVE TELL US?

The Jewish narrative highlights the survival of the Jewish nation under the domination of five imperial powers: Persian, Greek, Egyptian, Syrian, and Roman. Being governed by their own (Maccabees and Hasmoneans) also had its challenges. Being subject to these foreign powers facilitated exposure to their various languages, culture, religious doctrines and practices, moral values, and ways of life. Some of these were a challenge to Jewish culture and even threatened their identity. Others helped them to articulate their dogmas and communicate their views and values more effectively. The Greek and Latin languages served as effective tools for Jews to communicate Judaism to the Greco-Roman world.

God was not taken by surprise when the Jews came under foreign domination. He knew what was to happen to his people during this period. In fact, he had communicated through Daniel's prophetic visions that the Jews would be exposed to these foreign powers. The silent years saw the historical enactment of those prophecies through God's orchestration of the events of this period. God's orchestration was executed without making the participants in these happenings robots, but rather giving them the freedom to act of their own free will. They fell into God's schedule and fulfilled his plans without even knowing who God was or what his plans were.

God's lasting covenantal relationship with the Jews runs through their history.[34] For that relationship to last, the Jewish nation could not be destroyed. During the many challenges it faced during this period, God's plan was that the Jewish nation should survive. God did not want his chosen people merely to survive; there was a specific mandate in his covenant with them. He wanted them to be a light to the nations, not only within Jewish borders, but through the entire world (Isa 49:6, 42:6, 60:3). To carry out this mandate, they could not be closeted in their homeland but needed to be exposed to a wider world. The Roman Empire was that world. Rome had certain limitations in becoming the hub for the expansion of the empire. The Greek geographer Strabo noticed that Rome's location was not advantageous and did not have enough land of its own. Citing Strabo's observations, Goodman argues that this was a blessing in disguise.[35] Rome's limitations motivated Romans to build roads and aqueducts and this facilitated the movement and survival of the Jewish diaspora. God orchestrated the demographics of the world to expose the Jews to a wider world and thereby enable the Jewish nation to be a light to the nations. Did they fulfill the mandate? Despite Malachi's pleas and warnings, the Jews were not able to

---

34. Goodman, *Rome and Jerusalem*, xxviii.
35. Goodman, *Rome and Jerusalem*, 43–44.

fulfill the mandate, although they tried their best. Although God's chosen people failed, let us not be too judgmental. Would we have succeeded? It was not a Jewish failure, but rather a human default.

The Jewish narrative does not end on a bleak or depressing note. It anticipates with hope the arrival of the Messiah or the messianic age before the day of the Lord. Has the Messiah already arrived? This leads us to the Christian narrative.

THE CHRISTIAN NARRATIVE

The Christian narrative is centered on the conviction that the Messiah has come. It claims that "my messenger" and the "messenger of the covenant," who Malachi anticipated, have arrived as John the Baptist and Jesus, respectively. Before we find out how Jesus as Messiah brought about a paradigm shift in humanity's salvific quest, let us look into how the Intertestamental Period prepared the ground for such a paradigm shift.

When Malachi referred to the day of the Lord, he claimed that it would impact not only the Jews, but all people. If Jesus was to be the Messiah for all, God had to prepare the whole world for his advent. This happened during the silent years.

Long before the Intertestamental Period, the world at large was made aware that humans were in a predicament and needed to be redeemed. Karl Jaspers picked out sixth century BCE as the pivotal period of what he called the axial age (800–200 BCE).[36] The Intertestamental Period falls within the latter part of the axial age. In significant ways, the axial age was preparatory for Christ to accomplish his purpose. Why did he come? Let us investigate the three main reasons he came: Jesus came to redeem (1 Tim 1:15; Luke 5:32, 19:19; Matt 18:11), to reveal God to the fullest (Matt 11:27; John 14:9), and to mediate between humans and God (1 Tim 2:5). It is noteworthy that before Christ's arrival, during the Intertestamental Period, the world was dealing with issues pertaining specifically to these reasons.

Searching for the Problem

Jesus did not come to civilize people or to set up an ideal political system or even to reform religions; he came to save sinners. This is what he said about himself (Luke 5:32, 19:10; Mark 2:17) and what was said about him (1 Tim 1:15). If he came to redeem humans, the implication is that there was some problem with humanity. The Judeo-Christian world characterizes that problem as sin, which necessitated God's intervention. From the Christian

---

36. Jaspers, *Origin and Goal of History*. See also Jaspers, *Great Philosophers*, 99–105.

perspective, God had to send his Son to cure this disease. For the cure to work, the disease first needed to be diagnosed. It is in the diagnosis of the human disease that the axial age becomes relevant.

The axial age saw the rise of several major religious founders and seers, like Buddha, Mahavira, Lao Tzu, Confucius, Shinto seers, and Hindu reformists. They came from different countries and cultures covering an extensive geographical area. All of them identified the core cause of the disease as human default: human moral deficiency or spiritual bankruptcy. Buddha called it human craving; *Lao Tzu* called it flowing against the dynamic *Tao*; and the Hindu reformist *Sankara* identified it as ignorance of one's identity as part of the cosmic spiritual reality. Although their ways to cure the disease differed, they agreed on the diagnosis that the core cause of the human disease lies in humans.

The Greco-Roman world also identified human default as the cause of its predicament. Hellenism had a great impact in this world and Greek philosophy provided the conceptual framework. We should note that the demarcations among disciplines like philosophy, religion, and the physical and social sciences were not there at that time. All these disciplines were closely intertwined and came under philosophy. By the end of fifth century BCE, Athens had become the intellectual capital of the Greek world and the arena of philosophical discussion. A group of philosophers called sophists flocked to the city, wanting not only to make a name for themselves but also to make money through their rhetorical skills. Speaking on makeshift platforms in parks, these were the ancient equivalents of modern-era soapbox orators. To be successful both as orators and money makers, they had to please their audiences. Sounds familiar! They found that the philosophers who preceded them were caught up in a feud of conflicting views concerning the origin and nature of the world, resulting in confusion. This made the sophists skeptical of arriving at objective knowledge, so they adopted a subjective stance. Protagoras, a sophist, claimed that "man is the measure of all things," and therefore "truth is what appears to each one." Gorgias became famous for his sophisms like "What is, is not," and "If anything is, it cannot be known." Such subjective sophistry led to the dismissal of any objective standards to assess what is true, good, or right. Though sophistry led to relativism and subjectivism, it was a game-changer in that the sophists influenced their contemporaries to transfer their attention from speculating about the world to human issues, concerns, and challenges.

Socrates (470–399 BCE) was perturbed by the confusion that sophists were causing among their audiences, and he reacted vehemently against sophistry. Through his provocative dialogues with them, he identified the underlying cause of their confusion as intellectual depravity, which he called ignorance. This, according to him, resulted in subjectivism and relativism in the areas of knowledge and ethics. Athenians were confused as to what truth, good, or right were because of ignorance caused by sophist orators. Based on this diagnosis, Socrates came up with his curative dictum, "knowledge is virtue," which entailed "ignorance is vice." For Socrates, ignorance was the cause of the human predicament and knowledge was the cure.

Plato (429–348 BCE) agreed with Socrates's diagnosis. For him, all types of knowledge could not liberate, but only knowledge of the world of forms (ideas). The world of forms is the real world and the material world is an imperfect replica of it. The components of the material world are mere imperfect imitations of these ideal forms. Knowledge of such imperfect imitations, obtained through the senses, provided only opinion, which for Plato was pseudo-knowledge. Plato's way of freeing humans from their bondage of ignorance was through knowledge of the real world of forms, orchestrated through reason.

Aristotle (384–322 BCE) further developed the Socratic diagnosis and identified ignorance as the cause of the human predicament. To get rid of ignorance, he accommodated knowledge through reason as well as through the senses.

Socrates, Plato, and Aristotle, the key figures of the golden age of Greek philosophy, identified the core cause of the human predicament as ignorance and proposed knowledge as the way out of such a predicament. The Greek diagnosis of the human predicament provided the immediate conceptual context in which Jesus arrived. To proclaim that redemption of humans from their predicament could come only through relying on Christ and his death on the cross would have seemed foolish to the Greeks of this time (1 Cor 1:24).

Greek philosophers fell in line with the diagnosis of the seers of the axial age. Their diagnosis motivated people to search for a cure. Since humans had brought about their own plight, they could not get out of it themselves. They had to resort to something beyond them. This prepared the world of the time to understand the cure that Christ provided for sick humanity, since he, as cure, was more than human.

Searching Beyond the Human

The reliance on something beyond the human led to a search for God. The religious communities of the axial age were earnestly searching for God, even though their gods were multiple. Some religions began as nontheistic movements but later became theistic. For instance, Confucius considered himself as a teacher and did not resort to the superhuman nor did he claim to be God. After his death, Confucians deified him and built temples and even offered sacrifices to him. The Taoist founders, Lao-Tzu and Chuang-Tzu, downplayed the notion of deities. They could not prevent later Taoists from personifying *Tao*, deifying its founders, and introducing a hierarchy of deities. Gautama Buddha never claimed to be God and was silent when asked whether there was a God. Buddhists later elevated him to a transcendent being; Buddha came to be worshipped rather than venerated as a teacher. The metamorphosis that occurred in the life of these religions indicates people's search for and their need for God.[37]

From a Judeo-Christian perspective, humans are created in God's image. An image cannot survive without an original. The very makeup of the human being causes humans to search for God; they desperately need God to survive. Perhaps this led people to god-making, which has been one of the most lucrative industries in the religious market.

While making a scathing attack on Greeks for making gods in their own images, the philosopher poet Xenophanes (570–473 BCE) surmised that there had to be a transcendent divine being. His fragments contain pithy comments on Greek god-making (fragments B14–16); for instance, "mortals suppose that gods are born, wear clothes, and have a voice, and a body" (B14) and, "if animals like oxen and horses had hands and could draw, like people, horses would draw the shapes of gods to look like horses, and oxen would draw them to look like oxen" (B15).[38] Xenophanes observed that Ethiopians' gods were flat-nosed and black, while Thracians' gods had blue eyes and red hair (B16). Xenophanes also noticed that shaping gods in human images caused them to acquire human vices. Homer's gods were thieves, adulterers, and deceivers (B11, B12). While critiquing such god-making, Xenophanes surmised that the divine had to be perfect and transcendent. He characterized his god thusly: "One god, the greatest among gods and men, neither in form like unto mortals nor in thought" (B23).[39] Being so transcendent, he is unknown and unknowable. Xenophanes indicated that however perfect one's knowledge about God is, it would still be a matter of opinion, imagination, or guesswork (B34).[40]

Following Xenophanes, Anaxagoras (500–428 BCE) claimed that the order in the world could be attributed to a superior power, *nous*. For him,

37. Kulathungam, *Quest*, 126–28.

38. Burnet, *Early Greek Philosophy*, chapter 2. Burnet translates and numbers the B-fragments described by Diels and Kranz in *Die Fragmente der Vorsokratiker*. The only surviving quotations from the Presocratics are embedded in the works of later authors. These quotations are normally referred to by Diels-Kranz (DK) numbers.

39. Burnet, *Early Greek Philosophy*, 119.

40. Burnet, *Early Greek Philosophy*, 121.

nous was not an animistic spirit or an element of nature but best described as mind or reason. "All other things partake in a portion of everything, while Nous is infinite and self-ruled, and is mixed with nothing, but is alone, itself by itself."[41]

Socrates (470–399 BCE) was dissatisfied with the way Anaxagoras presented *nous* as giving order to the world. Socrates claimed that *nous* was not only one, but also the supreme intelligence that accounted for order in the world. He called it providence. Socrates gave personality to Anaxagoras's *nous*.[42]

Plato also attributed the order in the world to a supreme intelligence. For him, both the world of forms and matter were eternal. The world is made up of things that have both form and matter: they are matter that has been given order through forms. How did that happen? In the same way that a piece of marble needs a sculptor to turn into a sculpture, the world needs an intelligent designer to create the world. This was Plato's God. This God did not create out of nothing, but designed the world out of matter, modelling it on the forms. Forms were the model of his work. Plato's God was providence too, since he is the governing intelligence that renders order to the world.

Aristotle (384–322 BCE) noticed that the world was always changing. For him, movement was not merely something going from one location to another, but also from what was potential to what was actual. For instance, the germination and growth of a tree from a seed is movement from potential tree to actual tree. He saw that underlying every movement there must be a chain of events ultimately leading to something that moves others, but is itself unmoved: the unmoved mover. He called the source of all movement the prime mover, which is Aristotle's God. Such a God is perfect, eternal, immutable, and immaterial.[43]

Beginning with Xenophanes, Greek thinkers realized the necessity of a transcendent being to account for the order of the cosmos. Even though they described it as supreme intelligence, creator of order, prime mover, perfect, and unique, they could not name it. Naming implies knowledge of what is named. This God, though necessary to account for the world's order, was yet unknown!

While the acceptance of a single supreme intelligence became popular among the Greek intelligentsia, worship of multiple gods was still prevalent. Greek gods multiplied with the addition of Roman gods. Among such a

---

41. Burnet, *Early Greek Philosophy*, 259.
42. Gilles, *Evolution of Philosophy*, 10; Thonnard, *Short History of Philosophy*, 46–47.
43. Aristotle, "Metaphysics," 258–62.

medley of gods that catered to almost every need, there were altars to an unknown god. Why?

When we have more than one god, there lingers a doubt as to whether one has reached the perfect count. There could always be one more god: an unknown god. There is an interesting event associated with the unknown god. Around 600 BCE, Athens was devastated by a deadly plague and countless Athenians died. In desperation, some Athenians pleaded with the reputed prophet and philosopher-poet Epimenides[44] for help. When he arrived in Athens, he was shocked to see the roads lined with the idols of multiple gods. The prophet suggested that there could still be a god unknown to the Athenians but powerful enough to end the plague, if they would just invoke his help. The elders questioned him; how could they call upon a god whose name they did not even know? Epimenides responded that any god worth his name would disregard their ignorance and hear their plea, if they called on him. Epimenides chose a sign to determine whether such a god would respond to their pleas. He asked the elders to graze a flock of sheep on the slopes of Mars Hill. Then the prophet prayed to that god to show compassion and save Athens from the plague. He asked this god to reveal his willingness by causing at least some sheep to lie on the grass instead of grazing. The next morning, the Athenians were shocked to see some sheep had settled down to rest without grazing. These were separated and sacrificed to this god, who had shown favor through this sign. Within a week, Athens recovered from the plague. On Epimenides's suggestion, altars were built to *agnosto theo* (unknown god). Since then, altars to the unknown god came to exist in all the major cities of Greece. When Paul came to Athens (Acts 17), he was distressed to see the city full of idols, but noticed an altar for an unknown god. Athens housed the Areopagus, which was once the site of the council that governed the city-state. The council members considered themselves custodians of teachings that introduced new religions and foreign gods.[45] They found Paul's preaching about Jesus and the resurrection novel and strange, so they invited him for a meeting at the Areopagus.

It was clear that Paul was in controversial quarters, but he commenced his address in a manner that captured his audience's attention. He addressed them as being "religious," which in our scientific secular society would be taken as sarcastic. In Paul's day, when religion was part of philosophy and science, his comment would have been a compliment. He pointed out that the Athenians were religious because amidst the worship of multiple gods, they had even an altar to an "unknown god" (Acts 17:22, 23). Mentioning

---

44. Argubright, "To the Unknown God."
45. NIV Study Bible, footnote on Acts 17:22, 1683NTn.

the unknown god would have sparked the attention of both the intelligentsia and the common people. The philosophers' god, though needed to account for the world's order, was still unknown. The memory of the miracle on Mars Hill made Athenians still revere the unknown god. When Paul commenced his address by claiming, "So you are ignorant of the very thing you worship—and this is what I am going to proclaim to you" (Acts 17:23), the audience would have been curious to know what Paul had to say about this god. First, he told them that if they looked for this god, they would find him because he was not far from them. Paul introduced a quote from an Athenian poet: "For in him we live and move and have our being" (Acts 17:28). He was quoting Epimenides's *Cretica*, where Minos addresses Zeus:

> They fashioned a tomb for you, holy and high one,
> Cretans, always liars, evil beasts, idle bellies.
> But you are not dead: you live and abide forever,
> For in you we live and move and have our being.[46]

It is believed that Epimenides, whom Paul quoted, was the prophet of the miracle on Mars Hill, when the unknown god had freed the Athenians from the plague.[47] Paul tried to drive home the point that the god who was unknown to the Athenians was the one who was with them through the years.

Paul concluded by proclaiming that the god the Athenians worshipped as unknown was the one he was presenting (Acts 17:22); he was the one who revealed himself in Jesus, who rose again from the dead, and would be the judge of all humanity on the day of judgment. Naturally, many Athenians could not accept a God who not only came as a man but rose again. The Epicureans in the audience (Acts 17:8) did not believe in life after death. They could not accept Jesus' resurrection. Even though some sneered at Paul's proclamation, some were keen to know more about this unknown god, and some even became believers (Acts 17:33–34).

God's revelation in Jesus may be taken as divine response to the human search for God. Through Jesus, he made the unknown god known.

Through prophets, God had already revealed his awesome creation, miraculous interventions, divine guidance, and theophanies. He had yet

---

46. Longenecker, *Acts of the Apostles*, 476. In his *Cretica*, Epimenides called the Cretans "liars" since they took Zeus to be mortal, while Epimenides claimed him to be immortal. No works of Epimenides have survived. The *Cretica* quotation is given by Longenecker with a footnote: "The Syriac version of the quatrain comes to us from the Syr. Church father Isho'dad of Merv (probably based on the work of Theodore of Mopsuestia) which J. R. Harris translated back into Greek in *The Expositor*, 7 (1907)," 336.

47. NIV Study Bible footnote on Acts 17:28, 1683NTn

to reveal himself through himself. This happened in God's incarnation in Christ, when God became one of us. "Immanuel" is one of the many titles for Jesus that indicates his identity (Isa 7:14; Matt 1:22–23; Col 1:15; Heb 1:2; 1 Cor 8:6).[48] God not only had to reveal himself for humans to know him, but also make it possible for them to relate to him. This takes us to the search for intermediaries and how Jesus is the response to that search.

Searching for Intermediaries

Jesus came to mediate between humans and God (1 Tim 2:5). Relying on intermediaries to connect with a being beyond humans has been a prominent trend. This is evident both among the major religious communities and in the Greco-Roman world. Intermediaries like the Hindu *Ganesha*, the Taoist immortal *Lu-Ting-Pin*, and the Buddhist *Boddhi Sattvas* and *Dhiyana Buddhas*, have figured prominently among the religious communities.[49]

The Greeks introduced the concept of *Logos* to articulate connection with the divine. Heraclitus of Ephesus first introduced *Logos* in response to the question: "What renders unity and order to the world?" Logos literally means "word," but in the context of Greek philosophy it meant the thought behind the word, or what was in the mind prior to it becoming a word. By the time of Socrates, Plato, and Aristotle, Logos came to be taken as reason, both human and divine; it was a principle that transcended the world and yet resided in the human. Plato described it as a living entity. Aristotle developed logic as a science of rules of rationality based on Logos. Later, the Stoics proclaimed the precept of "follow nature" to lead people to a wholesome life. This precept was based on the view that the world is animated by the divine Logos. Stoics claimed that aligning with the Logos enabled one to align with nature. Greek philosophers came to see Logos as a divine rational principle, even sometimes as a living being. It served as an intermediary between the divine and humans.

Philo, an Alexandrian Jew (40 BCE—40 CE) and a contemporary of Jesus, belonged to a Greco-Jewish school originally founded around 150 BCE that attempted to align Judaism with Greek philosophy. As a Jew, Philo believed that God was one, transcendent and spirit. His very transcendence

---

48. Isaiah prophesied, "Therefore the Lord himself will give you a sign: The virgin will conceive and give birth to a son, and will call him Immanuel" (Isa 7:14). Matthew declares that this prophecy was fulfilled at the birth of Jesus: "All this took place to fulfill what the Lord had said through the prophet: 'The virgin will conceive and give birth to a son, and they will call him Immanuel' which means, 'God with us'" (Matt 1:22–23).

49. Kulathungam, *Quest*, 81–83, 128–30, 157. *Lu-Ting-Pin* is a divine being who incarnates; *Ganesha* is the god Shiva's son; Buddhist *Boddhi Satvas* are humans, while *Dhiyana Buddhas* are divine intermediaries helping people to be liberated.

made him unknowable. How could humans relate to him? Philo turned to the Logos. He proposed that there were several intermediaries, some angelic, between God and humans, and he called these "powers." The main one among them he called Logos. With its aid, humans could know and experience God. In the Greco-Roman world where God was unknowable, Philo's proposal provided the possibility for humans to know God. According to Philo, God created the world with the aid of the Logos. Philo proposed that the Logos was the highest among the intermediaries to relate humans with God and was involved in the creation of the world. Philo's proposal enabled the Greek world to understand Jesus as Logos (John 1:1–9), even though it could not handle the claim that he came in the flesh and was the one and only mediator between God and humans (1 John 1:2–3; John 1:10–18; 1 Tim 2:5).

Philosophy made a significant contribution in preparing the conceptual framework of the Greco-Roman world to comprehend, at least to some extent, Jesus' identity and role as intermediary. It also provided conceptual tools to articulate and help people understand the personhood of Jesus. For instance, Jesus as God the Son was a scandal and a stumbling block to monotheistic Jews. Greek Pythagorean mathematics enabled the articulation of God as one in three: one substance but three persons. In the Pythagorean number system, unlike in Arabic arithmetic, the numeral 3 is singular and taken to be the number 1 in perfect form.[50] During the early Christian period, Greek mathematics facilitated the formulation of the doctrine of trinity.[51] The terms "substance" and "person" came from the Greek philosophical vocabulary. They helped to present that Father, Son, and Holy Spirit, though distinct as "persons," could be one in "substance" as God.[52]

While Greece provided the conceptual tools, Rome gave the infrastructure that facilitated the spread of the gospel. Roman roads enabled Paul's extensive missionary journeys in Asia minor and Europe. The *Pax Romana* (Roman peace) provided a breathing space for persecuted Christians to live and spread the gospel.

During the silent years, the world was preoccupied with issues pertaining to the reasons Christ came, which helped prepare people to understand him and his advent.

---

50. Kulathungam, *Quest*, 25–37. This section of my previous book presents a more detailed explanation of Greek mathematics in New Testament times, the Pythagorean theory of numbers, and God as triune being through the Greek lens.

51. God as one in substance but three in persons was formulated at the Council of Nicaea, 325 CE.

52. Kulathungam, *Quest*, 29–31.

WHAT DOES THE CHRISTIAN NARRATIVE TELL US?

The Christian narrative revolves around the theme that the Messiah has already come in Jesus. In his letter to the Galatians, Paul points out: "But when the set time had fully come, God sent his Son, born of a woman, born under the law, to redeem those under the law, that we might receive adoption to sonship" (Gal 4:4–5).

It was God who sent Jesus, and he was sent "when the set time had fully come." The Greek word here is *pleroma*, which means "fullness," and Paul uses it in this sense (Col 2:9). This word is used about seventeen times in the New Testament and is a relative term, with its meaning being derived depending on the subject with which it is joined. Here it is joined with the word "time." Jesus being sent in the "fullness of time" would mean that time was fully ripe for him to come. As Ekstrand points out, "That little phrase 'when the fullness of time came,' gives significant application to these 400 years in a myriad of ways because of what God was doing—He was getting things ready for the most significant person and event in all human history . . . the coming of the Savior the Messiah; the Lord Jesus Christ into this world."[53] God, who sent Jesus to redeem the whole world, had to prepare the world to receive such a redeemer. This is what happened during the Intertestamental Period.

It is clear that Jesus came at the correct time, but was it a convenient time for him? It does not seem so! In fact, he came when the Greco-Roman world was at its most decadent and self-indulgent. Athens, once the intellectual hub of Greece, had turned into a city of multiple gods with diverse ways to reach them. The fusion of Greek and Roman cultures resulted in a confusing medley of world views, moralities, and rules of conduct. The dictum of the philosophers of the golden age, that knowledge frees one from the human predicament, was still prevalent, but several attractive alternatives had arisen. The Epicurean way, founded by Epicurus (341–270 BCE), proposed that pleasure was the supreme good. Though the Epicureans tried to stay clear of sensual pleasure, their proposal boiled down to, "eat, drink, and be merry, for tomorrow we die." Since they believed that life ended with death, they resolved to enjoy life while they could. The Stoic way, founded by Zeno of Citium (336–264 BCE), also believed that life ends at death. For Stoics, attaining a state of being perpetually untroubled would free one from the anxieties of life and postpone death. To achieve this, they advocated the precept "follow nature," which implied stringently following the laws of nature that were taken to be divine. Skepticism, founded by Pyrrho of Elis (360–275 BCE), initiated a trend that challenged the possibility of

---

53. Ekstrand, "Intertestamental Period and its Significance," para. 16.

objectivity in knowledge. Seeing contradictory views on truth, good, and right, Skeptics denied the possibility of any certitudes; only probabilities were possible. Eclecticism, whose principal proponent was Cicero (106–43 BCE), got its inspiration from Skepticism. Eclectics proposed that since one cannot claim that a particular stance—whether it be on moral conduct, religious doctrine, or views about the world—is absolutely true, one should not impose one's own stance on others but rather accommodate all.[54] Perhaps today's pluralism is a contemporary version of eclecticism.

Some of these salvific ways arose out of the world view that acknowledged nothing but the material world and that the human being decides human destiny. Jesus came into a multireligious, multicultural, materialistic, hedonistic, and egoistic world. Surely it was not a convenient time for Jesus but, in his wisdom, God sent his Son when the world needed him most.

THE LITERATURE OF THE SILENT YEARS

Intertestamental literature falls into canonical and noncanonical writings. The *Septuagint*, the Greek translation of the Hebrew Old Testament, is an important canonical work of this period. It is abbreviated as LXX, the Roman numeral for seventy, indicating that it was the work of seventy scholars from the third century BCE. It helped both Judaism and Christianity. The Bible in the Greek language helped those proficient in Greek to become familiar with Judaism. This helped in the spread of Judaism. Jesus himself quoted from the Septuagint. The Bible in Greek enabled new Christian converts to communicate their newfound faith to Greek-speaking people. Many converts to Christianity during the first century were Greek or spoke Greek (Acts 14:1, 17:1–4).[55]

The *Apocrypha*, *Pseudepigrapha*, and the Dead Sea Scrolls stand out as noncanonical works. They have been labelled as "outside writings," as they fall outside the divinely inspired Scripture. Nevertheless, they tell us much about the issues and concerns of the people of this period.

Apocrypha

Apocrypha was one of the "outside books," since it was not canonized and was therefore excluded from the Hebrew Bible, even though the Septuagint included it as an addendum.

Apocrypha was a set of about fifteen books. Thirteen of them, designated as Old Testament Apocrypha, dealt with Old Testament writings like

---

54. Thonnard, *Short History of Philosophy*, 152–65.
55. "Importance of the Septuagint."

Esther, Daniel, Jeremiah, and Ecclesiastes. There were also two books on the Maccabees (1 and 2), that cover the Maccabean revolt (167–143 BCE), discussed earlier in this chapter.

Whether canonized or not, the Apocrypha dealt with significant issues with which people of this era were grappling; these were issues that necessitated some connection with God. For instance, one of the Apocrypha's core themes was the problem of suffering. Daniel Harrington notes that, "Almost every one of the writings touches in some way on the mystery of suffering. How we can say that God is omnipotent and just, when innocent people are suffering? None of the books provides an answer to such questions."[56] In David Kraemer's book *Responses to Suffering in Classical Rabbinic Literature*,[57] he shows how the Apocrypha responds to the problem of suffering.

For the writers of the Apocrypha, suffering appeared to be a mystery. God did not and has not provided a theodicy of suffering in that he has not explained suffering. On the other hand, he has responded to it at times through immediate intervention, sometimes through what seems like delayed action, and sometimes through deafening silence. The Maccabee episode indicates how God did not give up on the Jews during the time of Syrian aggression. The Hanukkah miracle is a reminder of God's faithfulness. We may take what Jesus did on the cross as a response to the problem of suffering that vexed the writers of the Apocrypha.

Pseudepigrapha

The second set of noncanonical works, *pseudepigrapha* (200 BCE—200 CE), contains legendary histories, psalms, proverbs, and even some Christian additions. They affirmed belief in God's sovereignty amidst the challenges Jews were facing at that time. Scholars consider that these unknown writers were articulating a theology of hope amidst desperate conditions.[58] They seemed to be hoping for something to happen that would free them from their dispossessed plight. Was Jesus a disappointment or fulfillment of that hope?

Dead Sea Scrolls

Sometime between November 1946 and February 1947, a Bedouin shepherd named Muhammed edh-Dhib, his cousin Jum'a Muhammed, and another shepherd, Khali Musa, discovered seven scrolls in jars in a cave near what is known as the Qumran site. This discovery led to further discoveries of

56. Harrington, *Invitation to the Apocrypha*, 3.
57. Kraemer, *Responses to Suffering*.
58. Ekstrand, "Intertestamental Period."

scrolls that came to be called the Dead Sea Scrolls. They contain copies of the books of the Old Testament, commentaries on them, and sectarian works. There is controversy about whether the authors of these commentaries were Essenes of Qumran, as recorded by the historian Josephus. Some scholars have challenged the so-called "Qumran-Essene hypothesis," claiming that the authors living in Qumran were a splinter group from the Essenes. Tabor argues that the archaeological, historical, and textual evidence leaves little doubt that the scrolls were hidden away by a community of Essenes living at the desolate site of Qumran.[59] They are significant works of literature, regardless of who wrote them. They date from the mid-third century BCE to mid-first century CE. The commentaries on biblical texts show how the authors interpreted Scripture; for instance, how they thought the prophecies of Isaiah and Habakkuk would work out. Some scrolls provide insights into the life of the communities that lived near the Dead Sea, their rules of community life, and social and religious practice. *The Manual of Discipline*, for example, dealt with how one could fully participate in a community. The scrolls do not explicitly mention Jesus and yet they are relevant to him and his mission in two important ways. First, the scrolls contain copies of the Old Testament that speak about and anticipate the coming of the Messiah. The question is whether Jesus was that Messiah. To respond to this question, a scroll known as the Messianic Apocalypse (4Q521) is helpful. A list of miracles associated with the Messiah appears both in Luke 7:21–22 and in the Messianic Apocalypse. Talking to the disciples of John the Baptist in Luke 7, Jesus lists certain specific miracles like healing the sick, giving sight to the blind, and raising the dead as proof that he was the Messiah. The Messianic Apocalypse, written approximately 150 years before Luke's Gospel, states that the "Lord" who would come as Messiah would perform certain miracles. Interestingly, they are similar to what Jesus mentioned.[60] The source for both lists could be Isaiah 35 and 61. This resemblance between the lists of miracles that would accompany the Messiah, appearing both in the scroll and Luke's Gospel, provides some rationale to relate the Dead Sea Scrolls with the advent of Jesus as Messiah.

While the above-mentioned noncanonical writings do illuminate beliefs and practices of the Jewish community of that period, they also shed light in an indirect manner on Jesus and his mission. Jesus dealt with some of the issues that the writers of these works were grappling with and fulfilled some of their aspirations.

---

59. Tabor, "Who Wrote the Dead Sea Scrolls?"
60. VanderKam, "Dead Sea Scrolls."

WHAT DO THE SILENT YEARS TELL US?

Both the Jewish and Christian narratives highlight the significance of the paradigm shift that occurred during the silent years: that God was not silent but orchestrated history to carry out his plan. The beauty of it all was that he executed his plan without restricting human freedom. When Alexander the Great gloried over his success in creating the Greek Empire, he had the right to be proud, for it was he who accomplished this. His empire enabled the spread of both Judaism and Christianity, and so Alexander was very much in God's plan. Historical figures like Alexander and Pompey were not acting as robots manipulated by a mastermind, but were acting of their own free will and yet falling in line with God's sovereign plan. What was his plan?

From the Jewish perspective, God preserved his people amidst multiple challenges; the Jews had to survive to be the light to the nations, and eventually the Messiah had to come from them. After God spoke through the prophet Malachi, there was a long pause. At the time, his silence was deafening to the Jews. From a long-range perspective, God was orchestrating history to preserve the Jewish nation in order to send his Messiah, who would be a Jew.

The Christian perspective aligns with the Jewish in claiming that this period shows God's orchestration of history to preserve the Jewish nation for the advent of the Messiah. In the Christian story, the Messiah came in Jesus, at a time when the world was desperately in need of a savior. Historically, God seems to allow a desperate situation to develop before intervening. This pattern has recurred in Old Testament history, be it with Noah, Abraham, Moses, or Esther. The efforts of humans had to be frustrated before God would intervene. God simply allowed his people to exhaust their resources, and then he would manifest himself.[61] Jesus did not come during the golden age of Greek history, but waited until the Greco-Roman world was in a state of intellectual, moral, and spiritual decadence. The world was desperately searching, depending on multiple ways, multiple gods, and even worshipping an unknown god. This was precisely the correct time for God to send his Son as Messiah.

The silent years were not at all silent. They were a paradigmatic exhibition of God's relentless quest to relate with people, whether Jew or gentile, to orchestrate his redemptive plan.

---

61. Ekstrand, "Intertestamental Period."

5

The Salvific Revolution

My previous book, *The Quest*, looked at how major religious communities are striving to free themselves from the human predicament, and the role Christ plays in such a quest. They all attempt to provide a way of release from their predicament through self-effort with or without superhuman help. The human quest figures prominently in the salvific striving of these religious communities.

In the Judeo-Christian narrative, God's quest to relate with people stands out. It commenced in the Garden of Eden with Adam and Eve, who hid after they disobeyed God. He did not give up on them or forsake their descendants, who slipped into more and more sinful ways. At one time, God even regretted his own creation. Nevertheless, he rescued Noah from the flood and made a covenant with him. As we noted in chapter 3, God thwarted the effort of those who tried to reach heaven through building the Tower of Babel. During such folly, he called Abram and initiated a continuing covenantal relationship with him and the Jewish people.

In chapter 4, we saw that God's quest was not dormant during the Intertestamental Period, also referred to as the silent yars. God protected the Jewish nation when it was threatened by imperial powers. He preserved them because he mandated them to be a light for the nations and to birth the anticipated Messiah from among them. From the Christian perspective, that Messiah was Jesus and these years prepared the world to receive him. For both Jews and Christians, the silent years were very much in God's calendar.

God's quest to relate with people and redeem them from their problems—whether personal, communal, or national—has been characteristic of the Judeo-Christian narrative so far. With the advent of Christ, the Christian narrative deviates from the Jewish narrative in a significant manner. A new episode in the history of God's quest was orchestrated not through a teacher, prophet, priest, or king, but a Savior. Jesus, the Son of God, came not merely to protect and guide the chosen people, but to relate with and redeem all humans. Such an episode had no precedence in human history. From the Christian perspective, it was the apex of God's salvific quest, while in the Jewish world, as we will see in chapter 7, it was controversial.

Many scholars have identified the revolutionary nature of Jesus' life and mission. New Testament scholar N. T. Wright highlights the significance of Jesus' crucifixion as the "the Day the Revolution Began."[1] Pope John Paul II points out that God incarnate in Jesus highlights the centrality of salvation in the history of humanity.[2]

Such a revolution was centered on Jesus. Where he came from, the makeup of his personhood, his extraordinary birth, how he showed who he was, how he articulated his teachings, how he miraculously met the needs of the sick, raised the dead, died on the cross, and rose again were all geared to his revolutionary salvific mission. Characterizing his venture as revolutionary, however, makes it sound political. Was Jesus a political rebel? He is sometimes associated with the first-century Jewish political movement led by Zealots. They sought to overthrow the Roman government, resorting sometimes to violent tactics.[3] One of Jesus' disciples was named Simon the Zealot,[4] and some scholars associate Judas Iscariot with the Zealot movement. Can we brand Jesus as a Zealot rebel? The kingdom of God that he initiated may sound political, but it was not intended to replace the Roman Empire. His mission was not targeted to Jewish religious leaders or the Roman imperial powers. He revolted against a kingdom that was of an entirely different order. Paul reminded the followers of Jesus that: "our struggle is not against flesh and blood, but against the rulers, against the authorities, against the powers of this dark world and against the spiritual forces of evil in the heavenly realms" (Eph 6:12). Popular theologian and author Eugene Peterson states, "The gospel of Jesus Christ is more political than anyone

---

1. Wright, *Day the Revolution Began*.
2. John Paul II, *Crossing the Threshold of Hope*.
3. Zealots led the Jewish revolt that began in 66 CE. When the Romans overtook the rebels in 70 CE, a remnant of the Zealots took refuge in the fortress of Masada.
4. Matthew 10:4; Mark 3:18; Luke 6:15; Acts 1:13. The description of Simon as a Zealot may either be due to his religious zeal or a reference to his membership in the zealot party. See NIV Study Bible footnote on Matthew 10:4, 1452NTn.

imagines, but in a way that no one guesses."[5] Jesus was revolutionary, but not in the typical political sense.

Such a Jesus-centered revolution brought about a paradigmatic shift in the salvific history of humanity. Every facet of his life and ministry, from his birth until his death and resurrection, highlights the uniqueness of his personality and the revolutionary character of his accomplishments. The scope of his salvific mission went beyond traditional borders and how sinners could appropriate what he offered was also extraordinary. Even today, people find many facets of his life and mission unprecedented and difficult to accommodate, and react with strong emotions. Let us look at some examples that cause an exclamatory response.

SAVIOR'S HOME ADDRESS!

The Savior came from above. God, who had in the past revealed his will, directives, and warnings through prophets, priests, kings, and miraculous interventions, and related with his people through covenants, now revealed himself as God the Son. The main purpose of such a revelation was to redeem his creation: both humanity and the universe (John 3:16). God orchestrated his quest to save humanity in and through Jesus, his only begotten Son. He was God incarnate in human flesh. The redemption that Jesus orchestrated was so unique because it was centered on who he really was.

There is an interesting passage in Deuteronomy where Moses states, "The Lord your God will raise up for you a prophet like me from among you, from your fellow Israelites. You must listen to him" (Deut 18:15). The Lord further confirms to Moses, "I will raise up for them a prophet like you from among their fellow Israelites, and I will put my words in his mouth. He will tell them everything I command him" (Deut 18:18). Does this future prophet refer to Jesus? Citing certain passages in the Quran, like Surah 7:157, some claim that the future prophet refers to Muhammad. But the term, "fellow Israelites" clearly indicates that this prophet would have to be a Jew. In addition, the prophetic line came from Isaac, not Ishmael (Gen 17:21, 21:12).

We find that many considered Jesus to be a prophet (Matt 21:11; Luke 7:16, 24:19; John 4:19, 6:14, 7:40, 9:17). Stephen, just before being stoned to death (Acts 7:37), identified Jesus as the prophet Moses had prophesied about. When the crippled beggar was miraculously healed through Peter and John's ministry near the temple, people wondered how this had happened. Peter declared to them that they need not be surprised; it was Jesus' name and faith that comes through him that had healed the man (Acts

---

5. Peterson, *Reversed Thunder*, 117.

3:16). Then Peter told the puzzled crowd that Jesus was the one foretold by the prophets. Peter concludes by pointing out that Jesus was the one about whom Moses had said, "The Lord your God will raise up for you a prophet like me from among your own people; you must listen to everything he tells you" (Acts 3:22). Peter was trying to drive home to the crowd that it was listening to that prophet, Jesus, that raised the crippled beggar; it was listening that expressed itself through faith in Jesus' name. Peter's declaration not only indicates that he saw Jesus as the prophet spoken of by Moses, but also highlights how Jesus was different than Moses. No one prays in Moses' name. In fact, it would be blasphemous to pray this way in the Jewish context. But praying in Jesus' name brings about miracles!

Claiming that Jesus was the prophet foretold by Moses in Deuteronomy 18:15, Pope Benedict XVI notices that this passage "contains a promise that is completely different from the messianic hope expressed in other books of the Old Testament, yet it is of decisive importance for understanding the figure of Jesus."[6] The pope points out that Moses was a unique prophet and there has been no other prophet like him, because he knew God intimately (Deut 34:10). Nevertheless, he could not see God's face. He experienced only God's glory (Exod 33:20). On the other hand, only Jesus could see God and have the closest relationship with him, since Jesus was not only God's friend but also his son. As the pope points out, "What was true of Moses only in fragmentary form has now been fully realized in the person of Jesus. He lives before the face of God, not just as a friend but as a Son, he lives in the most intimate unity with the Father."[7] Jesus said that he did nothing on his own, but spoke what his Father taught him (John 8:28, 12:49). On several occasions, he called God his Father. Sometimes he went alone to pray, and such sessions were intimate conversations with his father, rather than prayer request sessions. God called Jesus his Son with whom he was well pleased (Matt 3:17). Jesus' filial relationship to God the Father provides the grounds to consider that it was he who fulfilled the promise given in Deuteronomy. Jesus, though like Moses, was much more than him.

It is Jesus as God the Son who orchestrated the salvific revolution. There have been several prophets, gurus, and leaders who have guided people in their strivings to obey God and fellowship with him. But for God, living as a human among people, to free them from their predicament was unprecedented. It was redemption that was wrought by *Emmanuel*, God with us. The word Emmanuel is a Greek rendering of two Hebrew words, *Imanu*, meaning "with us," and *El*, meaning "God," and is found three times in the

6. Benedict XVI, *Jesus of Nazareth*, 1.
7. Benedict XVI, *Jesus of Nazareth*, 6.

Bible (Isa 7:14, 8:8; Matt 1:23). Isaiah is the first prophet who talks about Emmanuel. "Therefore the Lord himself will give you a sign: The virgin will conceive and give birth to a son, and will call him Immanuel" (Isa 7:14). But who is this Emmanuel? Isaiah describes the characteristics of this person (Isa 8:10) but does not identify him. He is identified in the New Testament. Matthew, referring to Jesus and his birth, states, "All this took place to fulfill what the Lord had said through the prophet: 'The virgin will conceive and give birth to a son, and they will call him Immanuel,' (which means, "God With Us")" (Matt 1:22–23). This renders uniqueness to the salvific revolution wrought through Jesus. Though he was born and lived as a Jew, he was God. His home address was and still is heaven.

SAVIOR'S EXTRAORDINARY BIRTH!

The birth of Jesus is recorded in the gospels of Matthew and Luke (Matt 1:18–24; Luke 1:26–38) and is stated in the Apostles' Creed. This creed, though not written by the apostles, is the oldest creed of the church and has been the basis for subsequent creeds. Its earliest version, dated 140 CE, states that Jesus "was conceived by the Holy Spirit, Born of the Virgin Mary."[8] Such a pronouncement indicates that the belief that Jesus was born of a virgin was prevalent from early times and not a later development. Such a birth was miraculous as well as controversial. Although the belief that Jesus was born of a virgin has been acknowledged through the centuries, it is controversial because it is unusual. The virgin birth has been challenged on both theological and scientific grounds.

Let us first look at the theological reasons questioning the legitimacy of the event. Since most of the New Testament writings do not mention this event, it is surmised that the virgin birth did not occur. Does the historicity of an event depend on the number of times it is mentioned in Scripture? Adopting a historical-critical method of biblical exegesis, one could dismiss an event as theological opinion rather than historical happening. As we already have discussed in chapter 1, though the Bible is a historical narrative, its legitimacy does not depend only on empirical historical methods of verification. Some historical events in the biblical narrative, like the creation episode, are not amenable to historical assessment. The virgin birth episode is also an event that cannot be assessed on empirical grounds. Just because virgin births have not occurred in the past, does that mean that it cannot happen? Some question the translation of the term "virgin." They claim that virgin may be translated as "young woman." Here we must consider Joseph's reaction to the news that Mary was pregnant (Matt 1:18–19). Joseph did

---

8. Orr, "Entry for 'Apostles' Creed,'" para. 4.

not want Mary to be put to shame and thought of divorcing her. The Greek word *deigmatizo*, which literally means to expose or make a show of, is usually translated as "shame" or "disgrace." Why was Joseph so disturbed? Did he suspect Mary of being unfaithful to him? In that culture, giving birth to a child before marriage was a serious offense, not only against God, but also morally demeaning. Did Joseph realize that the child in Mary's womb was conceived by the Holy Spirit and was therefore overwhelmed with the holiness of the situation and the responsibility of being a stepfather to God's child?[9] Matthew's Gospel account presents Joseph as a just man. Whatever the reason, he was disturbed by the uniqueness of the birth of Jesus. The fact that the child was conceived through the Holy Spirit's intervention is beyond empirical assessment and it is this that makes the birth so rare and naturally controversial.

Some tend to dismiss the event as a myth since it is similar to pagan mythologies prevalent in the Greco-Roman world of that time. One cannot conclude that the biblical account was derived from pagan myths merely on the grounds of similarity. Most of the pagan stories referring to women having unnatural births do not explain why such births occur. They are taken to be mysterious! The gospel story does not merely stop with pointing out that Mary conceived in an unusual manner, but goes on to state that child was conceived by the Holy Spirit. This makes Jesus' birth unique, as this detail is not found in the pagan stories.

Virgin birth has also been challenged on scientific grounds. Based on biological reasons, virgin birth is dismissed as impossible. As we have already noted, the legitimacy of a historical event depends on whether there is at least some evidence that it occurred. Such evidence need not be always empirical.[10] J. Edward Barrett wrote about this topic in a *Bible Review* article, and the avalanche of responses to his presentation, both positive and negative, indicates how controversial Jesus' birth is.[11] It is controversial mainly because it is so unusual and therefore unbelievable on empirical and biological grounds. This is where faith clicks in. Certain events in the biblical narrative need to be accommodated on the grounds of faith. As we have already noted in chapter 1, the biblical narrative goes beyond historical traditional legitimacy. The virgin birth event is such an event, and one that

---

9. Aquinas, *Super Evangelium*, commentary on Matthew 1:16–21. St. Thomas Aquinas advocated for this view, which later came to be known as the "Pious Theory." Joseph had no suspicion of adultery for he knew Mary's purity and was aware that the virgin would conceive (Isa 7:14, 11:1). Did Joseph, being a just man, consider himself unworthy of such a role?

10. Kulathungam, "Scientific Understanding and Christian Faith."

11. Barrett, "Can Scholars Take the Virgin Birth Seriously?"

needs to be accommodated on the grounds of faith. The Apostles' Creed is a statement of faith and not a scientific proposal.

The virgin birth is an integral part of the biblical salvific narrative. It highlights that the Savior came from above and was not a product of human reproduction. As Karl Barth points out, the virgin birth is a "sign which accompanies and indicates the mystery of the incarnation of the son, marking it off as a mystery from all other beginnings of other human existence."[12] One would expect that a life that commenced so sensationally would bloom into publicity right away. But that did not happen!

SAVIOR'S SECRETIVE STRATEGY!

In our age so prone to showmanship, one would expect God's enactment of his salvific plan to take shape as a much-advertised pomp-and-glory show. Instead, the way the Savior revealed his true identity was clouded with secrecy. This is evident in how his salvific plan was initially conceived and how he carried out his plan. The plan of redemption was a proactive strategy conceived in utter secrecy before time began (Titus 1:2) and before the world's foundations were established (Eph 1:4). The Old Testament records several prophetic anticipations of the Messiah, but whoever expected the Messiah to be born as a carpenter's son in a lowly manger? Neither the Jewish clergy in Jerusalem nor the imperial headquarters in Rome were informed of Jesus' birth. A group of humble shepherds and pagan astronomers from the distant East received the news first. During that time, shepherds belonged to the lowest ranks of Jewish society and their testimony was not acceptable in a court of law. The Savior's birth was not broadcast from the temple in Jerusalem by the high priest, but by these shepherds on the outskirts of Bethlehem. The report of the wise men was disturbing to Herod, who wanted them to go and see the newborn "king of the Jews" and report to him secretly (Matt 2:7). They released the news neither to Herod nor to the Jewish clergy, but to the pagan world.

Secrecy also clouded over Jesus' identity. Mark's Gospel commences this way: "The beginning of the good news about Jesus the Messiah, the Son of God" (Mark 1:1). Such a declaration contains three significant facets of his identity. He was Jesus, meaning "Savior," the anticipated "Messiah," and the "Son of God." It is ironic that while Mark wants his readers to know that Jesus the Messiah was the Son of God, Jesus silenced many who declared who he really was. The demons who possessed a man in the synagogue in Capernaum confessed that they knew who Jesus really was, the Son of God. Jesus ordered the demons to keep quiet and then drove them out of the

---

12. Barth, *Church Dogmatics*, 1:207.

man (Mark 1:24–25). When Jesus asked his disciples who people said that he was, Peter answered, "You are the Messiah, the Son of the living God" (Matt 16:16). The term "Christ" means the anointed one, which in the Jewish context meant "Messiah." Jesus warned Peter and the disciples not to tell anyone his identity (Matt 16:20). Even when the devil tempted Jesus to prove himself as the Son of God, he did not (Luke 4:1–13). When mockers passing by the cross cried out, "Come down from the cross, if you are the Son of God," Jesus did not (Luke 27:40). He told the woman at the well that he was the Christ, but she was a Samaritan (John 4:25–26).

Jesus called himself "son of man" on many occasions. There has been much discussion in theological circles on the meaning and significance of the designation "son of man." Without deviating into such a controversy, let me suggest that perhaps Jesus wanted people to realize that even though he was extraordinary in many ways, he was really one of them. This may be part of his secretive strategy. The Roman centurion's declaration, when Jesus was dying on the cross, is a powerful vindication of Jesus' identity. Jesus' identity was publicly declared at the cross, when the Roman centurion declared, "Surely this man was the Son of God" (Mark 15:39)! The centurion's confession brings out Jesus' real identity; the Savior who was hanging on the cross for the sins of humanity was really God the Son! Let us remember that this declaration was made by a gentile military officer. The Jewish religious world would not have taken this seriously. Nevertheless, it was such a Savior who orchestrated the salvific revolution. This is what made the revolution so controversial both in the Jewish and gentile worlds of the time, and why it continues to be so even now. How is Jesus, the carpenter's son, the Savior and also God incarnate? This takes us to the unique blend in his personality.

SAVIOR'S DOUBLE PERSONALITY!

Jesus as the Son of God was unprecedented as well as unacceptable both in the Jewish and gentile worlds. In the Jewish context, as God incarnate, Jesus tampered with the very character of God: his spiritual make-up, his holiness, his transcendence, and his very identity. How can God, who is Spirit (John 4:24), become Immanuel, living with humans and becoming one with them? How could the holy God, who showed his presence only in the temple's holy of holies, mingle with sinful humans and even dine with them (Mark 3:13–17; Matt 9:10–17)? How could the transcendent God take up residence on earth? Acknowledging Jesus as the Son of God destroyed God's very identity: that he is one and there is no one beside him (Isa 45:5).[13]

---

13. There are approximately forty-five Bible passages stating that God is one.

The gentile world has also been searching for a way out of the predicament of human existence. Since the axial age, many philosophers, spiritual gurus, and religious leaders have attempted to articulate a way of redemption. As already noted, during the silent years such a quest became preoccupied with the search for a being beyond the human realm: the search for a "god." This god was different from the God who sent his only Son to free humanity. The Greek god, presented by philosophers like Plato and Aristotle, was one who brought about order to a chaotic world. This impersonal god had no intention to relate with humans, and did not seek to redeem people in bondage. The only option was for humans to find ways and means of relating to such a being. They resorted to intermediaries to connect with the divine. *Logos* figured as the most prominent intermediary—close to the divine, but not a god. On the other hand, John presents Jesus as Logos, who was there from the beginning and was not only with God but was God (John 1:1). The Greek Logos was a means for humans to relate with the divine being. Such a Logos was very much part of the human salvific quest. Jesus, as God's Son, was the Logos who came to relate with humanity. He was an integral part of God's personhood and indispensable in God's quest to save humanity.

Jesus as Logos was not a mere mental construct but a human in the fullest sense of the term. He was not a theophany having the appearance of a human but not a real human. He was truly human both in mind and body. Paul states, "in Christ all the fullness of the Deity lives in bodily form" (Col 2:9). He grew up to manhood (Luke 2:52). He was hungry and thirsty, slept and wept, was flogged and wounded at the cross, and died. When he rose again, he could say of his resurrected body, "a ghost does not have flesh and bones, as you see I have" (Luke 24:39). Martin Luther colorfully put it this way in a sermon, "Jesus did not flutter about like a butterfly but he dwelt among men. He had eyes, ears, mouth, nose, chest, stomach, hands, and feet, just as you and I do."[14]

Such a depiction of Jesus as Logos was unprecedented and unacceptable in the Greek world. The Greek Logos was purely mental construct or idealized reason. Such a depiction functioned within a two-tier system: the mental and the material. The material was viewed as inferior to the mental and identified as the root cause for the chaos in the natural world. The human predicament was traced to the overpowering of the mental by the physical, the body controlling the mind. When the mind is paralyzed by the fleshly desires of the body, ignorance occurs. Socrates's famous dictum

---

14. Martin Luther, as cited by Hardy and Richardson, *Christology of the Later Fathers*, 230–32.

that "knowledge is virtue" implied ignorance is vice. This is the cause of the human predicament. The cure for it is knowledge that is articulated by the mind. In this context, the physical was downgraded as being the cause for the world's chaos and the bondage in humans. Jesus, the Son of God, becoming a human being with both body and mind would have been distasteful to the Greek mindset. How can the Logos, taken to be pure reason and fully good, become evil by becoming physical? A world that downgraded the physical just could not accommodate Jesus as the legitimate intermediary, as the Logos. Such a world view impacted later developments of the critique of Jesus' personhood. The Doetists, for example, were a group led by Cerinthius, Ebion, Marcion, and Valentinius, who believed that the divine could never mingle with matter that is evil. They claimed that Jesus, as the Son of God, could not be born as a human, suffer, or die.[15] The underlying question is whether Jesus as God the Son could be totally human and yet able to save humanity. This dual personality was unprecedented both in the Jewish and Greek worlds of that time.

Out of the several roles Jesus played during his lifetime, let us examine two main roles: his role as teacher and as Messiah. As both teacher and as Messiah, he showed that he came from above and that his mission was salvific

SAVIOR'S UNCONVENTIONAL TEACHING!

Titles given to Jesus ranged from "Prince of Peace" to "Emmanuel," but his disciples and others who followed him called him rabbi. The word *rabbi* in Aramaic means "master." During the time of Jesus, when Rabbinic Judaism was not yet organized, rabbi referred to a teacher or master. After the first century, rabbi came to mean someone who had received *smikhut* (similar to ordination) and was authorized to decide questions of Jewish law.[16] When Jesus was called rabbi, he was referred to as a teacher and not one who had received *smikhut*. Even as a teacher, he was unconventional and this made him controversial. His unconventionality as a teacher lay in the way he taught and what he tried to convey through his teaching.

As a Jew, many of Jesus' teachings were based on the Torah. He made it a point to emphasize that he came not to abolish the law and the prophets but to fulfill them, and urged his student disciples to obey the law as given in the Torah (Matt 5:17–19). His manner of teaching from the Torah was unconventional. For instance, when Jesus used the parable of the wise and foolish builders to emphasize the importance of listening to his advice,

15. MacLeod, *Person of Christ*, 157.
16. Gruber, "Who is a 'Rabbi?'"

people were amazed that he taught as one who had an authority of his own, unlike their teachers of law (Matt 7:24-29). When he declared that not even the smallest letter of the law as given in the Torah would ever pass away (Matt 5:18), he also claimed that heaven and earth would pass away but his words would never pass away (Matt 24:35). Six times in the Sermon on the Mount, Jesus followed a sequence that exhibited an antithesis between what the Torah stated and his interpretation of it. He first states, "You have heard it was said . . ." and he follows it up with a quote from the Torah. Then he declares, "But I tell you . . ." and this is followed with his interpretation of the Torah passage. For scribes, Pharisees, and Sadducees, authority was founded on the Torah. To the Jews, it seemed that Jesus was placing his authority over that of Torah. By teaching in his own authority, Jesus was not a conventional Jewish teacher. How could a teacher dare to speak with the authority of God or to stand on the same level as God? Either he was a teacher who had missed his vocation, was utterly deluded, or was an unprecedented teacher with divine authority. This, as we shall see in chapter 7, was not only unprecedented but also controversial, especially in the Jewish context.

The way Jesus quoted from the Scripture and appropriated it was very different from the way Jewish teachers handled Scripture. One day, Jesus unrolled the scroll and while reading it (Luke 4:14-21) quoted from Isaiah 61:1-2: "The Spirit of the Lord is upon me, because he has anointed me to bring good news to the poor. He has sent me to proclaim release to the captives and recovery of sight to the blind to let the oppressed go free, to proclaim the year of the Lord's favor." Instead of explaining the passage, as rabbis typically would have done, Jesus sat down and declared, "Today this Scripture has been fulfilled in your hearing" (Luke 4:20). The Jews naturally would have viewed Jesus as a rabbi who had crossed the boundaries. How could he claim that he was the anointed one?

There was a spiritual overtone in Jesus' interpretation of the law as given in the Torah. As Pope Benedict claims, in spiritualizing the law, Jesus makes it the path to life for all; he universalizes the scope of the law.[17] In explaining the beatitudes, a conventional Jewish teacher would have highlighted how they applied to the Jewish community, but Jesus presented them as applying to both Jew and gentile. For instance, he pointed out that even when one is angry with one's brother, it amounts to breaking the law against murder. When referring to the law against committing adultery, he points out that even looking at a woman lustfully amounts to adultery (Matt 5:6-30). In giving such a spiritual overtone, he universalizes the scope of the laws given in the Torah. Such laws now become applicable to all, not

---

17. Benedict XVI, *Jesus of Nazareth*, 100-1.

just the Jews. We need to note that the law as interpreted by Jesus cannot be kept without God's help, whether one is Jew or gentile. In the Sermon on the Mount, Jesus addresses the Jews as the first bearers of God's promise. He also wanted them to realize that they belonged to a new family of God, drawn from both Jews and the gentiles,[18] from all those who experienced God's quest through his Son to seek and save all humans. In universalizing the scope of the Torah's laws, Jesus exhibited the unconventionality of his teaching.

A core message that Jesus conveyed through his parables and miracles highlighted him as Savior and emphasized the uniqueness of the redemption he offered.

Jesus was an expert in teaching through parables. Many listened to his parables but could not comprehend what he was trying to say. Some were too blinded by prejudice or too lazy to think. Jesus told his disciples that while he taught them in secret about the kingdom of God, he used parables to teach others (Mark 4:10–12). He was comparing his audience to that of Isaiah, who were "ever hearing, but never understanding . . . ever seeing, but never perceiving" (Isa 6:9–10). One may wonder why Jesus used parables to teach such an uncomprehending and stubborn audience. Would it not confuse them more? Interestingly, his use of parables was an effective way to communicate, though very unconventional. A parable tries to convey a point or two indirectly. The interpretation is left to the listeners. Jesus used everyday events and characters in his parables. They often had an unexpected twist or surprising ending that caught the listeners' attention. He wanted his dull audience to wake up and catch the point of the story. Here we see a master teacher handling a disengaged class using an unconventional but effective way to communicate his message.

His parables covered several topics like the kingdom of God, kingdom of heaven, God's love and mercy, Christian responsibility to care for those in need, stewardship, and persistence in prayer. One recurrent theme was God's salvific quest as orchestrated through the Savior. Some parables, like the parable of the lost sheep, the lost coin, and the prodigal son, highlighted the Savior's quest to go out of his way to save those who were lost. Some parables showed how people received what the Savior offered. An example is the parable of the two sons, only recorded by Matthew (21:28–31). Once a father asked his two sons to go out and work in his vineyard. The first refused to work but later changed his mind and worked. The other son immediately said that he would work but did not go. Jesus asked those who were listening, "Which of the two sons did what his father wanted?" They got the point

18. Benedict XVI, *Jesus of Nazareth*.

of the parable! Jesus made it to clear to them that sinners, like tax collectors and prostitutes, would enter the kingdom of God ahead of some others. The former group changed their mind while the latter group, depending on their bias, prejudice, or religiosity, refused the offer. Jesus, the master teacher, got his point across through effective use of an unconventional tool.

One may wonder why Jesus' ministry of miracles was an integral part of his teaching. Jesus performed many miracles, but none of them was for showmanship or cheap advertisement. His miracles were definitive enactments that exhibited what was unique about him as Savior and the scope of the redemption that he offered. It is significant that he performed some miracles citing Isaiah 35:3–5, which referred to the anticipated Savior. John the Baptist once sent his disciples to Jesus, asking him whether he was the one who was to come or whether they should expect another. Jesus assured them that he was the one by citing Isaiah 35:5–6: "Then will the eyes of the blind be opened and the ears of the deaf unstopped. Then will the lame leap like a deer, and the mute tongue shout for joy" (Matt 11:3–5). His citation from Isaiah was meant to show that the miracles he did were not only to help those in need, but also to indicate that he was the expected Savior. Some of his miracles indicate that he was in control of the worlds of nature, spirits, and humans. The miracles of walking on water or calming a storm indicate Jesus could suspend the laws of nature. When healing a paralyzed man, Jesus forgave his sins as well. This shocked the teachers of the law who watched the miracle. The Bible records that they were "thinking to themselves, 'Why does this fellow talk like that? He's blaspheming! Who can forgive sins but God alone'" (Mark 2:7)? Jesus knew their thoughts and told them clearly that he had authority to forgive sins (Mark 2:10). The redemption that he brought about covered all facets of the human being: the physical, the mental, and the spiritual. He not only healed the incurable and gave sight to the blind, but also freed the demon possessed, and even raised the dead. Jesus raised three people from the dead: the daughter of Jairus, the synagogue official (Mark 5:22–24, 35–43); the son of the widow of Nain (Luke 7:11–17); and his friend Lazarus, on the fourth day after his death (John 11:1–44). Seeing such miracles, many believed in Jesus but some plotted to kill him. Jesus' own resurrection from death, which we will examine later in the chapter, was the greatest miracle. It showed who was really in control of life and death! Jesus' ministry through miracles was an effective means by which he conveyed the uniqueness of his role as Savior and the redemption he offered. Moreover, some of his parables and miracles were centered on conveying to the world of his time the nature and scope of the kingdom of God or kingdom of heaven. This takes us to his role as the anticipated Messiah.

SAVIOR'S UNPRECEDENTED MESSIANIC ROLE!

Though the term *messiah* is not explicitly used in the Old Testament, eventually certain concepts and practices became associated with the role of messiah in the Jewish tradition. In this tradition, a messiah is not just a person blessed by God. The Hebrew word for messiah is *Mashiach*, which means "the anointed one" (Dan 4:6). When someone was anointed with oil (Exod 29:7; 1 Kgs 1:39; 2 Kgs 9:3), he or she was publicly acknowledged as being called by God for a specific job. Since kings and high priests were anointed with oil and called by God to do a specific job, they could be referred to as an anointed one, or a messiah. One of the core themes of prophecy highlighted in the Old Testament is the promise of a future age characterized by universal peace under God's sovereign rule.[19] These prophecies speak about a descendent of King David who will rule Israel during this age.[20] To distinguish this messiah from the previous ones, Jews call him *HaMashiach* (literally "the Messiah"). Since no one so far has perfectly fulfilled the portrayal of this Messiah, the orthodox sector of the Jewish world anticipates the coming of such a person.

The word "Christ" is a derivation of the Greek word *Khristos*, which means "anointed." Christ was originally a title, but later became identified with Jesus. Naming him Christ implied that he was the anointed one, the Messiah. As we have already noted, there was a cloud of secrecy over Jesus acclaiming himself as Messiah. It was not until the trial before his death, when the high priest questioned him: "Are you the Christ, the Son of the Blessed One?" that Jesus responded, "I am" (Mark 14:61–62). Other than Jesus' disciples, most Jews did not call Jesus the Christ. At first, even his disciples did not understand Jesus' messianic role.

Based on certain biblical prophecies, Jews viewed the Messiah as a God-anointed person called to establish an age of peace under Jewish leadership. But Jesus' messiahship went counter to such a view. He was not just a human being, but God the Son, and his mandate was not merely to free the Jewish nation, but to redeem all humanity from the bondage of sin. Both his divine identity and the universal scope of his salvific mission rendered his messianic role unique as well as controversial. The disciples expected that he would free Israel from bondage and establish an age of peace. His untimely death was a dead end to their anticipation. They felt so let down that when the woman reported to them that Jesus had risen and was not in

---

19. Isaiah 2:1–4, 32:15–18, 60:15–18; Zephaniah 3:9; Hosea 2:20–22; Amos 9:13–15; Micah 4:1–4; Zechariah 8:23, 14:9; Jeremiah 31:33–34.

20. Isaiah 11:1–9; Jeremiah 23:5–6, 30:7–10, 33:14–16; Ezekiel 34:11–31, 37:21–28; Hosea 3:4–5.

the tomb, they were very skeptical. When the risen Jesus met two men on the road to Emmaus, and asked them what they were concerned about, they told him their tale of woe. They had hoped that Jesus was the one who was going to redeem Israel. Disappointed with Jesus, Peter and some disciples returned to their former jobs as fishermen. The disciples, as well as the Jews of that time, shared the Jewish notion of the Messiah that was in vogue and were therefore frustrated when Jesus died before accomplishing his messianic mission. We find that only after the disciples were sure that Jesus had risen from the dead did they and other believers acknowledge Jesus as the Christ, the Messiah. They accepted him not as a mere God-anointed human being, but God the Son incarnated to save not only the Jews but also the gentiles through his death and resurrection. This is best seen when the followers of Jesus, mostly gentiles, were called Christians. This nomenclature indicates that these new believers accepted Jesus as Christ, as God's Son who was anointed to redeem them. This depiction of Jesus as the Messiah was controversial among the Jews. We will have occasion to consider the Jewish reaction to Jesus' messianic role in chapter 7. If Jesus is not only human but also divine, how can God die? This brings us to his death.

SAVIOR'S SHOCKING DEATH!

The ways of redemption in the Jewish and Greco-Roman worlds were woven around saviors like messiahs, prophets, philosophers, religious gurus, and revolutionary political figures. These saviors enthusiastically worked, convinced that they had a significant mission. They lived to propagate their way of redemption. Some even died for their convictions. For instance, the death of Socrates was well known at that time. He died for his conviction: that humans could be freed from the bondage of ignorance through knowledge. He was accused of corrupting the youth of his time through his salvific doctrine. The death of these saviors, however, was not shocking, for they were all humans.

Jesus came to die! His whole life and ministry targeted death. As John Stott puts it, "Although Jesus was brought to his death by human sins, he did not die as a martyr. On the contrary, he went to the cross voluntarily, even deliberately. From the beginning of his public ministry he consecrated himself to this destiny."[21] Once, when Jesus told his disciples that he must go to Jerusalem, suffer many things, and eventually die, Peter tried to correct him by pointing out that he would never die. Jesus turned to Peter and rebuked him in a rather harsh manner: "Get behind me, Satan! You are a stumbling block to me; you do not have in mind the concerns of God, but

21. Stott, *Cross of Christ*, 64.

merely human concerns" (Matt 16:20–23). Jesus did not want anyone, not even his disciples, to be a stumbling block to his destined end: death.

Jesus' mode of salvation was very different from that of the other saviors in that his way of redeeming humanity was centered on his death. Socrates, for example, was honored for his heroic death but it did not have any impact on his salvific dogma. Even if Jesus had lived an illustrious life, performed spectacular miracles, conveyed his dogmas through effective teaching, and was most loving and compassionate, but did not die as he did, his way of salvation would have been neither effective nor unique. Jesus' death was the indispensable core of his way of salvation. What is it about his death that made it so vital?

The human predicament caused by sin needed God's intervention. Here we see how serious the sickness of sin is. No human doctor could cure it, which is why God sent his only Son. But why should he die to redeem humanity? Jesus, being divine, could have easily redeemed humanity by destroying the cause of the human predicament, by ordering sin out of humanity. But instead, he adopted a strategy that was most difficult, even impossible: he chose to die.

Can God the Son die? This was the point of controversy. Death demeans the very nature of God, who is eternal. The God of the Jews is eternal. The medieval philosopher and Torah scholar Maimonides highlights that God is eternal in his Fourth Principle of Faith.[22] John depicts Jesus as the Logos who was there with God and was God from the very beginning (John 1:1–2). He was before all things (Col 1:17). These passages, and many others, indicate that Jesus was eternal. How then could he die? To claim that he was eternal and that he died is not only contradictory, but also degrades God's eternal nature. For it is only humans that die, not God!

"For the wages of sin is death" (Rom 6:23). Death caused by sin is not merely physical destruction but eternal separation from God, who is holy and sinless. For Jesus, the Son of God, to be associated with sin mars the holiness of God. The Bible puts it thus: "God made him who had no sin to be sin for us, so that in him we might become the righteousness of God" (2 Cor 5:21). The phrase "became sin" could also mean "became sin offering" (Rom 3:25, 4:25). Whether he became sin in a literal sense or acted as a sin offering, carrying the sin of all humans, to associate sin with the sinless is blasphemous. For humans to live with sin is natural and sometimes even comfortable and enjoyable, but for the sinless Son of God to carry the burden of sin was agonizing to say the least. This explains why he was in such agony in the garden of Gethsemane. It is with this burden that he went

---

22. Kaplan, *Maimonides' Principles*, 12.

to the cross. It was not the weight of the cross, but rather the burden of sin that made him so exhausted and depleted in his journey to the cross. This is the paradox of the Christian conviction; the sinless Son of God had to die carrying the sin of humans in order to redeem them.

Not only did Jesus die, but he died on a cross. The cross today has become a popular piece of jewelry, a symbolic stamp on Christian literature, and a prominent feature in the architecture of churches and Christian buildings. It is admired in paintings and sculpture, adorns the attire of popes and priests, and plays a melodramatic role in passion plays. During Jesus' time, the cross was not given any place of honor. The cross was reserved for heinous criminals and to be put to death on a cross was a curse. The Bible states, "Christ redeemed us from the curse of the law by becoming a curse for us, for it is written: 'Cursed is everyone who is hung on a pole (tree)'" (Gal 3:13; Deut 21:23). As we shall see in chapter 7, a person being crucified was detested and even mocked in Jesus' time.

Dying on the cross branded Christ as a terrible criminal under God's curse. Christ suffered on the cross, but what made it tortuous was the fact that he had to carry the sin of all humanity on the cross. It was in this predicament that "Jesus cried out in a loud voice, '*Eli, Eli, lema sabachthani*' (which means, "My God, my God, why have you forsaken me?")" (Matt 27:46; Ps 21:1). Theologians interpret this cry in different ways. As a nineteenth-century biblical scholar pointed out, any explanation that claims Jesus' cry on the cross as not representing the actual truth of his position should not to be entertained.[23] The cry was real. It must be noted that Christ on the cross carrying the burden of sin highlights the gravity of sin: that it separates the sinner from God. Does it mean that God the Father had forsaken his Son at this critical moment? The view that Jesus' agony on the cross was a punishment by a heartless Father presents the picture that God the Father had no part in the salvific episode at the cross. God the Father, who so loved the world enough to send his only Son to save humanity, did not give up on him at this critical juncture. Both God the Father and God the Son were very much part of the salvific episode at the cross. As the Bible puts it, "God was reconciling the world to himself in Christ, not counting people's sins against them" (2 Cor 5:19). It cost both God the Father and Jesus much more than we can ever imagine. God's salvific quest was at its peak at the cross.

---

23. Dale, *Atonement*, 61.

The Three Crosses (Digital Artwork by Raheel Shakeel, 2016)

The impact of God's salvific act on sinful humans is best seen in what happened at the three crosses. Two criminals hung on either side of Christ. One ridiculed him while the other cried out to Jesus, "Remember me when you come into your kingdom." Jesus responded, "Truly I tell you, today you will be with me in paradise" (Luke 23:42–43). Jesus agonized and died on the cross to save sinners. The responses of the two criminals beside Jesus poignantly portray humanity's response to what Jesus accomplished on the cross. One criminal rejected what Jesus offered while the other accepted it. Though God's salvific quest wrought through Christ reached its peak at the cross, it did not end there. This takes us to his resurrection, which is also equally unprecedented and controversial.

SAVIOR'S UNEXPECTED REAPPEARANCE!

The Christian narrative would have ended in an anticlimax if Jesus had not risen from the dead. He would have been like any other savior who did a great job when he was alive. Perhaps he would have been a living memory, but not a living reality. The resurrection episode provides the foundation of the Christian faith, which is centered on the conviction that Jesus saved sinners not only when he was living on this earth but also continues to save. Paul declares in his letter to the Corinthians:

> And if Christ has not been raised, our preaching is useless and so is your faith. More than that, we are then found to be false witnesses about God, for we have testified about God that he raised Christ from the dead. But he did not raise him if in fact the dead are not raised. For if the dead are not raised, then Christ has not been raised either. And if Christ has not been raised, your faith is futile; you are still in your sins. (1 Cor 15:14–17)

Paul first stresses that if not for Christ's resurrection, preaching Christ and believing in him would be futile. Then he reminds the Corinthians that if the resurrection did not happen, then those who declare it would turn out to be false witnesses. He concludes that if Christ had not risen, people would still be in the bondage of sin; Christ as Savior would only be a memory. In the Christian narrative, Christ's resurrection is presented as an event that really happened in history. Christ's resurrection is justified as a historical event based on certain evidentiary criteria. The event meets certain standard rules of evidence such as consistent eyewitness testimonies and multiple credible witnesses.

Paul stresses the indispensable role Christ's resurrection plays in Christian preaching and faith; for that to be the case, the event needs to have really happened. He establishes the historicity of the event in this way: "For what I received I passed on to you as of first importance: that Christ died for our sins according to the Scriptures, that he was buried, that he was raised on the third day according to the Scriptures, and that he appeared to Cephas, and then to the Twelve. After that, he appeared to more than five hundred of the brothers and sisters at the same time, most of whom are still living, though some have fallen asleep" (1 Cor 15:3–6).

Based on the study of Paul's early travels to Damascus and Jerusalem, biblical scholars date his letter to the Corinthians at about 55 CE. This means that the above passage was written a few years after the death of Jesus. This passage may be the earliest Christian creed that highlights the historicity of Christ's resurrection. Such a creed developed too quickly to be deemed as expressing a myth; a myth or a legend usually takes time to take shape. Paul was addressing a group of people, and among them some would have been witnesses to the resurrection. Paul's declaration was really a statement concerning an event that took place in the living memory of his audience. He cited witnesses who had seen the risen Christ: Peter (referred to here as Cephas), the disciples, and 500 people, some who were still living.

Jesus' disciples were not the only eyewitnesses to the event. Jesus appeared to some on more than one occasion. He first appeared to Mary Magdalene and to other women (John 20:10–18; Matt 28:8–10), then to Cleopas and his companion (Luke 24:13–32), to eleven disciples and others (Luke 24:33–49; John 20:19–23, 26–30, 21:1–14; Matt 28:16–20), and to the apostles on the Mount of Olives (Luke 24:50–52; Acts 1:4–9). The fact that Jesus appeared to 500 people all at once cannot be taken as a case of mass hypnosis. If so, when they had come out of their trance, they would have aggressively proclaimed that Christ's resurrection was a hoax. In fact, Paul told the Corinthians that some of these 500 were still living. Perhaps he wanted the Corinthians to check with the eyewitnesses as to the truth of his words.

Despite such eyewitness evidence of Jesus' resurrection, its historicity has been and still is contested. Even the most skeptical critic of Jesus' resurrection would admit the historicity of the significant growth of the Jesus movement, later called Christianity. How then can one explain the phenomenal growth of the early church as recorded in the book of Acts? What was the motivating factor for such a remarkable growth? Was it mere hallucination? Were the disciples projecting hallucinations of Jesus after his death from which they mistakenly inferred his resurrection? Hallucinations usually occur because of mental illness or drugs or through being infatuated with a preconceived idea. There is no evidence that the disciples used drugs or had mental issues. As Jews, they shared the Jewish view on resurrection and had absolutely no preconceived idea that Jesus would be resurrected. They anticipated a resurrection that would occur with the establishment of the kingdom of God, but such a resurrection would be general rather than individual. That was why the disciples were so shocked when they heard from the woman that Jesus had risen from the dead. At first, they refused to believe the women's report. Seeing Jesus alive went against their preconceived idea of the general resurrection of the dead. It seems clear that they were not hallucinating. Moreover, Jesus was seen not once but many times; not by one person but by several; not only at one place but at many locations; not only by believers but even by nonbelievers. How can such a diverse group of people be hallucinating? On these grounds, philosopher and theologian William Craig concludes that the hallucination theory cannot explain the spectacular growth of the Jesus movement.[24]

If the early believers were not hallucinating, what motivated them to spread the gospel, or the good news, so enthusiastically? What was so good about the good news? If not for the resurrection, the crucifixion would have been the final tragedy in the life of Jesus. He would have been another

---

24. Craig, "Contemporary Scholarship," 89–95.

martyred messiah who died for a noble cause. The believers would have been holy mourners and their tale of woe would not have attracted anyone. The book of Acts records the spectacular growth of the Jesus movement. The apostles, including Paul, preached about a living Savior and not a dead martyr. The reality of Jesus arisen was the motivating factor for the growth of the Jesus movement. Acknowledging the historicity of early growth and not identifying its motivating factor is like recognizing the sickness but ignoring its diagnosis.

The ultimate acid test of the historicity of the resurrection and the credibility of the eyewitnesses was that many—like Stephen, James the son of Zebedee, James the brother of Jesus, Peter, and Paul—courageously faced death without denying their testimony. Surely they were not so foolish as to die for a hoax. They died as martyrs, not for a novel religious doctrine, but for an unprecedented historical event: that the Savior, the Son of God who died on the cross, had risen and was very much alive.

Jesus, a Jew, died and was placed in a tomb in Jewish territory. It is not surprising that the first reaction to his resurrection came from the Jews. As already noted, they anticipated a general but not an individual resurrection. Jesus' resurrection went against their conviction. The earliest Jewish reaction to the proclamation of the resurrection was an attempt to explain away the empty tomb. The chief priests were the first to react. The report about the empty tomb from the guards disturbed the priests. They bribed the guards to say that the disciples had stolen Jesus' body from the tomb. Such a version of the resurrection story still presupposes that the tomb was empty. Since then, many have tried to explain away the empty tomb mainly based on their philosophical or scientific presuppositions.

One such presupposition is that what is believable is only what is historically valid. When something can be justified rationally or verified empirically it is taken to be believable. The Bible records that Jesus had a bodily resurrection. When Jesus was raised from the dead, his body was intact. His scars remained (John 20:27), he ate fish (John 20:12), he bodily ascended to heaven (Acts 1:9), and will bodily come again (1 Thess 4:16). But since such a resurrection flouts the laws of biology, some find it difficult to question Jesus' bodily resurrection. In an age when only what is scientific is considered believable, Jesus' bodily resurrection naturally appears as religious fiction.

As we have already noted, certain episodes of the biblical narrative fall beyond the scope of traditional historical assessment. The resurrection falls into this category. The Bible points out that all the members of the Trinity—God the Father, Son, and Spirit—were involved in the resurrection. God the Father brought Jesus back from the dead (Acts 2:32–33; Rom 6:4; Gal 1:1). Jesus himself rose from the dead, for it was impossible for death to hold him

(Acts 2:24; John 2:18–19, 10:18). The Holy Spirit raised Jesus (Rom 8:11; 1 Pet 3:18). Jesus' resurrection was orchestrated by the triune God: God the Father did the raising, Jesus was the one raised, and the Spirit was the agent who raised Jesus. It is the risen Christ, through the Holy Spirit, who gives his followers assurance of having life after death (Rom 8:11). Since the triune God is involved in the enactment of the resurrection, one cannot use the laws of biology to assess these actions.

Skepticism concerning the possibility of bodily resurrection was very much in vogue both in the Jewish and the Greco-Roman worlds. Among the Jews of that time, Sadducees totally rejected resurrection. Pharisees believed in the resurrection of the dead, but did not specify whether this resurrection included the flesh (Acts 23:8). The Essenes believed in the immortality of the soul but not in bodily resurrection. Impacted by the views of Plato and Aristotle, the Greco-Roman world believed in the immortality of the soul but not bodily resurrection. As already noted in chapter 4, the Epicurean and Stoic philosophers considered death as final, and ridiculed the idea of life after death as a religious superstition.

Despite the cloud of skepticism that surrounds Jesus' resurrection, it had to happen to render the salvific revolution a reality and not a mere historical memory. The resurrection shows that sin, its wages death, and the author of both sin and death did not have power over God the Savior. Imagine the celebration that Satan and the demons would have had between Good Friday and Easter Sunday, and the shock in store for them when Jesus reappeared on Easter Sunday.

Although the Jewish and gentile worlds did not expect Jesus' resurrection, it was a key part of God the Father's plan, enacted by Jesus his Son, and orchestrated by the Holy Spirit. Jesus knew that he would not only die, but rise again. His seven predictions about his death and resurrection (Matt 12:18, 40, 20:18–19, 26:32; Mark 9:30–32; Luke 9:22; John 10:17–22) indicate that the events of Good Friday and Easter Sunday were not surprising to him. They were part of his plan to offer humanity what it desperately needed. Jesus rose victoriously from death and left this earth, but he did not desert those who depended on him. This takes us to what he gave them before departing.

SAVIOR'S LAST WILL!

Usually a last will is written before a person dies. It helps someone at the brink of death rest in peace, while also informing his or her relatives and loved ones what they have inherited. But Jesus' last will came after his resurrection and before his ascension. He did not rest in peace after his last will but ascended in glory to his heavenly home. The inheritance that he left to his disciples and his followers included a unique gift, a command, and promise.

The gift was not the Jewish nation freed from Roman power or a structured religious dogma or code of moral conduct, but salvation orchestrated through the Son of God who died and rose again. Jesus assured his disciples and other followers not to lose heart for he, the risen Savior, would always be with them. Accepting him would redeem not only them, but also the world at large. Such salvation is a free but not a cheap gift. It cost God the Son a great deal to carry the sin of all humanity and die on a cursed cross. The risen, glorified Jesus interceding with his father on behalf of the penitent would be their ever-present Savior.

The command in the last will was to "Go but wait" (Matt 28:18–19; Acts 1:4). Jesus' great commission was a command to "Go" as well as to "Wait." He asked his disciples and followers not to keep the gift of salvation that they had received to themselves, but to make it available to both Jew and gentile. Jesus knew that this mission would be challenging. He was and still is what makes the salvation that God offers so controversial. We will see how both the Jewish and the gentile worlds found it difficult to accept Jesus as Savior (chapters 7 and 8).

Jesus knew that his disciples and followers were going to be challenged witnessing for him; they would soon become depressed and feel hopeless. They had to be instilled with hope and empowered to face the challenges ahead of them, which is why Jesus' last will ended with a two-pronged promise. Just before his ascension, he assured his disciples that he would come back the same way he was leaving. With his return as King of kings and Lord of lords, what was accomplished on the cross would be manifested in its fullest global dimension. The salvific revolution would climax with the establishment of the new earth and the new heaven. Until that happened, the disciples needed much more than mere bravery to be effective witnesses through the challenges they would face; they had to have superhuman wisdom and power. Jesus commanded them not to venture to spread the gospel before waiting for empowerment by the Holy Spirit (Luke 24:49). He did not want his witnesses to start such a difficult journey on an empty tank. Jesus assured them that he would baptize them with the Holy Spirit that his father had promised (John 14:15–20; Acts 1:7–8). He promised them that he would not leave them alone but would give them "another" one just like him. The Greek word used to designate this one is *Parakletos*, primarily a legal term, but with a wider connotation here. It means one who comforts, counsels, intercedes, empowers, and makes Christ real in a continuing, experiential manner. We will have occasion to look at this promise in our next chapter. The Savior's last will was a message of hope with an incredible inheritance rather than the depressive wish of a man about to die!

THE PIVOTAL POINT

The salvific revolution is the pivotal point of God's quest to redeem his creation. This revolution was centered on Jesus Christ. Every facet of his life and ministry was unprecedented. He orchestrated a revolution that crossed both boundaries of space and time. Its impact was not restricted to Judea but was extended to neighboring Samaria and to the ends of the world. Not only the Jews, but also the pagan gentiles came to be included as God's "chosen people." It became the catalyst to change the destiny of people, both individually and communally. Its scope covered the regeneration of not only the spiritual but also the mental and physical facets of human personhood. This revolution did not stop with Easter Sunday but continues today. The redemption that such a revolution rendered is not imposed but needs to be appropriated through human participation. Whenever someone repents and accepts Jesus as Savior, the revolution recurs and there is joy in heaven. For people to fully experience the redemptive life that the revolution offers and to enable them to spread the good news, God the Holy Spirit must enter the scene. This takes us to the next paradigmatic episode in the Christian narrative: the spiritual revolution.

6

The Spiritual Revolution

The salvific and spiritual revolutions are interconnected and complement each other. The blunder of the first humans not only disrupted the relationship between God and humans but also marred their spiritual nature and potential. God's persistent quest to meet the spiritual needs of people runs through history. This quest reached its peak on the day of Pentecost, which ushered in a revolutionary spirituality.

Spirituality is a universal human phenomenon that arises from the yearning to leap beyond the material and the mundane. It stems from the nature of human personhood. From a Judeo-Christian perspective, spirituality is ingrained in the very makeup of humans. Since God is spirit (John 4:24) and humans are created in his image (Gen 1:26–27), they are not mere physical organisms but have a spiritual component, however marred the image may be due to sin. The yearning to recover the lost image is evident in the spiritual history of humans. Just like an image is geared to reflect the original, humans, whether they believe in God or not, strive to retrieve what they lack. This provides the underlying motivation for human spirituality and accounts for multiple modes of spiritual expression. Even in our technocratic and materialistic world, spirituality is not dead.

Despite the demise of organized religion in modern times, one notices a significant global resurgence of religiosity that exhibits a pronounced spiritual overtone. It finds its way into many sectors of society, including the scientific, literary, artistic, musical, psychological, medical, and even ecological realms. Adherence to spiritual practices outside the ambit of religion may be referred to as secular spirituality. The volume *Spirituality and the Secular Quest* in the World Series on Spirituality acknowledges this brand of spirituality.[1] In the light of such an expression of nonreligious spirituality, Roger Housden claims that secular spirituality is not an oxymoron; it is possible to be secular and yet spiritual.[2]

The Judeo-Greco-Roman world, where the spiritual revolution occurred, highlights a desperate striving for spiritual fulfillment adopting multiple strategies. The revolution came at the time when it was needed most.

THE TIMING OF THE REVOLUTION

The pivotal moment of the spiritual revolution was the day of Pentecost, which is one of the most popular Jewish festivals. The festival was first called the "Feast of Harvest" (Exod 23:16), and later, "Day of the First Fruits" (Exod 34:22). It is popularly known as *Shavuot* or the Festival of Weeks (Lev 23:15–21; Deut 16:9), since *shavuot* in Hebrew means "weeks." The festival marks the completion of the seven-week period from Passover, which amounts to forty-nine days. *Shavuot* is celebrated the next day, which would be the fiftieth day after Passover. Greek-speaking Jews called the festival *Pentecost*, which is the Greek word for "fifty." Although it is essentially a harvest festival, Jews also commemorate the occasion when they were given the *Torah* on Mount Sinai and remember with gratitude how they were delivered from the bondage of Egypt at Passover.

Interestingly, the day of Pentecost falls fifty days after Easter. After Jesus had ascended, his disciples anticipated what he had talked about (John 17:7; Acts 1: 9–11) and spent many days at prayer in the upper room (Acts 1:14).

---

1. Van Ness, *Spirituality and the Secular Quest*.
2. Housden, "Secular Spirituality," para. 13.

Traditional site of the Upper Room, Jerusalem
(Photo credit: Ferrell Jenkins/BiblePlaces.com)

The upper room is believed to be the site of the Last Supper, and where the outpouring of the Holy Spirit took place on the day of Pentecost. It is known as the Cenacle, from the Latin for dining room, and is in the southern part of the old city of Jerusalem on Mount Zion. The current structure of the room dates approximately from the fourteenth century, which accounts for the existing Gothic-era columns. In May 2014, Pope Francis was permitted to celebrate mass in the Cenacle during his visit to Israel.

Those who gathered in the upper room on the day of Pentecost were mostly Israelite Jews and some Egyptian Jews who came to celebrate *Shavuot* and remember with gratitude God's gift of the Torah.[3] The outpouring of the Holy Spirit on the day of Pentecost was perfect timing in that it would have enabled these Jews to make the connection between Passover, Easter, and Pentecost. God, who had delivered their forefathers from Egypt (Isa 63:10–14), had freed them from the bondage of sin by raising Jesus from the dead, and was now pouring out the Holy Spirit.

---

3. This is claimed by Philo, the first-century historian. Levine and Brettler, *Jewish Annotated New Testament*, cites Philo's *On the Contemplative Life*, 65–66, in footnote to Acts 2:1–2, 223NTn.

THE SPIRITUAL REVOLUTION 123

Why did Jews have to wait so long for Pentecost?[4] Although the term "Holy Spirit" occurs only three times in the Old Testament (Ps 51:11; Isa 63:10–14), it does not mean that the Spirit was absent prior to the day of Pentecost. Expressions for the Holy Spirit frequently used in the Old Testament include "Spirit of God," "Spirit of the Lord," "my Spirit," "Spirit," "Spirit of Fire," "Spirit of Judgment," and "Spirit of Justice." References in the New Testament to the Holy Spirit's work in the Old Testament (Matt 22:43; Mark 12:36; Acts 1:16, 4:25, 7:51; Heb 3:7; 2 Peter 1:21) confirm that these Old Testament expressions refer to the Holy Spirit. Ivan Satyavrata identifies three roles of the Holy Spirit in the Old Testament: creative, enablement, and prophetic.[5] The Spirit hovering over dark and stormy waters (Gen 1:2) at creation portrays the Holy Spirit's creative role. The Spirit enabled certain individuals to accomplish God's purposes, as seen in the lives of Joseph, Moses, Gideon, Samson and the other judges, Saul, and David. The Spirit's prophetic role is prominent in the ministry of prophets like Elijah, Elisha, Isaiah, Ezekiel, and Malachi. The Old Testament records several instances where people experienced the Spirit. Both Jews and Christians acknowledge the ministry of the Spirit in the Old Testament. As we shall see in chapters 7 and 8, the controversy between Jews and Christians concerns the way Old Testament prophecies are interpreted, particularly those concerning the Messiah and the outpouring of the Spirit at Pentecost.

In his wisdom, God waited until the day of Pentecost to reveal the full identity of the Holy Spirit. God had brought the Israelites from Mesopotamia; a polytheistic, idol-worshipping world. He first wanted them to become committed to himself as the only God, who did not reside in idols. If he had revealed the Spirit as another divine person, the Israelites would have been confused, and may even have returned to polytheism. Describing the Holy Spirit as the "Spirit of God" was helpful to present God's uniqueness without confusing the Jews. Often, God reveals his character through object lessons. He waited for Jesus to be born into this world and interact with people to enable the Jews to accommodate Jesus as God the Son. Similarly, God waited for the Spirit to come, anoint, and empower them in order to reveal to them that the Spirit is the third person of the triune God. Although God has always been triune, he revealed himself as triune in stages so people could comprehend the complexity of his personhood to some extent.

---

4. "Pentecost" refers to the spiritual revolution that occurred on the day of Pentecost, unless otherwise indicated.

5. Satyavrata, *Holy Spirit*, 53–69.

In addition, Pentecost had to follow Easter. The baptism in the Holy Spirit, as Peter pointed out, was for those who repented and accepted Jesus as Savior (Acts 2:38). If one needs to be saved to be baptized in the Spirit, Jesus had to die and rise again. The outpouring of the Spirit had to follow Christ's resurrection; Pentecost had to follow Easter.

Pentecost occurred during the era when it was most needed. Although the Roman government provided stability, the social, economic, and demographic maps of the world at that time were undergoing drastic changes. The Greek city-state was no longer the hub of society. Athens, the intellectual capital, was replaced by the multicultural commercial port of Alexandria. The Greco-Roman society became very unsettled. Charles Puskas and Michael Robbins call this period "an age of anxiety and aspiration," and note that rapid changes in society often inspire new hopes but also arouse new fears. This paradox of aspiration and anxiety in the midst of rapid change was a key characteristic of the New Testament world.[6]

Such anxiety also infiltrated the Jewish community of that time. The freedom that the Maccabees had gained did not last. Jews were now under Roman imperial power, which allowed them to live in peace under a stable government but, on the other hand, the unpredictable maneuvers of Herod the Great were unsettling.

Gripped by anxiety, both Jews and gentiles resorted to various spiritual modes of release. Dismissing belief in gods and the afterlife as superstitions, philosophers like the Epicureans and Stoics[7] aimed to keep people stress free. Epicureans prescribed pleasure: "Enjoy life today for tomorrow we die." Stoics advocated "quietude" as the cure for stress. They believed that following the rules of nature would render quietude, because nature is permeated with a divine energy, known as *Logos*. Many others turned to multiple gods, even deifying Caesar. They needed gods that they could relate to, appease to get favors, and curse when they were silent. Paul was distressed when he saw multiple idols on his visit to Athens (Acts 17:16).

Alexander the Great's extension of his empire exposed the Middle-Eastern world to Eastern religions. Alexandria replaced Athens not only as the commercial capital, but also the location for the exchange of ideas between the East and the West. There was a comingling of races and religions in this cosmopolitan city. The exposure of Greco-Roman culture to Eastern religions resulted in various expressions of spirituality, including astrology, divinization, meditative methods, incantations, and ecstatic trances. Fatalism, so typical among the followers of these religions, also infiltrated the

---

6. Puskas and Robbins, *Introduction to the New Testament*, 4.

7. The Epicureans and Stoics confronted Paul when he visited Athens (Acts 17:18).

Greco-Roman mindset. To a society in distress, these were welcome ways of release.[8] People became enthralled with mystical experiences through intermediaries, initiations, expiations, and purifications to free themselves from their anxiety.[9]

Pentecost occurred in this context, where people were frantically trying to achieve spiritual fulfillment through various means. Pentecost occurred at the perfect time; it was what the world most needed. The events of the day of Pentecost differed quite substantially from the spiritualities in vogue at the time.

On that day, the Holy Spirit empowered the believers to witness (Acts 1:4–8) and to dwell with the community of believers (Ezek 36:27; John 14:15–17; 1 Cor 12:3). When viewed in this way, the day of Pentecost can be viewed as the birthday of the church. Luke records that the believers were "filled with the Holy Spirit" (Acts 2:4). It may be taken as the moment when "their spirits were completely under the control of the Spirit; their words were his words."[10] On that day, all these nuances seem to converge. The believers were empowered for witness. They were incorporated into Christ's body, the church, and were filled with the Spirit through yielding to him. That day sets the precedent and the parameters for this revolutionary brand of spirituality. What makes it so revolutionary?

THE SPIRITUALITY OF PENTECOST

God Initiated

This spirituality commenced with God. Its point of reference was not the human spirit, but God the Holy Spirit. It was not humans reaching out to the divine, but God reaching out to spiritually hungry humans.

What happened on that day epitomizes God's persistent quest through the ages to fulfill people's spiritual aspirations. Pentecost did not take the Judeo-Christian community by surprise. Joel, Isaiah, Ezekiel, and Zechariah of the Old Testament (Joel 2:28–32; Isa 44:3–5, 32:15–17; Ezek 36:26–27, 29; Zech 12:10) and John the Baptist of the New Testament (Matt 3:11; Mark 1:7–8; Luke 3:16, John 1:33) prophesied about the Holy Spirit. Joel prophesied about a day when the Spirit would be poured out on people (Joel 2:28–32). Peter declared in his sermon that the outpouring of the Spirit

---

8. Thonnard, *Short History of Philosophy*, 170.

9. Thonnard, *Short History of Philosophy*, 171; Saunders, *Greek and Roman Philosophy*, 2–5.

10. NIV Study Bible, footnote on Acts 2:4, 1645NTn.

was a fulfillment of Joel's prophecy (Acts 2:17–21).[11] Ezekiel highlighted a key promise of God's new covenant: "My dwelling place will be with them; I will be their God, and they will be my people" (Ezek 37:27). Jesus not only made definitive statements about the Spirit's personhood and mission, but also commanded the disciples to wait for his advent. These anticipatory pronouncements indicate that Pentecost was not an accident in history, but preordained to usher in a significant era in spiritual history.

The Bible records spiritual episodes both prior and subsequent to what happened on that day, but all these reflect a spirituality that commenced with God. The Holy Spirit portrayed as hovering over a chaotic earth (Gen 1:2) depicts how he was at work from the very beginning. Genesis 6:3 depicts God's Spirit striving with people who were deviating into sin. Deuteronomy 32:11 portrays God protecting his people like an eagle hovering over its young. These portrayals point out the creative and redemptive facets of God's quest that, as Steve Studebaker observes, are distinguishable though inseparable.[12] In the Old Testament, God through his Spirit enabled Bezalel to become the tabernacle's expert architect (Exod 31:1–5); settled upon leaders to administer effectively (Num 11:16–17); empowered warriors (Judg 6:34; 1 Sam 16:13); and anointed prophets like Isaiah and Ezekiel to proclaim God's word (Isa 61:1; Ezek 2:1–4).

Many spiritualities popular at the time featured humans striving to attain spiritual fulfillment. These spiritualities arose from different world views, which ranged from Greek Epicurean, Stoic, Greco-Egyptian mystics like Plutarch, and Greco-Jewish schools headed by Philo, to those offered by oriental religions like Hinduism and Buddhism. These world views may differ, but all of them belonged to a paradigm that propagated spirituality as an upward quest. This quest commenced with humans moving toward the reality of a distant God, an impersonal divinity, an exuberant experience, or even a psychological state of quietude. Such striving was articulated through various strategies to achieve a state or experience that satisfied people's spiritual thirst; many felt that they had arrived. As in all strategies based on self-effort, there tends to be a lingering doubt as to whether one has really arrived. The direction of such a spiritual journey was from human upwards. But Pentecost put a dead end on all who strove to ascend to spiritual heights, following the Babel way (Gen 11:1–9). God the Spirit took the initiative since humans were and still are unable to fulfill their spiritual

---

11. From the Jewish perspective, Peter's claim that what happened on the day of Pentecost was a fulfillment of Joel's prophecy is not warranted. We will consider this criticism in chapter 8.

12. Studebaker, *From Pentecost to the Triune God*, 67–78.

aspirations. This is because sin makes humans spiritually dead (Eph 2:4); dead people cannot strive!

It is here that the spirituality of Pentecost remedied the fallacy of the finite attempting to reach the infinite. For what happened at Pentecost came from God. Jesus asked his disciples to wait until they received what God the Father had promised: "power from on high" (Luke 24:49). It was not the power of human spirituality, but that which came from above as the Holy Spirit. The rushing wind[13] and the tongues of fire that settled on those in the upper room were not humanly engineered. The image of tongues of fire (Isa 5:24) and fire in general (Exod 3:2, 14:24, 19:18; Isa 5:24) symbolize divine presence.[14] Pentecost belonged to an entirely different paradigm.

Christ Centered

Some spiritualities in vogue at the time used intermediaries to reach their target. Philo of Alexandria (40 BCE—40 CE) postulated many intermediaries, called *Powers,* between the transcendent God and humans. They were identified as angels and the main one among them was Logos, the divine word. Philo saw Logos as nearest to God. Plutarch (50–120 CE), a popular mystic philosopher, believed in two realities: the principle of good as a transcendent impersonal divinity and the principle of evil identified as the material world. Between these two are intermediaries, some good deities and some wicked spirits. He advocated that one should rely on the good deities to reach God. Mystical modes would facilitate reaching God.

Pentecost too offered an intermediary, but he was neither one among many nor an angel, nor even Philo's Logos, nearest to the supreme god. He was God the Son. Pentecost highlights God's quest to fulfill people's spiritual aspirations through relating with them and is enhanced through the baptismal experience. This baptism was God the Father's promise (Acts 1:4), orchestrated by God the Son, gifting God the Holy Spirit. As Studebaker highlights, the three persons of the triune God—God the Father, Son, and Spirit—participate in the baptismal experience.[15] This characterization was unacceptable to the Jews who did not acknowledge God as triune.

On the day of Pentecost, Peter declared that it was Christ who baptized the believers with the Holy Spirit, promised by God the Father (Acts 2:32–33). When people asked Peter what they should do to receive this baptism, he made it quite clear that they had to repent and accept Jesus the risen

13. Wind signifying God's presence, as in Ezekiel 1:4 and Psalm 107.

14. Levine and Brettler, *Jewish Annotated New Testament,* footnote on Acts 2:3, 223–24.

15. Studebaker, *From Pentecost to the Triune God,* 2.

Savior (Acts 2:38, 4:12). This would have been scandalous to the Jews, who believed that only God could forgive sins. It would also have been strange for the gentiles. The Epicureans would have ridiculed the idea of repentance, for they claimed it stemmed out of superstitions like fear of death and fear of gods. Those impacted by Eastern religions advocated self-realization of one's spiritual potential as the way to spiritual fulfillment. Advocating self-realization rather than repentance was more popular, as who wants to admit one's faults?

A Personal Relationship

Pentecost occurred when people were striving to escape their anxiety through several spiritual modes. The Epicureans aimed to attain a state of pleasure, while Stoics advocated quietude through following the rules of nature. Those influenced by Eastern religions resorted to Hindu and Buddhist spiritual targets. The Hindu model aimed for a transcendental state of calm and peace by being united with cosmic consciousness *(Brahman)*, which though divine was impersonal. The Buddhist mode offered Nirvana, a state free from the bondage of cravings and cycle of rebirths reached through rigorous moral conduct and meditation. None of these spiritualities accommodated a relationship with a person, whether human or divine. The Greco-Roman polytheists strove for spiritual fulfillment by pleasing multiple gods through tortuous practices, sacrifices, and offerings. Though these devotees cultivated a sporadic love-hate relationship with the gods, they did not have a consistent personal relationship with them. The Judeo-Greek mystics like Philo resorted to Logos taken as reason amidst multiple intermediaries to connect with a transcendental god. But one could not have a personal relationship with Logos. Some mystics claimed to have exhilarating spiritual experiences, but these did not involve fellowshipping with a deity or even an intermediary. Jews acknowledged the Spirit of God at work in the life of humans, especially in prophets, kings, and leaders of the community. This indicated God's presence and direction. As we shall see in chapter 8, Jews found it difficult to accept having a personal relationship with the Holy Spirit, taken as the third person of a triune God.

These spiritualities were all human efforts to experience spiritual fulfillment but devoid of personal relationship with the divine. Those striving through such spiritual modes were either directed by a dogma, guided by a guru, helped by intermediaries, or were appeasing a god through offerings; an ongoing and intimate relationship with divinity as a person was significantly missing.

What happened to those in the upper room on the day of Pentecost went beyond an exhilarating experience. It was the Holy Spirit's entrance into their lives. He was not a formula to be mastered or a power to be manipulated or even an ecstatic experience, but rather a person; he was the third person of a triune God. The spirituality that commenced on the day of Pentecost retains this core feature: one that centers on the person of the Holy Spirit. David Barrett notes that the worldwide twentieth-century Pentecostal and charismatic renewals "share the experience of the infilling of the Holy Spirit, Third Person of the Triune God."[16]

The Spirit function as the third person of the triune God becomes clearer when we look at the trinitarian formulation of God, as articulated in the Nicene (325 CE) and Constantinople (381 CE) councils. Such a formulation, using the terms "substance" and "person," characterized God as a triune being: that God is one in substance and three in persons. In Greek vocabulary, substance is that which gives reality and identity to a thing. When we take Father, Son, and Spirit as one in substance, we consider them as having the identity of godhood. When they are described as persons, we need to keep in mind that person is a relative term. A relative term cannot stand on its own, but has to be in a relationship with something or someone. For instance, when we consider a fellow human, a pet, or even an inanimate object like a doll to be a person, we imply a relationship with it. It is this which makes it a person. God the Father, Son, and Spirit, though substantially one, acknowledge and relate to each other as persons. When Jesus was baptized, God the Father declared, "This is my Son, whom I love: with him I am well pleased" (Matt 3:17). Jesus addressed God in his prayers using "Father" in the sense of a loving son speaking to his father (Matt 11:25; Luke 10:21, 23:34, 46; John 11:41, 12:27, 17:1, 5, 11, 21, 24). In the garden of Gethsemane, he cried out in agony, "Abba, Father (patēr), everything is possible for you. Take this cup from me." (Mark 14:36). *Abba* is an endearing term like "Daddy." The terms "Father" and "Son" are relative terms. The Holy Spirit described as the Father's Spirit or the Spirit of Christ reflects the relationship between Father and Son to the Spirit. When Father, Son, and Spirit relate to each other, they function as persons within the Godhead. Peter Newman points out that Pentecostals look for an experiential spirituality that emphasizes immediate encounters with God through the Holy Spirit. Such an experience is mediated by the Spirit's work through Scripture, Christian tradition, and the broader cultural context.[17]

---

16. Barrett, "Worldwide Holy Spirit Renewal," 381.
17. Newman, *Pentecostal Experience*.

The baptism in the Spirit initiated a personal relationship between the triune God and the baptized. Being Spirit baptized was not a random provision to anyone in a crowd but an intentional act of the triune God directed specifically towards those waiting to be baptized. God the Father promised, God the Son baptized, and God the Spirit came to fellowship with the baptized (Acts 1:4–8). Those baptized turned out to be persons and not mere numbers in a crowd. When the baptized received the gift, they acknowledged and appreciated who the giver was, and what the gift was. It was a significant moment when the three persons of the triune God, acting in unison, enabled the baptized to appreciate the gift, but also the promiser and the baptizer as persons with whom they could relate in their spiritual journey.

Jesus wanted his disciples to consider the Holy Spirit not as a power but as a person. He made it clear to his disciples that they would receive power when the Spirit was poured out, implying that power comes from the Spirit, but he is not mere power (Acts 1:8). Jesus also comforted his disciples by telling them that he would send another advocate or counselor (*Paraclete*)[18] to be with them, empowering and guiding them (John 14:15–17). Using the word "another" before "counselor" implied that Jesus took the Holy Spirit to be a person like him. At Pentecost, the disciples experienced in a tangible manner what Jesus had told them about the Holy Spirit; he was a person, just like Jesus. The baptismal experience enhanced the relationship between the baptized and the Spirit. Such a relationship between the triune God and the baptized was not a one-time event, but an ongoing experience. This relationship is fully voluntary. A Spirit-filled person can grieve (Eph 3:20; Isa 63:10), quench (1 Thess 5:16–22), resist (Acts 7:51), or even blaspheme the Holy Spirit (Mark 3:29; Matt 12:31; Luke 12:10).[19] Pentecost offered an intimate and abiding relationship with a divine person: God the Holy Spirit, and through him with God the Father and Jesus the Son. Such a relationship was significantly missing in the spiritualities of the day.

For All, for All Times

Pentecost came in a world of many spiritualities but they were rather restrictive in the sense that several requirements had to be met to join them. Pentecost ushered in a spirituality that was open to all people. Not only the 120

---

18. *Parakletos* is a Greek term translated as "counselor," "comforter," "advocate," "friend," and "helper."

19. Blasphemy here is not to be taken as critiquing the Holy Spirit, but saying goodbye to Jesus the baptizer and God the Father who sent the Spirit, against the triune God; such a denial naturally falls beyond forgiveness.

people in the upper room, but also as many as 3,000 people who responded to Peter's sermon and received the Holy Spirit (Acts 2:38). The Bible records several Pentecostal occasions that followed that day (Acts 4:31, 8:14–17, 9:1–19, 10:45, 19:1–6). God lavished his Spirit on everyone, regardless of gender, culture, nationality, or ethnicity. This was what Peter alluded to in his sermon (Acts 2:15–21) as the fulfillment of Joel's prophecy (Joel 2:8–32). Moreover, the baptism of the Holy Spirit comes with an extended warranty. Peter proclaimed that Spirit baptism was not only for them, but also for their children, and those who were far off (Acts 2:39). In his survey of the explosive worldwide growth of Pentecostal spirituality, David Barrett notes three distinct but interrelated surges in the twentieth century Pentecostal-Charismatic renewal. He labels them as the first wave (the classical Pentecostal renewal), the second wave (the charismatic renewal), and the third wave (the neo-charismatic renewal). He points out that in all three waves, the Holy Spirit has impacted the lives not simply of a small number of individuals in scattered communities, but of millions across the globe.[20] He finds that such explosive growth was not only universal, but also multiple and diverse. Barrett notes that in today's Pentecostal world only 29 percent are white and 71 percent nonwhite, they are more urban than rural, more female than male, more children (under 18) than adults, more Third World (66 percent) than Western (32 percent), more living in poverty (87 percent) than affluence (13 percent), more family related than individualist.[21] Ewen Butler's book centers on the interaction between the Pentecostal Assemblies of Canada and the charismatic renewal movement. Despite some tensions between them, he shows how the Pentecostal-Charismatic partnership has contributed to the growth of Canadian Pentecostalism.[22] Peter's prophetic declaration that Pentecost is for all and for all times has been proved correct.

When a movement grows so rapidly and extensively with multiple and diverse expressions, deviations can occur. Even during biblical times, Paul was concerned with deviations that occurred among believers in the Corinthian church: "For if someone comes to you and preaches a Jesus other than the Jesus we preached, or if you receive a different spirit from the Spirit you received, or a different gospel from the one you accepted, you put up with it easily enough" (2 Cor 11:4).

Paul had pioneered the Corinthian church (Acts 18) and was concerned about the Corinthian believers deviating from what he had focussed on: Jesus, gospel, and the Spirit. For Paul, the day of Pentecost and other

---

20. Barrett, "Worldwide Holy Spirit Renewal," 381.
21. Barrett, "Worldwide Holy Spirit Renewal," 383.
22. Butler, *Canadian Winds of the Spirit*.

Pentecostal expressions recorded in the Bible set the precedents and parameters for subsequent spirituality. All of them were centered on Christ, gospel, and the Spirit. These should serve as the criterion to identify the authentic amidst the multifarious spiritual expressions that claim to be Pentecostal.

Gifted, Not Rewarded

On the day of Pentecost, those in the upper room and the thousands who responded to Peter's sermon were not rewarded but gifted. It was not a graduation ceremony for their spiritual accomplishments, but rather a gift presented fifty days after Easter! Being so gifted would have shocked the pharisaic Jews, the gentile gurus, and the mentors of that time, since for them spirituality was an achievement through self-effort. Philosophical spiritualists propagated that knowledge would make one virtuous. Polytheists believed that spiritual fulfillment could be achieved by pleasing the gods. Those impacted by Eastern religions resorted to worship of multiple gods, good works, and meditation. All these strategies were based on human effort. To claim that one could be spiritually fulfilled by receiving a gift with no strings attached would not have been well accepted in this context.

What made it truly controversial was that the gift was received in an unconventional manner. If what happened in the upper room was just a typical synagogue prayer meeting, the day would have ended without commotion. But, when people heard individuals speaking strangely, some thought that they were drunk, while others were utterly shocked and asked, "What does this mean?" Even today many ask the same question.

WHAT DOES THIS MEAN?

On April 19, 1906, the *Los Angeles Times* reported one of the worst and most powerful earthquakes in American history, killing many in San Francisco and destroying 514 city blocks. The paper also had an interesting front-page story of a spiritual earthquake that had hit Los Angeles in a little church on Azusa Street. The headlines read:

> Weird Babble of Tongues
> New Sect of Fanatics is Breaking Loose
> Wild Scene Last Night on Azusa Street
> Gurgle of Wordless Talk by a Sister.[23]

This is how the world first heard of the Azusa street revival that was to shake the Western spiritual world, much as the San Francisco earthquake

---

23. Synan, *Holiness-Pentecostal Movement*, 84.

had shaken northern California.[24] "Tongues"[25] made Pentecost controversial and continues to do so. If so, why retain tongues?

WHY TONGUES?
Integral to Human Personhood

The Bible characterizes "Tongues" in a literal sense as a physical organ (Mark 7:33; Jas 3:5) and in a figurative sense as language. In both respects, it is an integral part of human personhood. As a physical organ, it is indispensable for our bodily function. In the figurative sense, its role is significant. It could express one's emotional state as being joyful (Ps 126:2; Acts 2:26); could indicate one's cognitive capacities or deficiencies as being wise (Prov 12:18b), knowledgeable (Prov 15:2), or even lacking understanding (Job 42:2). It might signify a conative stance as stubbornness (Jas 3:8a), or submissive will (Isa 45:23; Phil 2:11). The moral caliber of a person may be identifiable through speech: whether one is perverse (Prov 10:31), a liar (Ps 120:31; Prov 12:19, 15:46), slanderous (Job 5:21), hypocritical (1 Tim 3:8; 1 John 3:18; Job 20:12), or adulterous (Prov 6:24). Human speech helps to categorize personality traits: as one being overtly arrogant (Prov 21:24; Ps 73:9), maliciously sarcastic (Ps 73:8), boastful (Jas 3:5), wisely protective (Prov 21:23), or lacking confidence, as with Moses' excuse (Exod 4:10). Speech could be divisive (Gen 11:9; Job 5:21; Ps 31:20; Isa 30:27; Jas 3:6–9) and could even indicate one's spiritual state. Speech could lead one to sin (Ps 34:13, 39:1) or to exalt God's righteousness (Ps 35:28). Speech could be prompted by sin (Job 5:5) and demonically bound (Mark 7:35). Renewed speech could be evident in a believer (Mark 16:17), while bold speech could indicate courage (Acts 4:31). The Bible views language and linguistic activity as being integral to one's personhood, intrinsically connected with human nature.

Recent linguistic research also stresses that language is an integral part of human personhood, playing a vital role that goes beyond verbal communication. It is much more than a tool by which humans learn to encode and communicate information.[26] Linguist and philosopher Noam Chomsky[27] claims language to be an integral part of human nature which enters into

---

24. Owens, "Azusa Street Revival," 39.

25. "Tongues," when placed within quotations, is to be taken as a collective noun, unless otherwise indicated.

26. The rationalist-empiricist view that Hobbes and Locke represent views language as a communication tool.

27. Chomsky, *Cartesian Linguistics*; Chomsky, *Language and Mind*; Chomsky, *Language and Problems of Knowledge*; Chomsky, *Logical Structure of Linguistic Theory*.

every aspect of human life, thought, and interaction; a species property.[28] In his recent book, *The Language Animal*, Charles Taylor claims that language plays a crucial role in shaping the very thought it purports to express; it does not merely describe but constitutes meaning and fundamentally shapes human experience.[29] It was George Orwell who pointed out, "But if thought corrupts language, language can also corrupt thought."[30] In Chomsky's view, though language unites communities, it can be divisive, even among those speaking the same language; people live in their own linguistic world. Ever since Chomsky, there has been a concerted effort by linguists to search for a generative grammar, a syntactical structure that underlies all languages.[31] Chomsky depicts a multiplicity of languages resulting in the loss of a universal language. He thinks that this led to not only dividing the human populace, but also depriving language of its core communicative efficacy.[32] With the hope that a common language would unify humanity, the search for the "unknown tongue" figures in the world of linguistics. What is really needed is a fundamental change in human nature, and this is where Pentecost becomes relevant.

Linguistically Legitimate

It is not uncommon to view "tongues" as a type of glossolalia; incomprehensible speech sometimes occurring in a trance state, an episode of religious ecstasy, or schizophrenia. According to the Merriam-Webster dictionary, "glossolalia" is a profuse and often emotionally-charged speech that mimics coherent speech but is usually unintelligible to the listener and is uttered in some states of religious ecstasy or in schizophrenic states.[33] The Oxford English Dictionary states that glossolalia is a phenomenon of (apparently) speaking in an unknown language, especially practiced by Pentecostal and charismatic Christians.[34] Taking "tongues" as a type of glossolalia, these definitions tend to view speaking in unknown tongues as a symptom of mental deficiency, since what is uttered does not qualify to be legitimate language.

Can we conclude that one who speaks in unknown tongues is mentally deficient? Is the speaker mentally deficient if what is spoken is not

28. Chomsky, *New Horizons*, 3; Chomsky, *Language and Problems of Knowledge*, 1–2.
29. Taylor, *Language Animal*, introductory comments on cover page.
30. Orwell, "Politics and English Language," 263.
31. Chomsky, *What Kind of Creatures are We?*, 4–10.
32. Chomsky, *Language and Problems of Knowledge*, 36.
33. *Merriam-Webster's Collegiate Dictionary*, s.v. "glossolalia."
34. *Oxford English Dictionary*, s.v. "glossolalia."

understood? It is possible that babbling may be a symptom of mental deficiency, but that does not warrant us to conclude that those who speak in tongues are all mentally deficient. Sometimes unable to fully express one's thoughts through language, people may resort to expressions that may be inappropriate or even nonsensical. This is because human language itself is limited in its expressive capacity and not because the speaker is mentally challenged. K. A. Smith notices that glossolalic prayer expresses a depth of dependency on God.[35] Is dependency on God and yielding to him considered mental deficiency?

Just because tongues are not comprehensible, does that mean that they are not a legitimate language? The Bible accommodates three types of tongues: "tongues of men," "tongues of angels" (1 Cor 13:1), and tongues which only God understands (1 Cor 14:2). An "unknown tongue" is unknown to the one speaking it. Nevertheless, it qualifies as language on the grounds of its intelligibility. The "tongues of men" may be intelligible to some but not to others. Both the Old and New Testaments record that humans understood whenever angels spoke to them. The language may have been Hebrew or Greek, but that does not mean that angels spoke only these languages. What about the conversations among them? Is Heaven a silent monastery? Even though the language spoken directly to God is not understood by anyone, it is intelligible to God and hence legitimate. An "unknown tongue" can be interpreted, which means that it is not meaningless babbling (1 Cor 14:4–5).

Those who were Spirit baptized on the day of Pentecost spoke in languages known to some who were there (Acts 2:8–10). Just because some people could understand some of the languages that were spoken, can we conclude that only languages known to humans were spoken on that day? Other languages, such as those of angels or those which only God understands, may also have been spoken. Perhaps that is why some who witnessed the event dismissed it as the babblings of drunkards. Both those who spoke on the day of Pentecost and those who continue to speak in tongues after that may be speaking in languages of angels or of God, which no humans understand. Since they are incomprehensible to humans, they may be categorized as a type of glossolalia; that does not mean that they are not legitimate languages.

Can we use the rules of human languages to determine the legitimacy of all "unknown tongues?" While "tongues of men" may be interpreted using the rules of language of a particular language, "tongues of angels" and "tongues spoken only to God" cannot be assessed using rules of human

---

35. Smith, *Thinking in Tongues*, 144.

language. That does not mean that they are meaningless, for they are intelligible to angels and God.

Even though speaking in tongues is primarily vocal, we cannot exclude sign language. Deaf people experience legitimate spirit baptisms, with unknown sign languages.[36] One example is the testimony of Sherry Burgoyne, who is deaf and experienced Spirit baptism. When she was sixteen, she committed her life to Christ at a Billy Graham crusade, but she yearned for more. In 1993, she began attending Deaf Shepherd Fellowship in Belleville, Canada, where she recommitted her life to Christ and was water baptized. In 1994, while praying, she experienced something new. While worshipping God, she began to "speak" in a language she did not know; it was not the sign language she had learned and used all her life. She says that her hands, from the elbow joints to her fingertips, began to move so fast that it reminded her of the wings of a hummingbird. It was all new and exciting. She was eager to find out what this experience was. Her pastor explained to her that she was Spirit baptized and spoke in a new language inspired by the Spirit. She realized with joy that she was baptized in the Spirit and speaking a sign language she did not know, an unknown tongue.[37] From that time onwards, she has worshipped God speaking both in sign language and in unknown sign language. Just because we cannot use traditional rules of language to determine its legitimacy, we cannot dismiss it as mere manual gymnastics! One cannot dismiss a language as gibberish only because it does not meet the requirements of spoken language.[38]

Deaf people can also minister in the Spirit through sign language. In 1990, Brent Shepherd[39] was admitted to McMaster Children's Hospital in Hamilton, Canada with acute lymphoblastic leukemia. His condition worsened during chemotherapy and he developed toxic shock syndrome. On November 21, he went into a coma that led to heart failure on November 24. Many prayed earnestly for his recovery through the night. Susan Graham, who is deaf, was awakened from sleep at midnight and began interceding for Brent in sign language. Susan's obedience, along with others across the

---

36. Taylor, "Deaf and the Initial Physical Evidence," 37–45.

37. Sherry Burgoyne shared her testimony with interpreter Adele Routliff, who sent me the account via email.

38. Walvoord, "Holy Spirit and Spiritual Gifts," 115–20; Pollock, *Modern Pentecostalism*. John Walvoord and A. J. Pollock challenge the legitimacy of "unknown tongues" because they fail to meet the syntactic and standards of language. They dismiss speaking in tongues as babbling gibberish.

39. Reverend Brent Shepherd is the youngest son of Reverend David and Connie Shepherd.

country, played a significant role in Brent's miraculous recovery from heart failure on the very same day.

From a biblical perspective, "speaking in tongues" is a legitimate linguistic activity at Spirit baptism (Acts 2:4, 10:45-46, 19:6), as a prayer language, or as a ministerial mode (1 Cor 12-14). Whether "tongues" is taken as part of the baptismal experience or as a gift, the difference is functional rather than qualitative. A common feature stands out when one speaks in tongues. Inspired by the Holy Spirit one speaks in an unknown language. This differs from regular linguistic activity in some significant ways. In a regular linguistic activity, the speaker uses a language that he or she knows. If the hearer also knows that language, then linguistic communication occurs. When one speaks in tongues, not only is the language spoken foreign to the speaker, but in many cases even the hearer does not know what is spoken. This creates a problem. Can there be linguistic communication when both the speaker and hearer do not understand what is spoken? The Bible presents speaking in tongues in three main modes: tongues of men, tongues of angels, and tongues that only God understands. In all three modes, the speaker does not know the language. In the case of "tongues of men," what is spoken is known to some people group (Acts 1:6-8). In the case of "tongues of angels," people do not understand what is spoken but angels do (1 Cor 13:1). In some cases, one may speak in a language only God understands (1 Cor 14:2; see also Rev 14:3). In that case, no one but God understands what is spoken, not even angels. But all three modes of tongues qualify as legitimate languages, since someone understands them. In all cases, speaking in tongues is not merely a physio-mental activity, but one where the supernatural is involved as the Holy Spirit enables (Acts 2:4).

The Bible renders three main roles for speaking in tongues: in the baptismal experience, as a prayer language that edifies believers, and as a ministerial gift edifying the church. The Holy Spirit distributes the gifts at his own discretion and the gift of tongues is one of them (1 Cor 12:7-11). All do not have the ministerial gift of tongues, while there are grounds to claim that "tongues" is integral to the baptismal experience.

Integral to Spirit Baptism

Even those who consider Spirit baptism as a legitimate spiritual experience are hesitant to accommodate tongues. It is sometimes taken as a gift wrap, perhaps meant to glamorize the gift but having no intrinsic connection to it; it is something one could discard after receiving the gift, since the gift wrap is separable from the gift. Tongues, then, is merely a sensational appendage to the baptismal experience. Spirit baptism as an act of giving also includes receiving. Let me suggest that speaking in tongues is an indispensable expression of receiving the gift and is therefore very much part of the experience of baptism in the Spirit; it is part of the package.[40]

Transformative

The significant role of tongues in the baptismal experience becomes evident when we relate Babel to Pentecost. At Babel, God recognized the corrosive effect of perverted human nature in orchestrating a universal language. He saw the builders' vain venture to construct a tower to reach the gods, to make a name for themselves, and to avoid being scattered (Gen 11:5–6). At Babel, people united by one language and enthused by a parochial sense of security strove to reach the impossible, hoping to become world renowned. In fact, God's dispersal by multiplying languages was a redemptive act to prevent such a catastrophic mistake. The day of Pentecost is God's response to Babel's blunder. On this day, he did not offer people a universal language but provided them a mode of linguistic articulation that united, edified, and empowered them to be his witnesses, not only in Jerusalem, their comfort zone, but in challenging and unfamiliar parts of the world (Acts 2:11, 1:7–8). On that day, the 120 people in the upper room glorified God and talked about his wonders (Acts 2:11). The miracle of Pentecost was not merely that the believers spoke in languages unknown to them, but in whatever language they spoke they were all glorifying God, quite unlike the self-glorifying language expressed at Babel: "so that we may make a name for ourselves" (Gen 11:4). The unity among the believers came not as the result of a universal language, but amidst a multiplicity of languages (Acts 2:9–11). The baptismal experience transformed the believers at their very core. It is here that speaking in tongues plays a vital role. What underlies and motivates such speaking is the willingness to yield to the Spirit. Such yielding is not imposed but is purely voluntary.

Expresses Yielding

Yielding is a voluntary act, unlike reflex action or reaction. A reflex action occurs when the body reacts to a stimulus automatically and often instantaneously "without reaching the level of consciousness and often without passing to the brain."[41] While reflex action is involuntary, reaction may be voluntary, though usually instantaneous.

---

40. Kulathungam, "Why Tongues?," 22–37.
41. *Merriam-Webster Dictionary*, s.v. "reflex."

When we say that we did something without thinking, that may be our unconscious mind at work. One may react to the Spirit in several ways. This has happened many times in many ways. In Barton Stone's autobiography, he lists the forms of religious ecstasy that he witnessed in camp meetings during his lifetime: falling, shaking, barking, dancing, laughing, and running.[42] These would be considered reactions, with the power of the Spirit as the stimulus. They may be sincere and a blessing to those involved, but they are different from yielding to the Spirit, which is a conscious act of will. Speaking in tongues is an expression of such yielding; one speaks as the Spirit gives utterance. Speaking in tongues is a response to the Spirit, rather than a mere reaction to the power of the Spirit.

Such a response is voluntary where both the conscious and unconscious parts of a mind are at work.[43] It is not mere reaction or an emotive outburst, but an act where one's will is the determining factor. The thousands on the day of Pentecost did not react to the noise that spread out from the upper room, but responded to Peter's sermon and decided to follow his instructions to experience the baptism (Acts 2:41).

The term "yield" sometimes has a negative connotation when taken as giving up control because one is forced to. The Holy Spirit is a gentleman and does not force himself into the life of a person or make one a slave. The one baptized in the Spirit can always backslide, choose not to continue speaking in tongues, or even deny their experience. What happened at Pentecost was a voluntary act of yielding to the Spirit through speaking in unknown languages. Such yielding may result in exuberant or ecstatic expressions; that does not mean that the whole experience is mere empty emotion. Jesus' analogy of what happens when a person receives the Holy Spirit—rivers of living water will flow from within them (John 7:38)—is helpful to appreciate what happens internally in Spirit baptism. The word baptism is derived from a root that connotes a complete overwhelming. When the word baptism is associated with the experience of Spirit baptism, it conveys the idea of saturation of the inner being of the one baptized in the Spirit. This happens when the believer who is already indwelt by the Spirit at salvation yields fully to him.[44] Of course, one could live a life yielded to the Spirit without speaking in tongues. What is stressed here is that Spirit baptism is an experience of yielding that is expressed through speaking in tongues.

42. Stone, "Piercing Screams and Heavenly Smiles."
43. James, "React vs Respond."
44. Holdcroft, *Holy Spirit*, 117.

Since speaking in tongues is a voluntary act there is always a possibility of misuse, such as pretending to speak in tongues, sensational vocalization for showmanship, and pseudoexpressions, some even manipulated by Satan. Tongues cannot be learned, but spoken as the Spirit gives utterance. Being preoccupied with the mechanics of tongue-speaking instead of yielding to the Spirit is putting the cart before the horse. Paul points out that those speaking in tongues without being motivated by love are merely making noise like a "resounding gong or a clanging cymbal" (1 Cor 13:1). Although the cymbal was used both in Greco-Roman and Jewish worship, it did not really create music but rather made noise.[45] When speaking in tongues is motivated by selfless love, it fulfills its intended role both in the baptismal experience, as well as a prayer language and as a ministerial gift.

Tongues and Spirit baptism may be distinguishable in meaning, but they are not separable in the experience of Spirit baptism. The Spirit is at work in the life of a person from the time of salvation and even before one becomes a believer. The Holy Spirit plays a vital role at salvation not only by regenerating those in sin, but also giving them the assurance of salvation; all these roles occur without tongues. One can be led and used by the Spirit in various ministries without speaking in tongues, but in the experience of Spirit baptism, tongues plays an indispensable role.

One may be led to believe that tongues is not integral to the baptismal experience since instances of Spirit baptism cited in the Bible sometimes mention tongues and sometimes do not (Acts 2:4, 1:46, 19:6, 8:15–17). The biblical stance is not based on statistical evidence. According to what happened on the day of Pentecost, the Bible portrays Spirit baptism as an occasion when one yields to the Spirit and articulates such yielding through speaking in tongues. In fact, the apostles and Paul saw the Spirit baptism that occurred on the day of Pentecost as the model to be followed. For instance, Peter ordered the gentiles who had been Spirit baptized to be baptized in water, since they had received the Spirit just as the apostles did on the day of Pentecost, by speaking in tongues (Acts 10:46–48). Considering Peter's view of Spirit baptism on the day of Pentecost as the ideal model to be followed, Luke does not need to mention tongues in every instance of Spirit baptism. In a statistically driven world, we try to validate our conclusions based only on statistics. Is this the only way to reach conclusions? The Bible highlights tongues as part of a package; speaking in tongues plays an integral and indispensable role in the experience of being baptized in the Holy Spirit.

---

45. Levine and Brettler, *Jewish Annotated New Testament*, footnote on 1 Corinthians 13:1, 345NTn.

Character and Role

When we take tongues as part of the baptismal experience, we should be careful not to mar the character and role of tongues. Categorizing tongues as merely physical evidence restricts its character. Speaking a language is not mere physical behavior since it involves the mental and emotional facets. When we view tongues as the audible evidence, we limit its scope. We exclude deaf people from being baptized in the Spirit for they use certain sign languages unknown to them, but which are not audible.

It is understandable why tongues has been viewed as the sign or evidence for Spirit baptism. Modern Pentecostalism had a difficult childbirth! The Pentecostal movement came out of a Christian world with a rich spiritual heritage, which was naturally skeptical about what Pentecostals claimed. The baptism of the Spirit was the main point of controversy. There were several types of spiritual experiences attributed to the work of the Holy Spirit in almost every facet of Christian life. The Pentecostals could not and did not deny the validity of such expressions of spirituality, but highlighted the legitimacy and distinctiveness of the experience of Spirit baptism and looked to the first Pentecost as the model to be followed. On the grounds of this model, they found that the best way to legitimize Spirit baptism as a distinctive spiritual experience was to pick out tongues as the sign or evidence of the experience. It turned out to be an apologetic tool. Highlighting tongues in this way has, on the one hand, rendered distinctiveness to Pentecostalism, but has also made it controversial.

Signs other than tongues have been cited for Spirit baptism, such as bold speech (Acts 4:31); miraculous ministry of signs and wonders (Acts 5:12); praise and worship (Acts 10:46); dreams, visions, and prophecies (Acts 2:17); unity among believers (Acts 2:42-47); love (Rom 5:5; 1 Cor 13); and the fruits of the Spirit (Matt 7:16; Gal 5:22-23). All of them are valid signs, but signs of what? We need to distinguish the experience of the baptism in the Spirit from the life in the Spirit that results from it. Just like the wedding ceremony is different from the married life that follows it, Spirit baptism is different from the life in the Spirit that follows it. After chapter 2, the book of Acts records how those who were Spirit baptized lived in the Spirit. They spoke boldly, did miraculous signs and wonders, praised and worshipped in the Spirit, had visions and dreams, ministered prophetically, exhibited unity as believers, and manifested the fruits of the Spirit in their life of witness. All these are signs of a healthy life in the Spirit. When Jesus, before his departure, told his disciples that they would receive power to witness in Jerusalem, Judea, Samaria, and to the ends of the earth (Luke 24:49; Acts 1:8), he was referring to life in the Spirit that results from being baptized in the Spirit. He commanded his disciples to wait for the baptism in the Spirit so that they would be able to live a victorious life in the Spirit.

We should also keep in mind that one may have a great baptismal experience, but then afterwards not exhibit the life of power that Jesus assured. Just as the gift of the Holy Spirit is voluntarily received by a believer, the life in the Spirit that follows Spirit baptism depends on the voluntary submission to the guidance of the Spirit. One may have a grand wedding but experience a miserable married life and even deviate from their marriage vows. Likewise, a believer could always turn away from God even after being Spirit baptized, as Paul noted of the Corinthian believers who had become worldly (1 Cor 2:14–15). We should not forget that speaking in tongues is not robotic but voluntary, so there is always room for turning away from God. However, speaking in tongues as a prayer language could prevent deviating. When one prays in tongues, one is edified (1 Cor 14:4) and this in turn prevents deviating or backsliding. Spirituality becomes a lifestyle rather than a series of sporadic experiences. Ron Kydd warns Pentecostals not to define spirituality only in terms of experiences. He calls for a spirituality of lifestyle, not of crisis.[46]

Indispensable to the Act of Gifting

When Spirit baptism is viewed as an act of gifting, it involves the giver, the gift, and the receiving of the gift. If any one of these is missing, gifting does not occur. On the day of Pentecost, God the Father was the giver, God the Son executed the giving, and God the Holy Spirit was the gift. The gift had to be received and this is where tongues entered the scene; it was part of the act of receiving the gift. The experience of Spirit baptism may include exuberant praise, penitent prayer, and devotional singing in one's own language, but speaking in an unknown tongue involves allowing the Holy Spirit to provide the language. It is an act of yielding oneself by faith to the Spirit. To speak in a known language needs linguistic proficiency, but to speak in an unknown language requires faith. It is only when that step of faith is taken that one experiences the baptism in the Spirit. The act of receiving the gift of the Spirit by yielding to him through speaking in tongues accomplishes the baptismal experience. Call it a sign, evidence, or whatever you wish, but tongues is integral to the experience of being baptized in the Spirit; it makes gifting possible. As R. E. McAllister points out in the first edition of the *Canadian Pentecostal Testimony*, "The mighty baptism was originally accompanied by speaking in other tongues as the Spirit gives utterance."[47]

---

46. Kydd, "Walking Straight in a Crooked World," 18–19.
47. McAllister, "Baptism of the Holy Ghost," 1.

Such a baptism revolutionized the spiritual life of those baptized on the day of Pentecost both individually and collectively. It changed Peter the denier, Thomas the doubter, and Paul the persecutor into powerful pioneers of the gospel. Collectively, Spirit baptism initiated a church which grew far and wide, amidst Roman persecution. Spirit baptism may be seen as the pivotal event that ignited a revolution and set the precedents and parameters for subsequent spiritual stances and practices. The spiritual revolution that commenced on the day of Pentecost continues to this day.

THE ONGOING SPIRITUAL REVOLUTION

The spiritual revolution was not just an exciting one-day event, but initiated a type of spiritual life that was novel and controversial. It drastically changed the practice of prayer, worship, and lifestyle among believers. All these were made possible through the enabling and abiding presence of the Holy Spirit.

Prayer and Worship

People have been praying throughout the ages. Pentecost came into a world where praying was very much in fashion. This period has been described as "the age of anxiety and aspiration."[48] Both the Jewish and gentile worlds yearned to be released from the anxiety of the age, and such help came on the day of Pentecost. On that day, a group of people gathered in the upper room and prayed. How they prayed we do not know. They were Jews and were accustomed to Jewish modes of prayer. Jesus had already tutored some of them about how to pray and had taught his disciples the Lord's Prayer. As Eli Lizorkin-Eyzenberg points out, the Lord's Prayer has Jewish liturgical roots.[49] The Spirit-baptized Jews may have prayed the Jewish way, but there was something novel about their prayer. Although they prayed in many languages, their prayer had a common theme. They all glorified God and remembered his wonders. We should remember that those who prayed came out of a world filled with anxiety. Anxious people, even when they sincerely pray, tend to concentrate on their own problems. The prayer of those Spirit baptized, however, was a refreshing breath in such a context, for it was a prayer that was rooted in God and his mighty acts. Those who were Spirit baptized prayed with enthusiasm to God, who kept his promise of sending the Spirit in the time they needed him most. Also, they did not stop praying after the excitement of the day of Pentecost was over. Prayer

---

48. Puskas and Robbins, *Introduction to the New Testament*, 4.
49. Lizorkin-Eyzenberg, "Does the Lord's Prayer?"

became a lifestyle, rather than a schedule to be followed at set times. They prayed and fellowshipped daily (Acts 2:42, 46–47).

Those who pray can become frustrated because their prayers are not answered. One reason may be that they are not praying according to God's will. Praying in tongues enables people to pray according to God's will; the Holy Spirit himself intercedes with groans that words cannot express (Rom 8:26–27). The Holy Spirit, who knows the believer through and through, intercedes according to God's will through such groans, even when the believer doesn't know what to pray.

A common hindrance to prayer is distraction. When praying in a known language, the words we use may themselves distract us. For instance, if one had been mistreated by his or her father, using Father to address God in prayer becomes a distraction. Also, it is possible for us to verbalize and yet be concerned about our daily chores and concerns; the Martha in us hinders our prayer life. Some forms of Eastern meditation have grasped the efficacy of meaningless expressions to empty one's mind from distractions.[50] Though speaking in tongues helps us to be free from distractions in our prayer life, it is very different from techniques that attempt to empty the mind. Praying in the Spirit does not empty the mind, but fills it with God's greatness and his blessings. In addition, when a believer speaks in a tongue known only to God (1 Cor 14:2), he or she is in a place of complete security, for only God understands the language; this could be considered "the shelter of the Most High" and resting "in the shadow of the Almighty" (Ps 91:1). Paul found the benefits of praying in the Spirit through tongues. He confessed that he spoke in tongues more than all the Corinthian believers (1 Cor 14:18). Praying in the Spirit added a new dimension to the practice of prayer, both collective and individual.

Praying that glorifies God naturally facilitates worshipping him, for worship is honoring or revering what one considers most worthy. Worship, like prayer, has been a religious practice through the ages. The Jews were a worshipping community and their center of worship was the temple. The worship that followed Spirit baptism was neither temple based nor priest led. In fact, Jesus told the Samaritan woman at the well that a time was coming when true worshippers would not be restricted to worship on Mount Gerizim[51] or in Jerusalem, but would worship God in Spirit and in truth and

---

50. Kulathungam, "Christian Meditation." Some Eastern meditational techniques use meaningless terms like koans in Zen Buddhist meditation and mantric repetitions like "Om" in transcendental meditation.

51. NIV Study Bible, footnote for John 4:21, 1598NTn. The proper place of worship had been a source of debate between Samaritans and Jews. Samaritans claimed Mount Gerizim to be the proper place and built a temple there in 440 BCE.

that such worship would please God (John 4:23–24). This is the worship that was enacted in the upper room. It was quite different from priest-led liturgical worship. Those who were Spirit baptized continued to worship and pray in the temple, and daily they gathered in the temple courts to pray (Acts 2:46). Peter and John healed the crippled beggar at the Beautiful Gate on their way to pray at the temple (Acts 3:1). The worship of the Spirit baptized was not restricted to the temple or synagogues. Whether they worshipped in the temple premises or at other locations, what characterized their worship was that it was corporate and participatory and not mere performance.

Worship was also very popular in the gentile world. Impacted by Greek and Eastern spiritual modes, some adopted knowledge, meditation, or worship of multiple gods. Those impacted by Greek philosophical trends turned to knowledge to enhance their quality of life. When they acquired such liberating knowledge, they were naturally exhilarated. Those impacted by Eastern religions experienced the excitement of worship when they realized that they were part of the cosmic divine reality. These modes, being founded on the conviction that self-effort could deliver the goods, were essentially individualistic. Each one, when excited by the success of their individual effort, naturally worshipped individually. The worship of those who were Spirit baptized at Pentecost appeared to be out of place and still continues to be incongruous. The heresy of individualism, as David Hazzard and Stacey McKenzie point out, breeds self-importance and self-reliance leading to self-arrogance.[52] In the contemporary context, where individualism has infiltrated into religious worship, Pentecostal worship appears out of place.

Worship that Pentecost introduced also became controversial, for it included singing and speaking in unknown tongues. This added an entirely new dimension to worship. Worship that accommodated tongues was not merely strange, but also tampered with the human ego. Tongues as a means of yielding to God is founded on the dictum, "He must become greater; I must become less" (John 3:30). Such a practice ran counter to the prevalent egoistic culture in a world that attempted to orchestrate worship to celebrate spiritual fulfillment through self-effort. Pentecostal prayer and worship continue to be controversial because egoistic individualism is still very much alive. When worship in the Spirit turns into performance-oriented showmanship, it will lose its efficacy.

Spirituality that Went Beyond the Spiritual

Pentecost came into a world where spirituality tended to either degrade or exclude the physical. This attitude about the physical was prominent in the

---

52. Hazzard and McKenzie, "Heresy of Individualism," 14.

mindset of people impacted by Greek philosophy and Eastern religions, and Pentecost ran counter to such a mindset. The fact that the Holy Spirit took residence in people highlights that the spiritual is not allergic to the physical human body. Paul urges the Romans to offer their bodies as living sacrifices and stresses that this is a spiritual act of worship (Rom 12:1–2). Moreover, life in the Spirit does not exclude the mental. In his letter to Timothy, Paul points out that God has not given us the spirit of fear, but of power, of love, and of a sound mind (2 Tim 1:7). In his view, the human body living in the Spirit could enhance the mind. One of the main gifts of the Spirit is the gift of healing. After the day of Pentecost, the apostles not only ministered to the spiritual needs of people, but also to their physical, psychological, and spiritual needs, even delivering those possessed by demons. Peter healed the crippled beggar at the temple gate (Acts 3:6–8). Peter's shadow healed several sick people as they lay on the streets. These acts indicate that the ministry of healing prominently figured after the day of Pentecost (Acts 3:1–10, 5:12–16). The spirituality that Pentecost offered did not separate the physiomental from the spiritual. Life in the Spirit encompassed every facet of human personhood.

Sometimes spirituality tends to make us so heavenly minded that we forget the world in which we live. Jesus advised his disciples to be in the world but not of the world (John 15:19, 7:14–16), which Paul also advocated (Rom 12:2; Eph 4:22–24; 1 Thess 4:1). This advice indicates that even though we should not be gripped by the world, we are not called to ascetic isolation. We are called to live in this God-fashioned earth and to appreciate it and take care of it. As we have noted in chapter 1, the blunder in the Garden of Eden flawed both humanity and the world. Both desperately needed help, and the help had to come from above. It came from God through Christ, who came to redeem both humans and the world (John 3:16). God the Spirit's care for the world commenced at the very beginning (Gen 1:2). Any strategy to solve the ecological problems of the world must be Christocentric and Spirit enabled.[53] It calls for believers empowered by the Spirit to go beyond being merely stewards taking care of the earth. God is not an absentee landlord. He is very much involved in the redemptive process and calls on humans to partner with him. Life in the Spirit encompasses taking care of God's creation.

Spirituality that Crossed Boundaries

The Holy Spirit that was poured out on the day of Pentecost and subsequent spiritual events went beyond the Jewish borders. Before his departure, Jesus

---

53. Kulathungam, "Christocentric Anthropocosmic Approach," 1–3.

told his disciples that they would be empowered by the Spirit to witness in Jerusalem, Judea, Samaria, and to the ends of the earth (Acts 1:8). To propagate such an explosive spirituality in a world of multiple spiritualities was both a challenge and an opportunity for the Jewish believers. For a Jew to minister to Samaritans and to the pagan gentiles worldwide was a rare, if not a real, challenge. Only the Spirit enabled Paul and the Jewish apostles to cross such boundaries. First, they needed to get out of their comfort zone and be exposed to the world at large. Paul's missionary journeys indicate the scope and effectiveness of Holy Spirit-empowered ministry that crossed several boundaries, countries, cultures, religiosities, and philosophies. The secret of Paul's success was that even though he crossed boundaries, he was careful to keep within the borders of the spirituality that Pentecost offered. He warned the Corinthians not to deviate from Jesus, the Spirit, and the gospel (2 Cor 11:1-4). The intertwining of pneumatology, soteriology, and Christology was that which rendered spirituality authentic and thereby relevant and effective to the spiritual aspirations of the people of that time. It is ultimately the Holy Spirit that enables one to fulfill the core aspirations of the spiritual quest of humans.

The spiritual revolution that reached its climax on the day of Pentecost is still continuing and is fast becoming global. Will such spirituality become outdated in this age of the technocratic digital revolution that is surging at high speed throughout our world? As long as humans survive and are not completely replaced by robots and nanobots,[54] let me suggest the spiritual revolution that occurred 2,000 years ago will not become out of date. Humans are not merely rational animals or mechanical constructs, but have a spiritual component in their very beings that motivates their spiritual quest. As long as Pentecost fulfills that quest, it will not become archaic. Those who claim to be part of Pentecost need to be authentic in their spirituality: Christ centered, gospel motivated, and Spirit empowered.

---

54. Cision PR Newswire, "Global Nanotechnology Market 2018–2024." Futurists predict nanobots will have diagnostic and creative abilities. Nanotechnology is an emerging and rapidly growing field, expected to exceed US$125 billion by 2024.

7

The Cross: Stumbling Block or Folly?

In writing to the Corinthians, Paul points out that: "Jews demand signs and Greeks look for wisdom, but we preach Christ crucified: a stumbling block to Jews and foolishness to Gentiles, but to those whom God has called, both Jews and Greeks, Christ the power of God and the wisdom of God" (1 Cor 1:22–24).

During Paul's time, the city of Corinth had a population of both Jews and Greeks. Although Corinth was not a university city like Athens, it was impacted by Greek culture. Many Corinthians were enthralled by Greek philosophy, which placed a high premium on wisdom.[1] There were prominent Jewish thinkers, like Philo of Alexandria, who attempted to articulate Christian dogmas by adopting Greek philosophical concepts. Like Athens, Corinth had many temples. The most popular ones were the temples dedicated to Aphrodite, the goddess of love; to Asclepius, the god of healing; and the temple of Apollo. At that time, most Corinthians were polytheists, but some leaned towards monotheism as articulated by philosophers like Plato and Aristotle. Like any large commercial city, Corinth was a center for open and unbridled immorality. The worship of Aphrodite fostered prostitution. So widely known was the immorality of Corinth that the Greek verb, "to Corinthianize," meant "to practice sexual immorality."[2] Both the Jewish and Greek cultures had an impact on the psyche and lifestyle of the people

---

1. NIV Study Bible, introductory notes on the book of 1 Corinthians, 1734NTn.
2. NIV Study Bible, introductory notes on the book of 1 Corinthians, 1734NTn.

of Corinth. This was the context in which Paul addresses the Corinthians. "Christ crucified" is not presented as mere dogma, but as the basis for a distinct way of life.

If Jesus had not gone to the cross, perhaps he would have been acknowledged as a knowledgeable though unconventional rabbi by the Jews, an eminent professor of great wisdom by the Greeks, and a compassionate miracle worker by many others. If he had gone to the cross but died and remained buried, he would have been acclaimed a martyr, like Socrates, who died for a great cause. But Jesus rose again! This makes him more than human. If he was indeed God, how could God die? As Paul points out, Jesus becomes controversial both to Jews and gentiles; Jesus was a stumbling block to the Jews and utter folly to the gentile Greeks. Let us first see how Christ was controversial in the Jewish world.

JEWISH REACTION

In his book, *A Rabbi Talks With Jesus*, Jewish research professor and author Rabbi Jacob Neusner places himself within the context of the Gospel of Matthew and imagines himself having a dialogue with Jesus. After listening to his Sermon on the Mount, Neusner engages with Jesus in a candid conversation about issues pertaining to Jesus' teachings. Neusner tries to understand and assess Jesus within the rabbinic tradition that is based on the *Torah* and supported by the *Mishnah* and *Talmud*. Though impressed by Jesus' teaching, Neusner is concerned about how incompatible the sermon's message is with his own convictions. He now retires for prayer and study with the Jews of a nearby town and starts a discussion with the master rabbi of that town. The conversation runs like this (*Note: "I" stands for Neusner and "He" for the master rabbi of the synagogue*):

> Citing the Babylonian Talmud, the Rabbi commences the discussion: "Six hundred and thirteen commandments were given to Moses, three hundred and sixty-five negative ones, corresponding to the number of the days of the solar year, and two hundred forty-eight positive commandments, corresponding to the parts of man's body. David came and reduced them to eleven ... Isaiah came and reduced them to six ... Micah came and reduced them to three ... Isaiah again came and reduced them to two ... Amos came and reduced them to a single one, as it is said, 'For thus says the Lord to the house of Israel. Seek Me and live.' Habbakuk further came and based them on one, as it is said, 'But the righteous shall live by his faith' (Hab 2:4)." (Babylonian Talmud Makkot 24A-B)

> "So," the master (Rabbi) says, "is that what the sage, Jesus, had to say?"
> I: "Not exactly, but close."
> He: "What did he leave out?"
> I: "Nothing."
> He: "Then what did he add?"
> I: "Himself."
> He: "Oh!"[3]

The exclamation at the end of the dialogue reveals the core point of controversy between Jews and Christians. Neusner listens to Jesus' sermon through Jewish eyes and considers the topics Jesus covers in the Sermon on the Mount, like the Beatitudes, Sabbath, the fourth commandment, and the kingdom of heaven. Eventually he reaches a conclusion about why the sermon did not convince him to follow Jesus. While treating Jesus with utter respect, Neusner points out that the core issue between Jews and Christians is Jesus himself. Why is Jesus so controversial?

Jesus was a Jew. He was born to Jewish parents and grew up as a Jew. In keeping with Jewish tradition, he was circumcised on the eighth day after his birth. He was baptized by a Jewish prophet, John the Baptist. He read from the Jewish Bible, the Old Testament. Even though he had some issues with the Pharisees and Sadducees, he worshipped at the temple in Jerusalem and participated in synagogue sessions. His disciples were all Jewish and he ministered mainly to the Jews within Jewish territory. In communicating to the Samaritan woman on certain important matters concerning worship, he spoke to her as a Jew (John 4:1–26). Even though accused of attempting to destroy the temple, that was not his desire. He was tried at a Jewish court, the Sanhedrin. He was buried and died as a Jew.

Joseph Klausner, an eminent Jewish scholar, affirms that Jesus of Nazareth was a product of pure Judaism without any external additives, and places him entirely until his last breath in the Judaism of his time.[4] Despite Jesus' Jewishness, he was and is a controversial figure in the Jewish world. Rabbi Dr. Barry Leff poses a question concerning Jesus:

> What is it about Jesus that gives Jews the "heebie-jeebies?" Is he a topic we shouldn't discuss?
> It's understandable why Jews have problems with Jesus. Centuries of anti-Semitism were carried out in his name. It's nice that Christians have apologized for that, but the Jewish cultural aversion to Christianity, Jesus, crosses, etc., runs very deep.

---

3. Neusner, *Rabbi Talks With Jesus*, 107–8.
4. Klausner, *Jesus of Nazareth*, 363.

> For Christians, Judaism is the root and source of their religion, so many Christians are comfortable talking about Judaism. For Jews, Christianity is not just heresy, it's a threat. It's heresy that has led to persecution and violence on the one hand, and assimilation and loss of identity on the other hand.[5]

In Leff's view, Christianity for the Jews is not just a heresy but rather a threat that led to their persecution and the loss of their national identity. They are understandably unable to forget the Holocaust, propagated in the name of Christianity, and anti-Semitism, which unfortunately seems to continue to rear its ugly head in subtle ways in our world today. Without being preoccupied with the polemics, let us consider the underlying threat that Christianity presents to Judaism. It stems from the core Christian dogma of Christ crucified. As Paul points out, this claim is the stumbling block to the Jews. A stumbling block is not a speed bump that merely slows down one's travel. It is not a stop sign that makes one stop at a red light and then proceed when the light turns green. A stumbling block puts an end to one's planned travel route and alters the schedule. The journey must either terminate or detour via an unexpected path. Despite concerted reconciliatory efforts through contemporary Jewish-Christian dialogues, "Christ crucified" continues to be a stumbling block to the Jews. It is perceived as shattering their travel plans. New Testament scholars like N. T. Wright, Mark Baker, and Joel Green prefer to use the word "scandal" to depict the Jewish and gentile reaction to Christ crucified during the time of Jesus.[6] Scandal, like stumbling block, has a disruptive effect. Later in this chapter, we will consider how the cross figured as an object of mockery in the gentile world. In such a context, scandal poignantly expresses the attitude of mockery. Whether the cross is depicted as a stumbling block or a scandal, it was a formidable roadblock. The cross and the one who died on it became controversial to the Jews in more than one way.

---

5. Leff, "Jewish View of Jesus," paras. 3–4.
6. Wright, *Day the Revolution Began*; Baker, *Proclaiming the Scandal*; Baker and Green, *Recovering the Scandal*.

The Controversial Rabbi

Jesus and the Rabbis (section of a larger painting by Isaak Asknaziy, 1879)

As noted in chapter 5, the word *rabbi* in Aramaic meant "teacher" or "master." During Jesus' time, a rabbi did not have official status and was not authorized to decide issues pertaining to Jewish law—the term simply referred to a Jewish teacher. It was in this sense that Jesus was referred to as a rabbi. The Pharisees, who were fastidious in keeping to the letter of the law, found Jesus the rabbi controversial.

Jewish scholar Lawrence Schiffman clarifies some points of controversy between Jesus and the Pharisees.[7] He notes that Luke portrays them as addressing Jesus with respect (Luke 5:17, 9:39), inviting him to dine with them (Luke 7:36, 11:37, 14:1), and offering him help when he was in trouble (Luke 13:31). But Schiffman goes on to point out, "The Gospels overwhelmingly portray the Pharisees in a negative light. They are often pictured as ready to challenge Jesus, entrap him or test him" (Matt 12:36; Mark 8:11; Luke 11:53–54).[8] Jesus also criticized pharisaic practices such as not harvesting grain (Matt 12:1–2), healing on the Sabbath (John 9:13–17), and refusing to eat with sinners and tax collectors (Mark 2:15–16). In defending the Pharisees, Schiffman claims that they did not disdain or reject the poor,

---

7. Schiffman, "Pharisees," 619–22.
8. Schiffman, "Pharisees," 621.

but opposed people transgressing the Torah's commands and thereby collaborating with the Roman Empire.⁹ He identifies the underlying issue the Pharisees had with Jesus: it was over the Torah, how it should be interpreted, and what role it should play in Jewish doctrine and practice. The Pharisees fully acknowledged the authority of the Torah when interpreting it and evaluating Jewish traditions. For instance, it was not pharisaic practice to harvest grain on the Sabbath. Jesus criticized the Pharisees, giving examples from the Old Testament and implying that they misapplied the Old Testament law regarding harvesting on the Sabbath to the actions of his disciples (Matt 12:3–7). This made the stance of the Pharisees appear hyper-legalistic and tradition bound. When Jesus drove the merchants and the money changers from the temple (Matt 21:12–17; Mark 11:15–19, Luke 19:45–48; John 2:13–16) it appeared to the Jews that he was attacking one of the sacred practices in the temple: the sacrificial system. The merchants were selling animals for sacrifice and the money changers were enabling people to pay the merchants in Jewish currency.[10]

Christ Driving the Money-Changers from the Temple
(Oil on panel by Garofalo (Benvenuto Tisi), c. 1540–50 CE)

[9]. Schiffman, "Pharisees," 622.

[10]. Matthew 21:12–13, Mark 11:15–18, Luke 19:45–46, and John 2:13–17. Money changers changed the Greek and Roman money for Jewish currency to be given to the merchants.

Was Jesus really attacking the sacrificial system prevalent in the temple or rather the exploitive profit-making of merchants? Was he not concerned that the house of prayer was becoming a commercial center? No matter his intent, Jesus' criticisms and actions appeared harsh and even derogatory to pharisaic Jews.

In the Jewish context, a rabbi is expected to take the Torah as the authority in his teaching. Jews found that Jesus taught as one who had authority and not as their teachers of law (Matt 7:24–29). The Jews thought that Jesus was making himself the final authority to interpret the Torah. We have already referred to Jesus teaching in the synagogue on a passage from Isaiah 61. Jesus' application of that prophetic passage to himself disturbed the Jews. No Jewish rabbi would have done that. Not surprisingly, the Pharisees viewed Jesus as a controversial rabbi who had crossed boundaries. He became even more controversial when he was acclaimed as Messiah

The Controversial Messiah

One recurrent theme in Old Testament prophecies was the promise of a future age of universal peace under God's sovereign rule. Traditionally, Judaism claimed that such an age will be brought about by a God-appointed person called the *Mashiach* (Messiah). Based on one of Maimonides's (1135–1204 CE) thirteen Principles of Faith—"I believe with perfect faith in the coming of the Messiah, and though he may delay I will wait daily for his coming"—many Jews pray daily, "May the offshoot of your servant David soon flower."

Jews have been inundated with many claiming to be Messiah. To distinguish the legitimate one from such claimants, Jews came to call him *HaMashiach* (literally, The Messiah).

The Jews during Jesus' time had endured and survived under several imperial powers. They hoped that the freedom they obtained through the Maccabean Revolt would last, but it did not. They came under the power of Rome. Their frustration gave birth to the hope of deliverance and many Jews longed for messianic deliverance.

Josephus names the Pharisees, Sadducees, and Essenes as prominent and influential Jewish groups during Jesus' time. Of these groups, the Sadducees did not have any explicit doctrine concerning the Messiah. Pharisees believed in a Messiah who would be a human being with superhuman powers mandated by God to set up his sovereign rule. Like the Pharisees, the Essenes were very meticulous in obeying the law of Moses. Their interpretation of the Torah was based on the views of their "Teacher of

Righteousness,"[11] and only his interpretation of the Scriptures was seen as valid. The Essenes are noted for their life of seclusion and for preserving the Dead Sea Scrolls. Even though they did not believe in bodily resurrection, they had strong messianic anticipation. Although it is not clear whether the Essenes believed in one or many messiahs, their anticipation of the Messiah was very definitive.

The Zealots could also be included as another prominent group advocating messianic deliverance. They wanted to break away from Roman domination, but their means of achieving this was through violence. They hoped that the Messiah would overthrow Roman power through military means.

Jesus came to a world where messianic anticipation was pronounced in certain sectors. Was Jesus the anticipated Messiah? Some Jews accepted him, while many rejected him. Why? There are many reasons why the Jewish world found Jesus as Messiah not only a disappointment, but also a stumbling block to their anticipation of *HaMashiach*. If the Messiah had already arrived, why anticipate?

The name given to Jesus ignited the controversy. In Hebrew, "Jesus" has the same root as the names Joshua or Isaiah.[12] It means "Savior" or "Lord who saves" (Matt 1:21). The term "Christ," on the other hand, is of Greek origin and means "anointed" or "chosen." It should be noted that the Hebrew word *Mashiach* (Messiah) also means "anointed." The Hebrew word *Mashiach* in Romanized Greek was *Christos* (Christ). Both the Hebrew *Mashiach* and the Greek *Christos* referred to a person who was anointed by God. In a world where Greek culture was so widespread, the name Christ was adopted much faster than Hebrew-derived Messiah. In the Greek-oriented world of the time, Jesus Christ became more popular than Jesus the Messiah in referring to Jesus. Jesus Christ referred to the historical figure who was both Savior (Jesus) and Messiah (Christ). It is precisely this reference to the historical Jesus as both Savior and Messiah that made him so controversial in the Jewish world. "Savior," as characterized by Christians, and "Messiah," as depicted by Jews, were strange bedfellows!

As noted in chapter 5, the Savior in the Christian narrative is God incarnate, not merely human. He was miraculously born, displayed a unique authority to interpret the Scriptures, forgave sinners, was crucified but raised from death, and will come again as King of kings and Lord of lords. His mission on earth was to save all humanity and ultimately redeem all

---

11. The "Teacher of Righteousness" is a figure found in some of the Dead Sea Scrolls at Qumran, which refers to the origin of a sect, probably the Essenes. The scroll talks about God raising a teacher of righteousness to guide them.

12. The biblical meaning of "Isaiah" is "The salvation of the Lord."

creation. To associate such a Savior with the Jewish depiction of Messiah raised many questions, to say the least.

Jesus Christ as the Savior-Messiah became controversial in the Jewish world; his birth, his messiahship on the grounds of his genealogy, his claim to authority that belongs only to God, his fulfillment of messianic prophecies, his death, and his resurrection were all controversial.

From the Christian perspective, for Jesus to be Savior, he had to be conceived by the Holy Spirit and not through normal reproductive processes. Anyone born in the normal way is born in sin and therefore cannot save sinners. The Jews challenge this claim on the grounds that "born of a virgin" could also be interpreted "born of a young woman" (Isa 7:14). To establish that Jesus was the Messiah, his genealogy was traced from David, but this claim is not valid according to the Jews.[13]

Jesus' way of interpreting the Scriptures went beyond the methods of other rabbis. He appeared to the Jews as one claiming authority to interpret the Scriptures: an authority only possessed by God. As a human, the Jewish Messiah would interpret the Scriptures like any other rabbi. In Jesus' interpretation of the Scriptures, it appeared that he had authority over God's word, the Torah, and this the Jews could not accept. We need to remember that the motivating factor in Jesus' strategy was to universalize the scope of the law so that it would be a path for all. To make the law amenable to all, he had to go beyond its restrictive literal meaning by highlighting its spiritual connotation.[14] In adopting such a strategy, Jesus appears as the Savior who had divine authority.

Jews saw fulfillment of Old Testament messianic prophecies as one of the main requirements of a legitimate Messiah.[15] These prophecies highlighted that the Messiah would initiate an age of world peace (Isa 2:1–4) under the kingship of God (Zech 14:9).[16] In establishing such a world order, he would gather all Jews to the land of Israel (Isa 43:5–6) and build the third temple (Ezek 37:26–28). For the Jews, Jesus did not fulfill these prophecies and is therefore disqualified. Referring to Jesus, Maimonides observes that

---

13. Jews claim the Scriptures state that a person's genealogy is transmitted exclusively through one's father (Num 1:18; Jer 33:17). He must be a direct male descendent of King David (1 Chr 17:11; Ps 89:29–38; Jer 33:17; 2 Sam 7:12–16) and King Solomon (1 Chr 22:10, 2 Chr 7:18). Therefore, Jesus cannot possibly be a descendent of the tribe of Judah or of King David and King Solomon.

14. Benedict XVI, *Jesus of Nazareth*, 100–1.

15. Levine and Brettler, *Jewish Annotated New Testament*, footnote e on 1 Corinthians 1:22, 324NTn.

16. See also: Isaiah 32:15–18, 60:15–18; Zephaniah 3:9; Hosea 2:20–22; Amos 9:13–15; Micah 4:1–4; Zechariah 8:23, 14:9; Jeremiah 31:33–34.

"all of the prophets spoke that the Messiah redeems Israel, and saves them, and gathers their banished ones, and strengthens their commandments. And this one (Jesus) caused (nations) to destroy Israel by sword, and to scatter their remnant, and to humiliate them, and to exchange the Torah, and to make the majority of the world err to serve a divinity besides God."[17] On these grounds, Jews believe that Jesus did not fulfill the messianic prophecies, so he was not the anticipated Messiah. The Christian response that all the prophecies would eventually be fulfilled when Jesus returns does not convince the Jews. From the Jewish perspective, the Messiah will appear in history only once and that would happen after all the messianic prophecies are fulfilled.

Jesus' death on the cross and his resurrection are two other major reasons for the Jewish rejection of Jesus as Messiah. The first followers of Christ in Antioch, called Christians, were convinced that Jesus was the Messiah who saved humanity through his death and resurrection. But who killed Jesus, and did he really rise again?

The Controversial Accusation

Accusing the Jews for Jesus' death is another issue that has caused a great divide between these two communities. But who killed Jesus? Is accusing the Jews for the crime based on a misunderstanding? Peter refers to those who killed Jesus as Israelites (Acts 2:23, 4:10), members of the Sanhedrin (Acts 5:30), and people in the country of the Jews (Acts 10:39). Stephen referred to them as stiff-necked and disobedient Jews (Acts 7:15). Paul addresses them as "people of Jerusalem and their rulers" (Acts 13:27–29). The Gospels and Acts claim Jesus' death was according to divine plan (Acts 2:23, 3:18, 4:28, 13:28; Luke 4:24–26) and that the Jews acted in ignorance (Acts 3:17, 13:27). Due to these comments that seem accusatory, the Jews feel that they have been unfairly accused of killing Jesus. Jewish scholar Amy-Jill Levine points out that this is an instance of Christians misunderstanding the Jews.[18] This misunderstanding may be due to how one understands the term "Jew." Does it refer to the Jewish race or nation, the Jewish religion, or the Jewish rulers? The Greek term *Ioudaios* and its variations appear in the Gospels many times, originally thought to refer to residents of Judea. Dr. Eli Lizorkin-Eyzenberg thinks that John refers to the Jews responsible for killing Jesus in this restrictive sense; as referring to Judeans (John 1:11).[19] Jewish commentary records that by the second century BCE, the term *Ioudaios*

17. Rudin, *Christians & Jews*, 128–29.
18. Levine, *Misunderstood Jew*.
19. Lizorkin-Eyzenberg, "Why Don't Jews Believe?"

was used to refer to Jews in general. Based on the wider reference of the term, the Jewish commentators claim that the New Testament writers and Christians in general accuse the Jews in an unqualified sense for the death of Jesus.[20] The Judeo-Christian controversy concerning who killed Jesus still lingers.

Several persons and people groups have been accused of killing Jesus. They are the Roman soldiers, Pilate, Herod, Jewish masses, Pharisees, scribes, Zealots, and priests. All of them fall within the orbit of the trial that occurred in Jerusalem. Going beyond the legalities, we may put the blame on the sins of all humans, both Jew and gentile, both past and present. Going yet beyond the human realm, we may blame Satan and his accomplices for Jesus' death. In fact, the Bible reports in two places that Satan entered into Judas Iscariot prior to his betrayal of Jesus (Luke 22:3; John 13:27). Does that mean that Satan gets credit for killing Jesus? Who is in control of history: God or Satan? As already noted in chapter 4, the silent years indicate that God is the Lord of history. He did not surrender his power to Satan at the critical juncture of Jesus' death. As we noted in chapter 5, the triune God—Father, Son, and Spirit—was very much involved in Jesus' death and resurrection. God the Father, who gave up his Son, was very much a participant in Jesus' death (Rom 8:32; Isa 53:10). Paul states in Colossians: "For God was pleased to have all his fullness dwell in him, and through him to reconcile to himself all things, whether things on earth or things in heaven, by making peace through his blood, shed on the cross" (Col 1:19–20). In fact, Jesus went to the cross voluntarily and deliberately. Comparing himself to a good shepherd who lays down his life for his sheep, Jesus said "I lay down my life . . . no one takes it from me, but I lay it down of my own accord" (John 10:11, 17, 18). When his disciples, especially Peter, tried to block his journey to the cross, he sternly rebuked them (Matt 16:22–23).

There are two ways of looking at the trial and death of Jesus. From the human perspective, many people had a part in killing Jesus. In fact, they are all to be blamed for all are sinners and it was sin that took Jesus to the cross. From God's perspective, what happened to Jesus on the cross was the peak of his salvific quest and he orchestrated history to accomplish his plan. He was in control. In responding to the question "Why did Jesus Christ die?," John Stott states that Jesus "did not die but was killed" as well as "he was not killed, he died, giving him up voluntarily to do his father's will."[21] When we take into consideration the seriousness of human sin that took Jesus to the cross and God's strategy through his Son to save humanity from sin, it is

20. Reinhartz, "Introduction to the Gospel," 172; Garroway, "Ioudaious," 596–98.
21. Stott, *Cross of Christ*, 65.

polemical to blame the Jews for the sacrificial death of the Savior. This takes us to the way he died.

The Controversial Cross

During the time when Jesus came, many Jewish groups anticipated the Messiah. They all anticipated one who would first show his mettle by overthrowing Roman bondage. The hyper-legalistic Pharisees hoped for a revolutionary change in Judaic practice through replacement of Roman law with Jewish law. This was to be orchestrated by the Messiah. The Essenes went further to form an isolated society in Qumran fully based on keeping the law. They hoped that the universalization of such a society would usher in the messianic age, free from Roman domination. This would be led by a Messiah with superhuman powers.[22] The Zealots also anticipated the Messiah, but thought he would use military power to overthrow the Roman Empire. In the light of such expectations, Jesus was a great disappointment. He was sentenced to be crucified based on Roman authority and hung by Roman soldiers on a Roman cross!

From the Jewish perspective, Christ's death on a Roman cross indicated the failure of his messianic mission, and such a death was demeaning in God's sight. Writing to the Galatians, Paul states, "Christ redeemed us from the curse of the law by becoming a curse for us, for it is written: 'Cursed is everyone who is hung on a pole'" (Gal 3:13). Paul is citing Deuteronomy 21:23, which states that the body of the one dying on the cross is cursed by God and should be buried immediately in case it defiles the land. Christ's death on the cross was much more heinous than undergoing a Roman punishment. It was unthinkable for the Jews at that time to accept a Messiah who died in a way that was cursed by God.

The Christian claim goes further in highlighting that this death was necessary for humans to be freed from their bondage of sin and sickness (1 Pet 2:24). For this to be accomplished, the Messiah had to be sinless, and only God is sinless. The Messiah was not merely a human with superhuman powers, but divine in his very nature. In the Jewish context, it was idolatrous for the Messiah to be God, and for him to become sin (2 Cor 5:21) and die mars his essential holy and eternal character: it amounts to blasphemy.

Circumcision was another factor that made Christ's death controversial. For Jews, the covenant of circumcision is the sacred act of affirming the Abrahamic covenant. Paul's emphasis that circumcision is not merely an outward act but a matter of the heart (Rom 2:29) is understood by the Jews.[23]

22. Shanks, *Ancient Israel*.

23. Levine and Brettler, *Jewish Annotated New Testament*, 291 (note on "Circumcision of the Heart").

What is controversial is whether circumcision becomes redundant because of Christ's sacrifice on the cross. Paul's claim that in Christ we are freed from sin by the circumcision that came through the shedding of his blood on the cross seems to imply that circumcision is no longer needed (Col 2:11–14). Circumcision includes a surgical incision, followed by minor flow of blood, completed with bandaging of the wound. Jewish scholar Lawrence Hoffman claims both Jews and Christians agree that "blood saves" on the grounds of two significant events recorded in the Old Testament (Ezek 16:1–6; Exod 12:7).[24] Christians emphasized the shedding of Jesus' blood, depicting the *paschal* or Passover lamb as the way for salvation. Jews deemphasized the paschal blood, but made the circumcision blood fundamental.[25] They believe that circumcision is a significant event in the life of Jew in that it has the power to render freedom from sin through the blood at circumcision. Paul's claim that circumcision is not needed undermines the very identity of Jews as chosen people of the Abrahamic covenant. Jews trace the root of the challenge to Christ's death on the cross.

Jesus' death served not only as a sacrifice to save sinners but also as a ransom to justify them. Both Jewish and Christian traditions acknowledge there is a rift between humans and God. The process by which such a broken relationship is mended is called atonement. In its widest sense, atonement is an act of making amends, offering expiation, or giving satisfaction for a wrong or injury; atonement is an act to repair a wrong.[26] In the Judeo-Christian context, atonement is an attempt to reconcile the broken relationship between humans and God, caused by sin.

Both Jews and Christians identify sin as the cause of the rift between humanity and God. Though sin is understood differently in these traditions, they both acknowledge that humans need help and this help must come from God. In the Jewish context, sin is interpreted as *hata*, or going astray; a "wilful disregard of the positive or wilful infraction of the negative commands of God as proclaimed by God."[27] As we previously noted in chapter 2, Christians agree with the Jewish depiction of sin, but the main point of controversy is over "original sin." The Jews reject original sin, and this differentiates the Jewish and Christian ways of atonement. Both Jews and Christians agree that sin entails guilt, so there is a need to be declared innocent. Through Jesus' death as a "ransom" (Matt 20:28), he removed the guilt

---

24. Hoffman, "Circumcision," 674.
25. Hoffman, "Circumcision," 674.
26. *Merriam-Webster Dictionary*, s.v. "atonement."
27. Jacobs and Eisenstein, "Sin," para. 1.

THE CROSS: STUMBLING BLOCK OR FOLLY?   161

of humanity. Judaism does not find the need for the ransom that Christ's sacrificial death provides.

Before the destruction of the temple, the sacrificial lamb without any blemish was the ransom to reconcile one with God. Jews meticulously orchestrated sacrifices to be atoned for their sins. When sacrifices ceased with the destruction of the temple, how was atonement still possible?

Some Orthodox Jewish scholars, like David Berger and Michael Wyschogrod, stress that when sacrifices are possible they need to be done with a broken spirit to be effective. When sacrifices are not possible, repentance is equally effective.[28] Rabbi Shamuel Kegan notices that when the people of Nineveh sinned and Jonah showed them their sin, they fasted and prayed and were forgiven. In the book of Esther, Jews living in Persia repented of their sins and were forgiven. Kogan points out that these historical citations indicate that when there was no temple, sincere *teshuvah*, or repentance, was all that God demanded.[29] In the light of a forgiving God, Jews do not find the need for anything or anyone beside him to be forgiven and reconciled. As Amy-Jill Levine notes, Jesus is unnecessary or redundant for Jews; he is not needed to save from sin or death, since Judaism proclaims a deity ready to forgive repentant sinners.[30]

The Jewish reluctance to accommodate Jesus' shedding of blood as ransom boils down to the questions: Was his death vicarious? Did he die for the sins of all humanity?

Today, Reform Judaism considers Jesus' vicarious death to be archaic and barbaric. This is the reason that Reform Judaism has omitted reference to sacrifices in its prayer book. The Orthodox Jews repeatedly pray for the restoration of the temple and sacrifices, but bypass Jesus. The Conservative prayer book proudly remembers the sacrifices that were once offered in the temple but do not pray for them to be reinstated.[31] Instead of the ransom of Jesus, Judaism recommends prayer, repentance, charity, suffering, and even exile as means to receive forgiveness.[32] For the Jews, Jesus' vicarious death as ransom is redundant as well as ineffective. No human can die for the sins of others, and Jesus was merely a human Jew. In the Christian context, on the other hand, what Jesus accomplished on the cross was both effective and necessary. He was more than human and could die for the sins of others. He was more than human since he not only died but rose again.

---

28. Berger and Wyschogrod, *Jews and "Jewish Christianity,"* 58–59.
29. Kogan, "Atonement in the Absence?"
30. Levine, *Misunderstood Jew,* 18.
31. Adopted from Telushkin, *Jewish Literacy,* 62.
32. Summarized in Mishkin, *Jewish Scholarship,* 105n379.

The Controversial Resurrection

The Empty Tomb (Photo credit: Loria Kulathungam)

The Christian story does not end with the cross but climaxes with the empty tomb. Jesus died, but also rose again. It is this that provides the grounds to claim that Jesus is more than a rabbi, a human Messiah, and a martyr who died on a cursed cross. The hope of the early followers of Jesus that the resurrection of the dead would happen one day was strengthened by the fact that Jesus rose again after being dead for three days. As N. T. Wright claims, it is Jesus' resurrection that gave force and shape to the Christian hope in bodily resurrection.[33] The Jewish world, however, could not accommodate such a claim. If Jesus' resurrection is a historical fact, then Jesus must be more than a human. On the other hand, Jesus' resurrection becomes uncomfortable, if not controversial, in the Jewish world. Perhaps encouraged by the prophecies of Isaiah 26 and Ezekiel 37, and belief in a Messiah that would redeem the Jewish nation, the Jews during the time of Jesus hoped for a resurrection that would occur on the day of judgment: a collective resurrection encompassing God's chosen people. The individual resurrection of Jesus, who they considered to be human, was unbelievable.

33. Wright, "Jesus' Resurrection and Christian Origins," 615–35.

David Mishkin's *Jewish Scholarship on the Resurrection of Jesus* is a recent, well-researched, comprehensive work on Jesus' resurrection.[34] He points out that "the resurrection of Jesus is the main focus of the Gospels, the content of proclamation in the Book of Acts, and the foundational event to all of Paul's theology."[35] He meticulously examines literature pertaining to Jewish reactions to Jesus and places them in several categories: historical fiction, Jewish histories, biographies, and researched presentations. Even though some works are purely fictional, and some categorically dismiss the historicity of Jesus, some do accommodate Jesus as a historical figure while remaining hesitant to acknowledge his resurrection. In Hugh Schonfield's bestselling book about Jesus' resurrection, *The Passover Plot,* the author claims that Jesus believed he was the Messiah and orchestrated a plot to show that he died and rose again. Schonfield acknowledges the historicity of Jesus but dismisses his death and resurrection as fantasy.[36] Michael Alter, in his book, *The Resurrection: A Critical Inquiry,* acknowledges some of the key events in the life of Jesus: he was a Galilean who lived in the first century, spoke Aramaic and Hebrew, chose twelve disciples, engaged in controversy about the temple, and was crucified outside of Jerusalem during the reign of Pontius Pilate. It is interesting that Alter bypasses Jesus' resurrection and claims that after his death his followers formed themselves into an "identifiable movement" that was resisted and even persecuted.[37] Here is an example of Jewish scholarship acknowledging the historicity of Jesus but not his resurrection. If his resurrection had really happened, it would mean that Jesus was much more than human. This would qualify him to be both Messiah and Savior.

Though controversial in the Jewish world, Jesus' resurrection provides the climax to what Jesus accomplished on the cross. Andrew Lloyd Webber and Tim Rice's 1970 rock opera, *Jesus Christ Superstar,* was both applauded and criticized by the media. The most significant criticism is that the film stops with Jesus' crucifixion and thus omits his resurrection. In defense of his creation, Webber commented in a March 18–25, 1987 cover story in the *Christian Century* that the film was only about the last seven days of Jesus' life and including the resurrection would have affected its dramatic impact.[38] Surely Jesus' last seven days makes him a "star," but what really makes him

---

34. Mishkin, *Jewish Scholarship on the Resurrection.*
35. Mishkin, *Jewish Scholarship on the Resurrection,* 118.
36. Schonfield, *Passover Plot.*
37. Mishkin, *Jewish Scholarship,* 199.
38. Polkow, "Andrew Lloyd Webber."

a "superstar" is his resurrection. If this was included in the musical, it could have been true to its title!

If Jesus had died as a human, the Jewish world of his time would have accommodated him, perhaps as another failed messiah or a courageous martyr who underwent a cruel death. But to claim that he was the long-anticipated Messiah and God-incarnate Savior who, through his death and resurrection, saved sinful humanity was surely a stumbling block to the Jews.

GENTILE REACTION

Christ came into a world that was not only Jewish but also predominantly Greco-Roman. Such a world worshipped wisdom and resorted to knowledge to be freed from the bondage of ignorance. Socrates was acclaimed a savior who provided a way out of the human predicament. His death was lauded as an expression of a hero giving up his life with nobility for the cause of freeing humanity through knowledge.

The Death of Socrates (Oil on canvas painting by Jacques-Louis David, 1787)

In this context, Christ's death on a disgraceful cross was seen to be utter folly. The cartoon below graphically makes a mockery of worshipping a crucified one.

THE CROSS: STUMBLING BLOCK OR FOLLY?

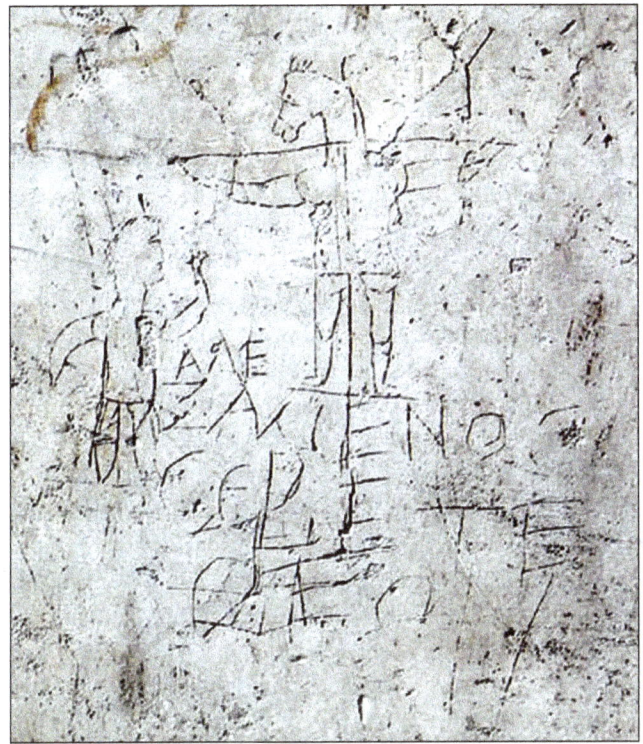

Palatine graffito of Alexamenos

The *Alexamenos Graffito* was an inscription carved on a wall in a room near Rome's Palatine Hill, which can now be found in the *Museo Palatino* (Palatine Museum) in Rome. It is believed to be one of the earliest pictorial representations of the crucifixion of Jesus, from around the second century CE. In the cartoon, a man named Alexamenos is worshipping someone on a cross who has a donkey's head. The cartoon depicts how foolish it is worship one who is crucified.

John's Gospel becomes relevant when dealing with the Christian presentation of Jesus to the Greco-Roman world. Scholars differ in their views of John's intended audience, and question whether he wrote specifically to Jews, to Greeks, or to all people. All these views are acceptable since the Gospel shows evidence that it was written to Jews as well as to the gentile world. John's claim that God sent his Son to save all humanity (John 3:16, 20:31) indicates that John had not only the Jews but also all people in mind when he presented Jesus as the Son of God who would save anyone who believes in him. John introduces his Gospel this way: "In the beginning was the Word, and the Word was with God, and the Word was God" (John 1:1).

The key term here is "Word," which is *Memra* in Aramaic and *Logos* in Greek. This term prominently figured in both the Jewish and Greek languages. Lizorkin-Eyzenberg points out that the idea of the Word (*Logos/Memra*) possessing extraordinary qualities and functioning in relationship to God was not new to Second Temple Judaism.[39] This conclusion is reached on the strength that Logos is found in the Jerusalem *Targum*, when translating the original Hebrew of Genesis 3:8 and 19:24. Lizorkin-Eyzenberg also cites Philo of Alexandria's use of the term Logos. Philo, an Alexandrian Jew impacted by Greek philosophy, attempted to articulate Judaism through Greek concepts. One such concept is Logos, which figured very much in Greek philosophical vocabulary. Logos is not to be confused with "word," taken as part of the vocabulary of a language. The Greek term used for that is *lexis*. But Logos refers to the word that is latent in one's mind even before it is expressed in language: an inward thought or reason. Five hundred years before Christ, the Greek philosopher Heraclitus realized that the ever-changing universe had an order. For him, this was neither by chance nor the mere interplay of material things, but governed by a universal force of reason, which he called Logos. Since Heraclitus, Logos has figured in Greek thought as the principle of reason that renders order to the universe and governs human actions. It eventually acquired divine qualities, like eternity. When applied to the universe, it referred to the rational principle that gave order to all things and events in the universe, including human actions.

As noted in chapter 4, Philo placed Logos above several intermediaries (powers) and claimed that it was nearest to God. Lizorkin-Eyzenberg notices that Philo interprets Logos through allegory. Regarding Logos, Philo claims that "the most universal of all things is God; and in the second place the Word of God. (Allegorical Interpretation, II, 86)," and that ". . . the shadow of God is His Word, which He used like an instrument when He was making the world . . . (Allegorical Interpretation, III, 96)."[40] We should note here that Philo interprets Logos as having divine qualities, nearest to God, and second to God, but not God. John's Logos, though close to Philo's Logos, was different.

When John uses the term Logos, both Jews and Greeks would have been familiar with the term. It provided a common ground to relate Christ in a vocabulary familiar to them. The Greeks would have found no problem accepting it as having divine qualities and providing order to the universe. But the problem begins when John presents Logos as not only being with God, but that Logos *was* God (John 1:1), and in the subsequent verse Logos

---

39. Lizorkin-Eyzenberg, "Jewish Logos Theology."
40. Lizorkin-Eyzenberg, "Jewish Logos Theology," para. 2.

is referred to as "He"; "He was with God in the beginning" (John 1:2). John depicts Logos as a person and not as a mere impersonal force. He then goes on to claim that this divine person created the universe (John 1:3) and was the source of life that enlightens humans (John 1:4, 9). This Logos incarnated and "became flesh" (John 1:14). Such a depiction of Logos was not what the Greeks would have expected. For them, Logos was impersonal. There were several creation stories in the Greek world, but God as a personal being who created the world was not a viewpoint that was in vogue. The god of Plato who created the world, modelling it on the world of forms, and Aristotle's "unmoved mover" who commenced the flow of the universe, came closest to the view of God creating the world. The god of both these philosophers was impersonal. Moreover, Logos as the "true light that gives light to all men" (John 1:9) challenged the popular Greek view that reason enlightens people, leading them to liberating knowledge. In the Greek world, where the mental is separated from the physical and the material is degraded, to claim Logos incarnated and became flesh was revolutionary. The Greeks could not comprehend John's depiction of Logos. In contrast to Philo's Logos, John claimed that Logos, though a distinct person, was God, that he incarnated in human flesh, and that he was the historical Jesus. Logos, as referring to Jesus, is found only four times in the New Testament: twice in John's introduction to his gospel (1:1, 1:14), in John's epistle (1 John 1:1), and in Revelation 19:13. This depiction of Jesus as Logos was foolishness to the Greeks. When we do not understand something, we usually hesitate to acknowledge our cognitive limitation but rather blame it on the topic and dismiss it as nonsense! Jesus as Logos was incomprehensible to the Greek world and therefore appeared nonsensical.

Moreover, Greek pundits were astounded at Jesus' teaching, not merely because of its content but because of the way he taught. His teaching style reflected an authority that did not come from anything external; he was his own authority. Greeks believed the authority of any legitimate teaching should be founded on human reason. Jesus' teaching, based on his own authority, sounded too subjective and foolishly presumptuous.

The Greek philosophical world considered the human being to have two distinct parts: the physical body and the immaterial mind. At death, the immaterial mind survived death, but there were several views as to what happened to it after death. Those impacted by Eastern religions believed that after death, the immaterial soul migrated into another body. When the soul that was caught up in the cycle of rebirths was finally freed, it was rid of the physical. The physical was therefore taken to be the cause of human bondage and the mind had to be freed from its bondage. The Epicurean and Stoic philosophers of Paul's time (Acts 17:16–34) believed that death was the end. When then they heard Paul talking about resurrection of the dead in Athens, they were curious to understand his strange ideas. As noted in chapter 4, when he was invited to speak at the Areopagus, he made his presentation using vocabulary that the Greek audience would understand. He made it quite clear that his God was not one worshipped as an idol in Athens, but that the "unknown God" they worshipped was the God who created the universe, who did not live in temples, and who would one day judge humanity through his appointed one, Jesus. Paul concluded by pointing out that the one who would judge is the one God raised from the dead. This claim would have shocked the audience that was skeptical of resurrection. Homer, who was greatly respected in the world of ancient Greece, thought of life after death as bleak. In his famous work, *The Odyssey*, Odysseus's journey to the underworld hardly encourages readers to suppose that death will take them into a better world.[41] Plato thought that there was a chance of a blissful afterlife, at least for those who had an insight into the ideal "world of forms" through reason. This was not central to his thought. In the Greek world, although the possibility of the survival of the rational part of a human was accepted by some, bodily resurrection was denied. Such a view is best expressed in Aeschylus's popular play, *Eumenides* (647–48). In this play, during the founding of the court of the Areopagus, Apollo declares that when a man has died, and his blood is spilled on the ground, there is no resurrection.[42] When Paul spoke about Jesus' bodily resurrection, likely some people in the audience were curious to find out more about his ideas, but many sneered for they did not believe in bodily resurrection and dismissed it as nonsense.

For those who received Paul's proclamation of Christ crucified, whether Jew or gentile, it was the power and wisdom of God—the power to be free from the human predicament and divine wisdom—that liberates one from ignorance. Such power and wisdom could be obtained only through acknowledging one's helplessness and resorting to God's help. This strategy went against the several modes of redemption which figured predominantly in the Greco-Roman world. They were all based on the conviction that human effort could be redemptive. As noted in chapter 4, the silent years saw the rise of multiple ways of salvation based on different world views. Besides the popular mode of salvation through knowledge initiated by Socrates, several alternative modes arose, like the Epicurean resort to pleasure, the Stoic state of quietude through following the laws of nature, and the eclectic

---

41. Homer, *Odyssey*, Books 10 and 11. Hades, the abode of the dead, is a place of shadows where one may just about remember what life was like, but not much more.

42. Wright, "Jesus' Resurrection and Christian Origins," 615–35.

stance that generated religious pluralism. The fusion of Greek and Roman cultures led to an influx of the worship of multiple gods. As Paul observed, Athens had become a city of gods. Even though gods became agents of salvation, to achieve it one had to please these gods through offerings, sacrifices, tortuous practices, good works, and faithful temple attendance. Even the so-called theistic modes of redemption were based on human effort. All these modes of release arose out of the conviction that humans, through their own efforts, could shape their own destiny. On the other hand, Paul proclaimed that humans were helpless and required help, and that this help could come only by committing oneself to Jesus, who came to save sinners. For this to happen, it was essential to acknowledge one's utter helplessness and realize that human effort in itself was inadequate. Such a declaration did not merely belittle the value of human effort, but also touched on a very sensitive area to humans: human pride. The people of the Greco-Roman world could not handle a way of redemption that toppled their salvific strategies and demeaned their self-worth. To be freed from the human predicament on the grounds of God's unmerited favor or grace, appropriated through acknowledging one's utter helplessness, was too cheap, if not an insult to the potentiality of human capability. It is not surprising that they branded the way of Christ crucified as folly.

The salvific revolution that centered on Jesus' accomplishment on the cross turned out to be a stumbling block and a scandal to the Jews, and complete folly to the people of the Greco-Roman world. "Christ crucified" continues to be controversial; it is a stumbling block to those who find him blocking their religious routes and folly to those who find their own salvific strategies more sensible.

8

Pentecost: Blasphemy or Off Track?

THE SPIRITUAL REVOLUTION THAT climaxed on the day of Pentecost occurred in a world that was thirsting for spiritual fulfillment. Pentecost was a timely response to such a thirst. The book of Acts records many Jews and gentiles accepting this new spirituality enthusiastically. History also shows that it was not well received by either the Jewish or gentile sectors, and this hesitancy continues. Why? Let us look at the Jewish and gentile reactions to the spiritual revolution. The Judaic world considered Pentecost[1] as blasphemous, while the gentile world saw it as being off track.

THE JEWISH REACTION: THE BLASPHEMY OF PENTECOST

Judaism, though exhibiting a legalistic bias, is a religion that gives an important place to spirituality, both in its dogmas and practices. When we look at how the Jews reacted to Pentecost, we need to keep in mind that this reaction came out of a rich spiritual tradition. We should also remember that this spiritual revolution had its roots in Judaism. In fact, what happened on the day of Pentecost is taken as a fulfillment of prophecy as recorded in the Hebrew Bible (Old Testament). Peter and Paul, who articulated the meaning and significance of the revolution, were Jews, and used Jewish concepts in their presentation. The first participants of the revolution were mostly Jews. Controversy about Pentecost is a family feud rather than a downright

---

1. "Pentecost" is here taken as the spirituality that climaxed on the day of Pentecost.

condemnation. To understand the full scope of the Jewish reaction, we should also consider reactions to Pentecost that came because of subsequent developments in the Jewish world.

Adopting a framework that accommodates both the immediate and subsequent reactions, we can look at the Jewish response to the spiritual revolution within three domains: the traditional, the radical, and the mystical. These domains are not Judaic sects but represent different articulations of spirituality within Judaism. They all categorize the spiritual as indispensable to Judaism but differ as to how one could achieve spiritual fulfillment. All three domains are hesitant to accommodate the spirituality of Pentecost.

The Traditional Domain

Judaism is noted for its commitment to commandments—there are believed to be 613—which include the Ten Commandments and regulations based on the teachings of the *Torah*, the *Talmud*,[2] and *Halakhah*.[3] These laws and regulations are meant to guide the practice of Judaic worship, festivals, and dietary habits. They provide guidelines for worship and prayers, the most essential being the *Shema*,[4] devotional reading of the Torah, keeping the Sabbath, maintaining a kosher diet, and participating in commemorative festivals. Traditionalists stress that, despite the legalistic bias, there is a spiritual undertone in keeping the law and participating in rituals.

Presenting the traditionalist stance, Rabbi Jonathan Magonet points out that: "In Judaism 'spirituality' is an expression of subsuming one's will to God. Seeking the nearness of God in one's life, is traditionally expressed through the symbolic language of 'mitzvot,' 'commandments.' Essentially it is about a life regulated, conducted and defined within a particular framework of practices, rituals and actions."[5] This way of life carries with it certain challenges, as it could turn into a life burdened with laws and rituals. On the other hand, when these are done faithfully to follow God's will, they could become divine service. Magonet observes that although such a lifestyle

---

2. The body of Jewish civil and ceremonial law comprises the Mishnah and the Gemara. Two versions of the Talmud are the Babylonian Talmud (dates from fifth century CE, but includes earlier material) and the earlier Palestinian or Jerusalem Talmud.

3. The word *halakhah* is usually translated as Jewish Law, or more literally as "the path that one walks."

4. *Shema/Sh'ma Yisrael* is translated as "Hear, [O] Israel," the first two words of a section of the Torah that provides the title—*Shema*—of a prayer that serves as a centerpiece of daily morning and evening Jewish services.

5. Magonet, "Spirituality and Scripture," 93. Rabbi Jonathan David Magonet is a British theologian, an eminent Jewish scholar, and vice president of the World Union for Progressive Judaism.

seems to be determined by external factors, it has its own rich inwardness, which turns one's thoughts constantly to God.[6] It is this inwardness that makes traditional Judaism spiritual. Traditional spirituality is Scripture based and regulated. Rabbi Tzi Freeman stresses that all aspects of Jewish spirituality are deeply rooted in God's revelation at Mount Sinai that gave Jews the core commandments.[7] This is found in the Torah, which provides the underlying foundation of spiritual dogma and practices. The Torah is made up of both the written *Torah Shebikhtav*, and oral *Torah Shebe'alpeh*. Traditionalists view the oral Torah as a commentary on the written one. This commentary continues as a seamless chain of tradition from Moses to the pharisaic and later rabbinic teachings. "Scripture" here refers not only to the Torah in the Hebrew Bible, but also the oral Torah located in other Jewish writings commencing with the *Mishnah*, the earliest extrabiblical clarification of Jewish oral law. The *Talmud* (Babylonian and Palestinian) is an extensive commentary to the Mishnah. *Halakhah* is the body of Jewish law and tradition. The nonlegal material (*Haggadah*) of the Hebrew Bible is explored in various rabbinic writings, the *Midrash*. Traditionalists claim that Torah and the traditions that ensued from it as contained in the *Talmud* and *Halakhah* provide the parameters for spirituality. Rabbis feature as the gurus orchestrating spirituality to keep within Jewish tradition. In the traditional domain, not only the Torah, but many other writings provide directives to the proper practice of Jewish law and rituals. Spirituality in the traditional domain is given shape through such practice.

As in all religions, keeping the law and following ritualistic practices could turn into mere formalities over time, and Judaism is no exception to such a trend. The development of nonorthodox denominations like the Conservative, Reform, and Reconstructionist exhibited a softening of rigid adherence to Jewish laws and rituals. Even among such liberalizing and divisive trends, there have been determined efforts to sustain and revitalize Judaism and make it more acceptable to modern times. Some of these developments gave birth to a rather radical version of Jewish spirituality.

The Radical Domain

Rabbi Lewis Solomon best represents the radical stance in contemporary Judaism. In his ground-breaking but controversial book, *Jewish Spirituality: Revitalizing Judaism for the Twenty-First Century*,[8] Solomon claims:

---

6. Magonet, "Spirituality and Scripture," 93.
7. Freeman, "What's Up With Jewish Spirituality?"
8. Solomon, *Jewish Spirituality*.

> When we think about Judaism, we usually focus on mechanical repetition and cookbook-like observances and rule. We think that Judaism is synonymous with an almost mindless performance of ceremonies and rituals, particularly with respect to observing the Sabbath and the dietary law. The rituals have taken on a life of their own. Yet the ceremonies, rituals and all the accompanying rules and regulations (Jewish religious law, or Halakah) are the byways of Judaism, not its highways or its essence.[9]

Solomon is convinced that a new approach is needed to revitalize Jewish spirituality. For him, traditional Judaic spirituality that is rigidly structured around laws and regulations cannot deliver the goods. He claims that laws and rituals, though designed to open and touch the spiritual dimension of humans, often block their spiritual life and vitality. In his view, "In the twentieth century, Jewishness has rested on three pillars, adherence to God's law as revealed in the Torah; second, a collective reaction to anti-Semitism; and third, faith in the restoration of Zion, which for the past fifty years has meant support of Israel."[10] He argues that these foundations, on which twentieth-century traditional Judaism stood, are crumbling.[11] Solomon's views on traditional Judaism raise a number of controversies. We will not get into the family feud among Judaic sectors over the spiritual efficacy of laws and rituals, fear of anti-Semitism as a key to Jewishness and Zionism, and the state of Israel as "a beacon of Judaism." In his view, the crumbling of these foundations has led to the liberalization of Judaism but has not filled the spiritual vacuum. He attempts to offer a "vision of a personal intimate experience of a living God, as the source of health, joy, love, abundance, and wholeness."[12] Solomon's version of liberal spirituality downplays rigid adherence to laws and rituals and stresses the necessity of personal experience, and yet, as we shall see, it is hesitant to accommodate the spirituality of Pentecost.

Traditional and radical spiritualities represent two perspectives on how spirituality could be practised by the Jewish people. The Torah played an indispensable role in the spirituality of both traditionalists and radicals, and both considered it to provide doctrinal basis for their practice of spirituality. They differed in the way they understood the content of the Torah and how it could serve as the criterion to discern the legitimate from

---

9. Solomon, *Jewish Spirituality*, 5.
10. Solomon, *Jewish Spirituality*, 13.
11. Solomon, *Jewish Spirituality*, 13–28.
12. Solomon, *Jewish Spirituality*, cover leaf.

pseudospirituality. The radicals were more liberal than traditionalists in interpreting the Torah. According to the traditionalist view, the Torah, along with the Talmud and other rabbinic writings, provide the biblical foundation for spirituality. The latter (the Talmud and rabbinic writings) are accommodated as formulating Jewish tradition. Traditionalists reference the Talmud and Halakhah as the norm for spiritual practices.

Though the radicals accommodate these works, they do not want spirituality to be restricted by tradition. They strive to conform to the changing spiritual aspirations of the Jewish populace. They find the traditionalist spirituality rather restrictive. As Rabbi Solomon observes, making Judaism more liberal does not always lead to spiritual fulfillment. What he envisions is better realized in Jewish mysticism.

The Mystical Domain

Rabbi Jonathan Magonet succinctly characterizes "the core features of traditional Jewish spirituality as the *mitzvot*, commandments, as tangible expressions of Israel's covenant with God; study, as the continuing searching out of God's will in all its manifestations; and worship, as the human response, the personal self-revelation to God."[13] He observes that these interwoven elements indicate people's response to God's quest. To experience spiritual fulfillment, it is necessary to go beyond obeying laws. It is here that mysticism enters the scene.

Kabbalism and *Hasidism* feature prominently as expressions of Jewish mysticism. Both these movements were impacted by the prophet Ezekiel's chariot-throne vision (Ezek 1). Ezekiel, a widowed priest in the temple prior to its destruction, was in Babylon with the Jews in exile. Like other exiled Jews, he felt that God had given up on them and that they were a forsaken nation. Most unexpectedly, God appeared to Ezekiel outside the land of Israel and beyond the precincts of the temple. There are many controversies concerning the meaning of the vision, but the most significant impact it had on Ezekiel and the Jews who heard about it was that God had not given up on them. They realized that God's presence was not restricted to the temple in Jerusalem or to the boundaries of their holy land. Prior to this event, the Jewish world had assumed that God's presence could be experienced only within the portals of the holy of holies in the temple and that only the priestly elite could ever experience his presence. Ezekiel's vision shattered this restrictive elitism[14] and geographical limitation. Since then, Jews have

---

13. Magonet, "Spirituality and Scripture," 97–98.
14. Dedopulos, *Kabbalah*, 10.

aspired to experience God the way Ezekiel did. The Kabbalah and Hasidic mystics led the way in this endeavor.

"Cleaving to God," or *devekut* in Hebrew, has played a vital role in Judaic spirituality. Originally, *devekut* referred to the close relationship Adam and Eve enjoyed with God before they sinned. After their fall, humans lost that intimate connection with God. To regain what was lost, Judaic spirituality resorted to "cleaving to God." In traditional Jewish circles, one could cleave to God through obeying laws, sincere devotion, and faithful ritualistic practices. To experience spiritual fulfillment, there is a need to go beyond rigid obedience to laws and regulations. Kabbalah and Hasidic mystics strive to have such a spiritually fulfilling experience. *Devekut*, in the mystic domain, enables the mystics to experience union with the divine.

The Kabbalah Endeavor

The word *Kabbalah* is derived from a Hebraic root word meaning "to receive" or "to accept." *Kabbalah* may be traced to *Merkavah*, the main strand of early Jewish mysticism. These mystics strove to experience Ezekiel's vision of the divine chariot (*Merkavah*) based on the rabbinic literature of Talmud and Midrash and mystic texts, *Heikhalot*.[15] Motivated by Ezekiel's vision, *Merkavah* and then *Kabbalah* mystics claimed that the glory of God's presence could be experienced not only by the priestly elite but also seekers outside the temple. Over the centuries, these mystics had attempted to find ways and means to experience God. The *Zohar*, a collection of commentaries on the Torah, is foundational to *Kabbalah* doctrine and practice. It is intended to guide Kabbalists in their spiritual journey, and experience union with the divine (*unio-mystica*). Opinion differs among Kabbalist scholars concerning the extent to which such union occurs. Gershom Scholem, representing the moderate stance, claims that the mystic who experiences such union still preserves his or her individuality.[16] Moshe Idel, on the other hand, refutes such a moderate stance by proposing that *devekut* involves some form of obliteration of the human personality when the mystic experiences union with the divine.[17] Both these stances stress that *devekut* serves as a means for the mystic to enter into the divine sphere and experience divine presence.

---

15. An ancient commentary on biblical text. The earliest Midrashim come from the second century CE, although much of their content is older.
16. Scholem, *Messianic Idea in Judaism*, 203–7.
17. Idel, *Kabbalah*, 3–4; Idel, "Universalization and Integration," 33–38.

The Hasidic Venture

Hasidism is derived from the Hebrew word *hasid*, meaning "pious," and referred to those whose spirituality went beyond merely meeting the requirements of Jewish law as given in the Torah.

Like *Kabbalah*, *Hasidism* was also inspired by Ezekiel's vision and claimed that anyone could personally experience God. Hasidism has its roots in twelfth-century Germany, but really became recognized as a mystical movement through the leadership of eighteenth-century Polish preacher Israel ben Eliezer, popularly called *Baal Shem Tov* (Master of the Good Name) or "the Besht" for short. In the 1730s, he gathered a group of followers and they referred to themselves as the *Hasidim*, "the pious ones." Like the *Kabbalists*, *Hasidic* mystics placed a high value on *devekut* (cleaving to God) by means of ecstatic worship through *kavanah* (intention and focus). Hasidic mystics, like Rabbi Menachem Mendel of Vitebsk, Belarus, advocated that when one totally cleaves to God, one is self-annihilated and loses individuality.[18] The Hasidic viewpoint about experiencing union with the divine became controversial when they took it a step further. They claimed that a seeker could experience God through ecstatic prayer, even without the aid of the sacred texts, and that one could become aware of hidden truths beyond the revealed aspects of the Torah. Experiencing the divine was open to anyone, even the uneducated. This open-ended, anti-intellectual spirituality was controversial among traditional spiritualists.

Both *Kabbalah* and *Hasidic* mystics claimed that people could relate to God experientially, since God himself desired to relate with humans. *Kabbalism* and *Hasidism* represent the Jewish quest for a spiritual experience that goes beyond obeying commandments and practicing rituals, an encounter that accommodates a personal experience with the divine.

All three domains in the Jewish world—the traditional, radical, and the mystical—give significant weight to spirituality, though they differ as to how such spirituality is achieved. Why are all three hesitant to accommodate the spiritual revolution that climaxed on the day of Pentecost?

WHY IS PENTECOST PROBLEMATIC?

The Jewish controversy concerning Pentecost centers on three core issues: whether it fulfilled prophecy, was Christ centered, and orchestrated a personal relationship with God the Holy Spirit.

---

18. Mendel, *Pri ha-Aretz*, 64.

Event that Fulfilled Prophecy

The spiritual revolution that occurred on the day of Pentecost was not a historical accident, but the fulfillment of prophecy. Peter proclaimed in his sermon on that day (Acts 2:15–21) that the spiritual outpouring was a fulfillment of Joel's prophecy (Joel 2:28–32). As Levine and Brettler suggest, rabbinic literature understands Joel as referring to the world to come (Num. Rab. 15.25; Deut. Rab. 6.14; Tanh. Miqqetz 10).[19] In the book of Acts, Peter notes the events that would occur in the last days would happen in the outpouring of the Spirit (Acts 2:17). Rabbinic literature points out that Luke adds the phrase, "in the last days," and that he is "presenting the plan as now realized in the giving of the Spirit."[20] Such an event includes people from "all orders of society,"[21] and not merely those filled by the Spirit. From a Jewish perspective, Peter's proclamation, as presented by Luke, is based on a misinterpretation of Joel's prophecy, which is centered on the "day of the Lord" and what would happen in conjunction with it. In the Jewish context, this day needs to be understood only in terms of what the Old Testament says about it. Within such a framework, the day of the Lord refers to the end of the world as we know it and the climax of God's sovereign rule. This day will be preceded by God's judgment, punishment, and blessing. Before that day occurred, many things would have to happen. Most importantly, the Messiah would appear, with Elijah appearing prior to that. From a Jewish perspective, since these events had not yet happened, Peter's claim that events of the day of Pentecost were a fulfillment of Joel's prophecy is not merely false, but heresy. It falsifies the true meaning of a section found in the Bible that, for the Jews and especially the traditionalists, is God's word in written form. It is sacred, and discrediting the sacred script is heresy. Pentecostal spirituality is blasphemous to the Jews, since they consider it to be founded on heresy.

Christ-Enabled Experience

Judaism's core dictum is that God is one (Deut 6:4) and there is no other God beside him (Deut 4:35, 39, 32:39). *The Thirteen Principles of Jewish Faith*, compiled by Moshe ben Maimon, summarizes the foundational beliefs of the Jewish religion. The principles commence with the declaration

---

19. Levine and Brettler, *Jewish Annotated New Testament*, 224 (footnote on Acts 2:14–36).

20. Levine and Brettler, *Jewish Annotated New Testament*, 224 (footnote on Acts 2:14–36).

21. Levine and Brettler, *Jewish Annotated New Testament*, 224 (footnote on Acts 2:14–36).

that God, who is the creator of all (principle 1) is one (principle 2), and is Spirit (principle 3).[22] The Jewish confession of faith, "Hear O Israel *(Shema Yisrael)*: G-d is our L-rd. G-d is one" (Deut 6:4), is the first line and the core of the *Shema* passage, which is the most important prayer in Jewish corporate worship. It is recited three times daily as well as in the Sabbath service. It is the final prayer of Yom Kippur, the holiest day of the year, and is traditionally a Jew's last words before death. It is usually recited with the right hand covering the eyes, to prevent any distraction. The dictum, "God is one," figures as the cardinal principle of Jewish doctrine and spirituality. Those who seek God with the conviction that he is one will experience spiritual fulfillment. This fulfillment is articulated through traditional, radical, or mystical avenues; all these ways are founded on the belief that the God who is able to render spiritual fulfillment is one and there is no God beside him.

The spirituality of Pentecost also commences with God, but it is a triune God. God the Father, Son, and Spirit are involved in the outpouring of the Holy Spirit. The baptism in the Spirit is God the Father's promise; the baptizer is Jesus, God's Son; and the gift is God the Holy Spirit. This enactment of spirituality appears idolatrous in the Jewish context. Acknowledging a God beside the one and only true God would demean God, so the spirituality of Pentecost, due to this idolatry, is viewed as not merely pseudospiritual, but blasphemous.

Christ becomes controversial not only in being identified as the second person of the triune God, but also in his indispensable role in Spirit baptism. John the Baptist, the forerunner of Christ, stirred up controversy among the Jews by his provocative prophetic declaration. He proclaimed that they would soon see the occurrence of a pivotal event, orchestrated by a significant person. Both the person and the event he mentioned were controversial. He proclaimed: "I baptize you with water for repentance. But after me comes one who is more powerful than I, whose sandals I am not worthy to carry. He will baptize you with the Holy Spirit and fire" (Matt 3:11).

Christ is indispensable to the experience of Spirit baptism. To receive the baptism in the Spirit, Peter declared one had to repent and be baptized in the name of Jesus Christ. Jesus is controversial to the Jews for they see him neither as the Son of God nor the anticipated Messiah. Since Jesus is controversial, the baptismal experience that he facilitated becomes questionable.

Christ figures in this experience not as a mere facilitator but as Savior. Peter declared one had to repent to receive the Spirit. Why should one

---

22. ben Maimon, "Thirteen Principles of Jewish Faith."

repent, and why repent to Christ? This takes us to how the human being is characterized in Judaism and Christianity. The Bible records that God created humans in his image (Gen 1:26, 27). Since God is spirit (Maimonides's principle 3), humans created in his image possess a spiritual component and they reflect God. Humans are not merely physical organisms or mental constructs, but also spiritual, or at least possessing the potential to be spiritual. As God's image, everyone has the signature of God within them. This provides the grounds for humans to be spiritual. Both Jewish and Christian spiritualities agree on this. The controversy is over the extent to which sin mars the human capacity to be spiritual. From the Christian viewpoint, humans are sinful by nature since they inherited the sin of the first humans. The seeker in the Jewish context needs only a forgiving God, but in the Christian context, the seeker is dead in sin (Eph 2:1) and needs the divine grace of a Savior to be brought back to life. The apostle Paul writes, "In the same way, count yourselves dead to sin but alive to God in Christ Jesus" (Rom 6:11).

Judaism proposes that humans sin by commission or omission. In this context, one only needs to repent of sins committed or omitted. Lewis Solomon, articulating the Jewish stance, claims that for humans to actualize their spiritual potency, they need to accept and fully live their spiritual identity. In his view, humans are not created flawed but are an extension of God and share divine attributes. Since they are not depraved beings inherently sinful by nature, they do not need a Savior.[23] Considering this depiction of human identity, Peter's declaration on the day of Pentecost that to receive the baptism of the Holy Spirit one had to repent and be baptized in the name of God the Son, Jesus, would not be acceptable. From the Jewish perspective, Peter's depiction of the human being as helpless and in need of a Savior is sacrilegious, for God's creation is sacred. The spirituality of the day of Pentecost is controversial because of the pivotal role Christ plays in it. The controversy does not end here. It moves on to how the Spirit baptism that Christ provides is experienced by the one baptized.

Experience that Facilitated a Personal Relationship

The pivotal event of Pentecost was the baptism in the Holy Spirit, a baptism that was unprecedented in the Jewish world. The word baptism (*baptizo*) is a Greek word and does not appear in the Hebrew Bible. The Jewish purification and consecration rites called *Tvilah* have similarities to baptism. *Tvilah* is the act of immersion in water, *mikva*, that comes from natural sources. According to rabbinical teachings, in addition to circumcision and sacrifice,

---

23. Solomon, *Jewish Spirituality*, 31.

Tvilah was a necessary ritual to be performed to convert to Judaism.[24] *Tvilah* enabled one to be purified so they could experience the presence of God's glory.

Although in some biblical passages seeking means inquiring about God's will or how to keep his commandments (Ps 119:45, 94, 155), the Bible takes the act of seeking as more than an attempt to get information. It involves an attempt to relate to God experientially. This experience is not merely wishful thinking, but possible since God is waiting for his people to seek him (Ps 14:2; 1 Chr 28:9). The possibility of having such an experience of God provides the occasion for spirituality in Judaism that facilitates experiencing God's presence and sharing his glory.

Being incorporeal, God is not restricted by space and time; he is everywhere all the time (Ps 139:51–52; 1 Kgs 8:27). There are occasions when he is just here, even though he is also everywhere. When this occurs, God is believed to relate with humans by being present. We also find the term "glory" used along with God's presence. When God is present, his glory is seen. Eventually, the term *shekinah* came to be linked with "glory." Although *shekinah* is not found in the Bible, there are allusions to it (Isa 60:2; Matt 17:5; Luke 2:9; Rom 9:4). *Shekinah* means "that which dwells," and is derived from the Hebrew verb *shaken* or *shakhan*, which means "dwell" or "reside."[25] This definition of *shekinah* highlights the glory that emanates when God is present. In Jewish literature, *shekinah* has also been used to describe the mystical presence of God in the tabernacle and later, in the First and Second Temples.

The *shekinah* glory of God's presence was experienced by certain prophets and, at other times, by all people. When the Israelites were in the wilderness, the glory of the Lord appeared to all the people on more than one occasion (Lev 9:23; Num 16:19, 17:7, 20:6). The book of Deuteronomy applauds thusly: "The Lord our God has shown us his glory" (Deut 5:21). The glory was often revealed in a cloud, fire, storm, or in lightning (Exod 24:15–17, 40:34; 1 Kgs 8:11). We should not confuse the glory of God with its manifestations, since they provide the setting for the glory, but not the glory itself.[26] God fulfilled the spiritual aspirations of Israelites who sought him through sharing his presence, yet did not give up his transcendence in the process. Whenever God is present, his glory is seen, but that does not mean that God's glory is the same as God in his fullness. As Heschel correctly points out, "The glory is the presence not the essence of God; an act

---

24. Kohler and Krauss, "Baptism."
25. Orr, "Definition for 'Shekinah,'" para. 1.
26. Heschel, *God in Search of Man*, 81.

rather than a quality; a process not a substance."[27] God sought the Israelites by showing them the *shekinah* glory of his presence on several occasions and in many ways. Let us look at several episodes in Jewish history that reflect this.

God's Presence at Mount Sinai

When Moses came down from Mount Sinai with the tablets containing the Ten Commandments, his face was so radiant that Aaron and those with him were afraid and could not look at such radiance. Moses had to cover his face with a veil (Exod 34:29–35). Why was his face radiant? Moses appealed to God to show his glory (Exod 33:18). Perhaps Moses' face was reflecting God's glory from being in his presence. Moses was assured of God's presence in the wilderness (Exod 33:14) and he had the privilege of experiencing God's glorious presence, but he could not see God face to face for that would have been death for Moses (Exod 33:20). God's glorious presence is not the same as God.

God's Presence in the Tabernacle

After their miraculous escape from Egypt, the Israelites would have expected to step into the promised land right away. Instead, they had to journey in the wilderness for many years. They were frustrated and needed assurance that God was still with them. God assured them that his presence would go with them on their journey (Exod 33:14), but he warned Moses that seeing God's face would prove fatal (Exod 33:20). How could the holy God dwell among sinful people? God had an alternate plan: the tabernacle. Though God was present among his people during their departure from Egypt (Exod 13:17–18, 21–22), he went further by being present in the tabernacle[28] (Exod 25:8). The tabernacle (tent of meeting) served as a portable place where God met with the Israelites during their forty-year journey in the wilderness. Specifically, the ark of the covenant in the tabernacle served as the location of his presence (Exod 25:22). It should be noted that the tabernacle was God's idea, initiative, and design (Exod 25–40). "The Israelites had done all the work just as the Lord had commanded Moses," and Moses inspected their work and was satisfied with it and blessed them (Exod 39:42–43). The tabernacle was not a structure designed by humans, for God does not live

---

27. Heschel, *God in Search of Man*, 82.

28. Keyser, "Yehovah's Shekinah Glory." The word *mishkan*, a derivation of *shakan*, is often translated "tabernacle." The Hebrew word for tabernacle is more often simply *ohel*, or "tent". *Mishkan* means "dwelling place."

in temples built by human hands (Acts 17:24). When the Israelites travelled through the wilderness, they needed a portable place for God's presence to go with them. The tabernacle served as a place of God's protective presence wherever they went (Exod 40:36–38). The next location of God's presence was the temple.

God's Presence in the Temple

Eventually, the holy of holies within the temple of Jerusalem became the location of God's presence. The rabbis highlighted God's presence by referring to his glory filling the temple (2 Chr 7:1). The holy place contained three items: the golden candlestick, the showbread table, and the altar of incense. Just behind this altar was a thick veil separating the holy place from the holy of holies, which contained the ark of the covenant, upon which rested the mercy seat and the cherubim. The *shekinah* glory of God's presence was believed to rest on the mercy seat (Lev 16:2–34). Since God is holy, humans could not enter that place of holiness. It is mind boggling to think that God, who transcends time and space, was present in a specific locale. Nevertheless, the holy of holies enabled people to relate to him in a nonthreatening way; the veil was to protect them rather than prevent them from experiencing God's blessings. God's presence facilitated, on the one hand, for God not to forego his transcendence and, on the other hand, for people not to be overwhelmed by his holiness.

Experiencing and being blessed by the glory of God's presence, while experientially enhancing and spiritually fulfilling, seemed rather restrictive. As we have noted, during the sojourn of the Israelites in the wilderness, the glory of the Lord appeared to all the people more than once. Most of the time, however, only priests, prophets, and a few chosen by God had the opportunity to experience God's presence firsthand. Several were spiritually edified through the priestly and prophetic ministry of these leaders, but there were many who yearned for firsthand spiritual exposure. The Jews needed a grassroots-level, broad-based spirituality.

The Jewish yearning for God's presence is evident to this day. Eli Lizorkin-Eyzenberg claims that: "Jewish prayer is the heartbeat of Judaism. In the very center of its elaborate liturgical experience lies one prayer that stands out among others—the *Amida*, literally, 'the standing.' The main idea behind its name ('standing') is the worshipper's entrance into the presence of the 'seated' Heavenly King. God has granted the ultimate audience to the humble worshipper."[29] Such a prayer indicates that the Jews want to experience God's presence in an intimate manner.

29. Lizorkin-Eyzenberg, "To Pray as a Jew," para. 1.

The baptism in the Spirit that occurred on the day of Pentecost met such a need, for the baptism was open to all. It was not immersion in water for purification, but rather being immersed in God the Holy Spirit to fellowship with him. This type of baptism orchestrated a personal relationship with the Spirit. It is precisely this that disturbed the Jews. Judaism stresses that God, in his essence, does not mingle with his creation. Humans cannot handle such an overwhelming encounter. For the Holy Spirit, the third person of the triune God, to take up residence in those baptized not only went against the Jewish conviction of a transcendent God, but also bordered on blasphemy. The idea of God residing in human vessels demeaned his holiness.

Traditionalists accommodate the spiritual, but they articulate it through relying on the Torah and rabbinic directives, faithful obedience to laws, adherence to rituals, and participation in commemorative festivals. Radicals downplay such modes of articulating their spirituality. Both traditionalists and radicals find it difficult to accept the baptism in the Holy Spirit at Pentecost, which orchestrates an indwelling personal relationship with God the Holy Spirit.

Kabbalah and Hasidic mysticism claimed that people could relate to God experientially based on the conviction that such an endeavor would not be in vain since God himself was eager to relate with humans.

Kabbalah mystics seemed to have recognized God's quest. This is evident in their presentation of key concepts, such as God as *Ein-Sof*, the ten *Sephiroth*, and the *Otz Chiim* (tree of life). According to Kabbalah, God in his essence is known as *Ein-Sof*, which means "without end or limits." Since he is not limited by boundaries, he can connect with the universe even though he is transcendent. He does this through ten emanations known as *Sephiroth*. Though these ten emanations originate from God, they also connect with the universe and humanity, making them immanent in a sense. On the other hand, God in his essence (*Ein-Sof*) is not part of the universe or humanity. This characterization is in keeping with the Jewish belief that God is transcendent and, in his essence, cannot become part of his creation.

The famous Kabbalah *Otz Chiim*, or tree of life, is taken to be the blueprint that underlies everything, from the structure of the universe to the composition of the human personality. It maps out God's route to humans and the world, commencing with his act of creation, and shows the route that humans can take to approach God.

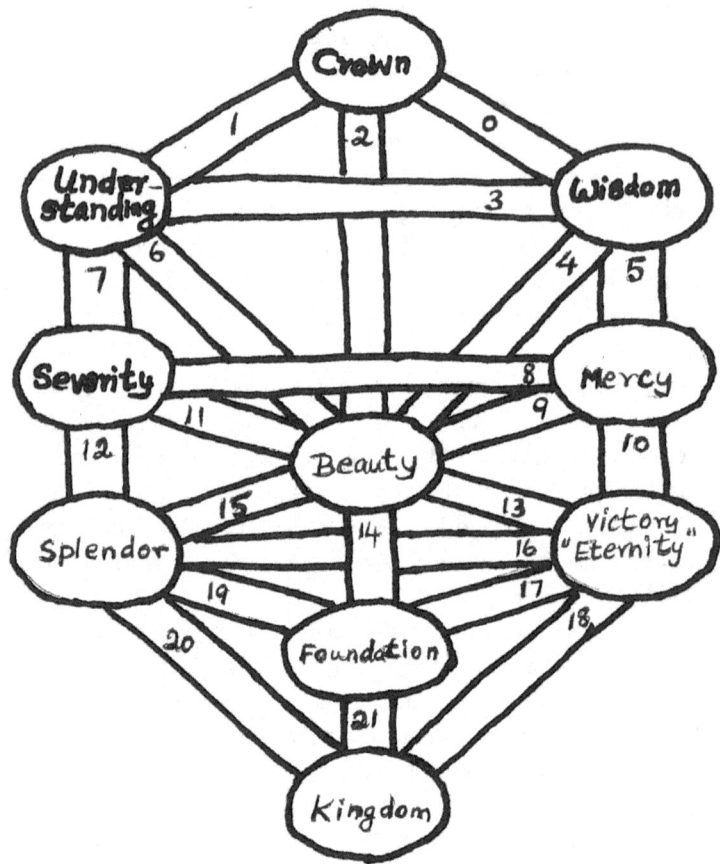

Sketch of the Tree of Life (*Otz Chiim*)

The tree of life represents different levels of reality that are all linked. The diagram consists of circles, representing spheres (*Sephiroth*), and lines (*Nitivoth*), which are paths linking the circles. Each sphere represents a core quality that constitutes the universe. The lines are the paths of the tree and the struts that interlink the spheres, providing conduits by which the qualities in the spheres can balance and interweave. The diagram shows the different levels of reality and how they are linked. Both the spheres (circles) and the paths (lines), when taken together, are believed to exhibit the pattern that reflects the wisdom of God in creating the universe. The tree shows how "the spark of divinity became the substance of the universe. It is the route from energy to matter, from God to man."³⁰ It may also be seen as portraying how transcendent God became immanent.

It is not surprising that there are various interpretations of the diagram's meaning. Let us not be bogged down by these! Despite the controversies, there seems to be agreement that the tree of life maps two main routes. The first route shows God creating the universe and then relating with it. By winding its way down from sphere 1, the divine energy of God winds its way through the spheres of creation, until it reaches the end of creation at the bottom, sphere 10. The second route portrays the human ascent to reach divinity from sphere 10 to sphere 1.

Those who structured and orchestrated the tree of life did not want its meaning and message to be restricted to the enlightened mystics. They believed that anyone who would at least try to understand would benefit. They claimed that "gaining some familiarity with the *Sephiroth* is enough to bring about a better understanding of life and the design of the universe."³¹ Moreover, the second route that portrays the human path to God is believed to enable people to experience the spiritual fulfillment they are yearning for.

How can humans approach God, who is so transcendent and holy? Rabbi Aryeh Kaplan, a Kabbalist scholar, responds to this question by pointing out that there is a more perplexing question to be answered first. He claims that, "God's simple essence is so powerful that it must be hidden if creation is to exist at all."³² Creation would cease to exist if God withdrew himself and, if that happened, nothing could exist. Kaplan suggests that the question is not, "How can the ONE interact with the MANY?," but "How can MANY even exist?" "How can creation exist?" Based on the Jewish distinction between God's essence and his presence, he responds to the question, claiming that God introduced a "spiritual dimension" to relate with humans. On one hand, this domain enables the universe to exist; it is made up of every basic concept to create and sustain the universe. On the other hand, it is through this spiritual domain that God interacts with his creation. It forms a bridge between God and creation and acts as a "step-down mechanism which prevents creation from being overwhelmed by God's essence, while still being infused by it."³³ According to the Kabbalists, it is this spiritual domain that makes it possible to speak about God's multifaceted relationship to the universe without violating his unity and his simplicity.³⁴

30. Dedopulus, *Kabbalah*, 28.
31. Dedopulus, *Kabbalah*, 30.
32. Kaplan and Sutton, *Innerspace*, 7–8.
33. Kaplan and Sutton, *Innerspace*, 8.
34. Kaplan and Sutton, *Innerspace*, 21–23.

It is through this spiritual domain that one comes to know God. It also provides the key to understand how the prophets of the Bible connected with God.[35] This domain is like a "spiritual computer," programmed to fulfill God's ultimate purpose of bestowing good upon his creation, through his presence.[36]

To further clarify the mediating role of the spiritual domain, Kabbalists adopted the concept of *devekut* (cleaving to God) to articulate the spiritual journey of a seeker. It served as the means for the mystic to enter the divine sphere (spiritual domain). It enables the mystic to cleave to God and become like him.

Devekut also facilitates a salvific transformation in that it gives the mystic the peace of being with God and the assurance of eternal life, since only God is eternal and anyone rooted in him has eternal life. The ways to orchestrate *devekut* could be through esoteric practices or meditation. Some moderate kabbalists accommodate obeying God's commandments as a way to orchestrate cleaving to God.

Judaic spirituality, especially that orchestrated by Kabbalah and Hasidic mystics, is essentially a way to God through human effort. The spiritual domain provides the arena for the seeker to experience God's peace and presence without in any way becoming one with his essence, which would be fatal. This strategy also falls in line with the foundational Judaic dogma that there could be a fulfilling relationship between God and humans, without God foregoing his transcendent holiness, and that humans could be blessed by the divine presence without trying to become one with God.

Kabbalism and Hasidism show the quest of Jews for a spiritual experience that goes beyond rigid legalistic ritualism and leads to a personal experience with the divine. It is here that the spirituality of Pentecost becomes relevant, for it meets such an aspiration, but why is Jewish mystic spirituality not able to accommodate Pentecost?

For the Kabbalah and Hasidic mystics, the mode of orchestrating *devekut* (cleaving to God) may be in one of two ways. For many Jewish mystics, Kabbalah is not an alternative to their traditional methods. For instance, Rabbi Shlomo ben Avraham ibn Aderet and Rabbi Joseph Karo claim that Kabbalah's real contribution was in raising the awareness of the Jew to the ultimate goal of Jewish spirituality.[37] These Kabbalists "regarded the attainment of *devekut* not as a mystical value per se but as the culmination of their

---

35. Kaplan and Sutton, *Innerspace*, 8.
36. Kaplan and Sutton, *Innerspace*, 34–35; 191n33.
37. Idel and McGinn, *Mystical Union and Monotheistic Faith*, 54.

observance of the commandments."[38] On the other hand, as an alternative to following commandments and rules, some devout Kabbalists advocated mystical techniques like recitations of letter combinations and divine names together with breathing exercises and incantational practices.[39] Both these modes strive to experience the divine on the grounds of self-effort.

Conversely, Pentecostal spirituality is founded on the dictum that self-effort is not enough; we need help and that help must come from God. Those who heard Peter's sermon about the baptism in the Holy Spirit asked Peter and the disciples, "Brothers, what shall we do" (Acts 2:37)? They were eager to have the experience of the baptism in the Spirit that the disciples spoke about. In response to their query, Peter insisted that they needed to repent and be baptized in the name of Jesus Christ and then they would receive the "gift" of the Holy Spirit (Acts 2:38).

Peter's reply would have shocked Jewish traditionalists, radicals, and even mystics. First, Peter was opening the invitation not only to the chosen people, but to anyone who sincerely repented. In the Kabbalist world, where one could experience spirituality only by entering the spiritual domain through arduous esoteric practices or through meticulous observance of Jewish laws, Peter's invitation would have been too open ended. Peter presented the baptism in the Holy Spirit not as a reward for human effort, but rather as a gift of God's grace.

From the perspective of Jewish spirituality, the revolution that climaxed on the day of Pentecost presented a spirituality that bordered on blasphemy on more than one count. The centerpiece of such spirituality was the baptism in the Holy Spirit since, to receive that gift, the Jews had to go through Jesus Christ. Jesus here is taken to be God, for only God could forgive sins. The requirement to receive the gift was to accept Jesus as Savior God, but that was viewed as idolatry.

The most controversial issue was that the experience of Spirit baptism highlighted a personal relation with the Holy Spirit. The baptism in the Spirit at Pentecost does not merely take one into a spiritual domain, however exhilarating that may be, but facilitates a relationship with the Holy Spirit, who is a divine person rather than a spiritual computer. Those baptized in the Spirit were not merely blessed by the *shekinah* glory of God's presence, but they experienced the fellowship of God the Spirit through yielding to him. It was not merely a sensational moment, but the start of an ongoing relationship and an intimate fellowship with the Holy Spirit. Jewish

---

38. Idel and McGinn, *Mystical Union and Monotheistic Faith*, 55.

39. Idel and McGinn, *Mystical Union and Monotheistic Faith*; see also Idel, *Kabbalah*, 96–103.

spirituality could accommodate seekers experiencing God's presence, but it was blasphemous to think that God could reside in human vessels.

Even though the spiritual revolution has Jewish roots and there are many meeting points between Jewish and Pentecostal spiritualities, there are certain lingering controversial issues such as whether Pentecost was the fulfillment of prophecy, whether authentic spirituality should be founded on Christ the Savior, and whether it could be orchestrated through personal relationship with God the Holy Spirit.

THE GENTILE REACTION: PENTECOST OFF TRACK

At the time of Pentecost, the gentile world was filled with anxiety which gave rise to several types of spiritualities that addressed the malady of the age.[40] These spiritualities differed in significant ways from the spirituality that Pentecost offered. They described the spiritual journey by how it commenced, the direction it took, how it equipped its seekers, and where it took the seekers. In light of such a track, which is still very popular, Pentecost becomes controversial.

Wrong Starting Point

The starting point of many gentile spiritualities was the human being. The human being was depicted as essentially good or even divine, and having the potential to achieve spiritual fulfillment through human effort. For instance, the Greek Epicureans considered human beings capable of achieving spiritual fulfillment through pleasure, which freed them from the superstitious fears of deities and death. The Greeks, following Socrates, claimed that humans could acquire knowledge that would make them virtuous, provided they freed themselves from ignorance. Although they were impacted by ignorance, they were not incapacitated by it; humans have the potential to free themselves through acquiring knowledge. The Greeks and Romans, who worshipped multiple gods, considered themselves good enough to receive divine blessings, provided they pleased their gods through sacrifices, offerings, and good deeds. As noted earlier, after Alexander the Great's expansion of the Greek Empire, people were exposed to Eastern religions that brought with them several modes of spirituality. Hindu spirituality viewed humans as divine. The cause of the human predicament is that humans do not realize their divinity; ignorance of their real identity incapacitates them. They

---

40. Abhayananda, *History of Mysticism*, 98–109. Swami Abhayananda notes that the Greco-Roman era had several philosophers whose philosophies exhibited mysticism: philosophers like Pythagoras, Heraclitus, Xenophanes, Socrates, Plato, Aristotle, Zeno of Citium, and Philo of Alexandria.

needed a way to enable them to realize their identity, which was provided through the help of gurus, divinization, meditative methods, incantations, and ecstatic trances. It is noteworthy that most of the popular spiritualities considered the human being, the seeker after spiritual fulfillment, to have the potential to attain it. The spirituality that Pentecost initiated, however, went against such a depiction of human identity. In his sermon, Peter insisted that one should repent to receive the Spirit (Acts 2:38). Repentance implies that humans need repair work, in fact, a total overhaul. The starting points of the spirituality of Pentecost and that of other popular spiritualities were far apart. These other spiritualities saw Pentecost as having missed the mark for its starting point was off track.

Wrong Track

If a spiritual journey was to reach its target, it needed to be on the right track, and moving in the right direction. Most spiritualities of the time began with the human being trying to achieve spiritual fulfillment and assuming that humans could reach their goal. They carved out a track that commenced with the human on a journey to spiritual fulfillment that was orchestrated through self-effort. The Hindu transcendental meditational strategy depicts this type of journey. This mode views God as cosmic consciousness (*Brahman*), which includes the human soul (*athma*). Deceived by spiritual illusion (*maya*), we are not aware of who we really are, as part of the divine. This spiritual blindness results in bondage. Transcendental meditation frees us from this predicament by enabling us to realize our true divine identity. The following diagram presents the Hindu track.

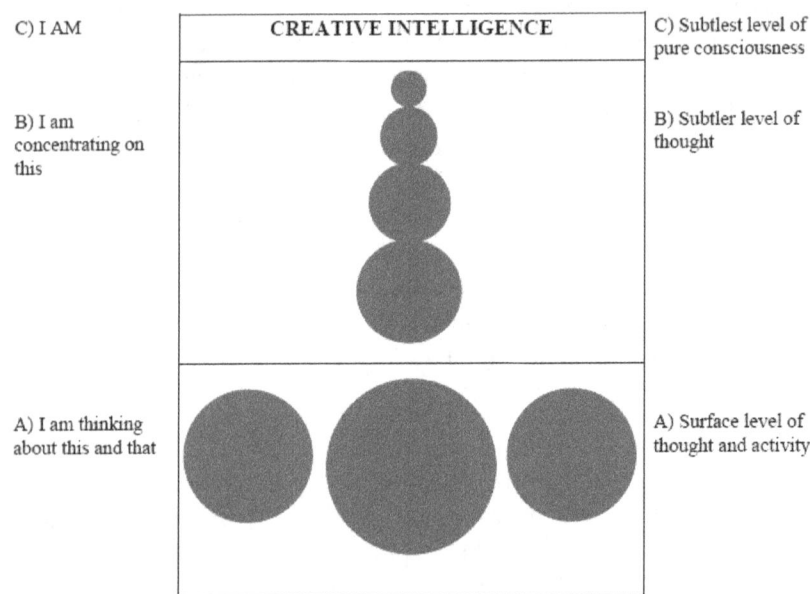

The Transcendental Meditation Track

The circles in the first (bottom) level indicate our restless preoccupation with this and that; the confused state in which we begin at the surface level. When we attempt to concentrate on a single thing among several others, we begin our journey, taking us to the second level. Through concentrating on that single thing, we gradually lose awareness of even that one thing. The shrinking size of the single circle in the second level of the diagram shows this. Finally, we end up in a state of being fully aware, but not of anything in particular, which is the subtlest level of pure consciousness. Even the single thing we were concentrating on (the circle) is gone. The absence of circles in the third (top) level of the diagram indicates this. When we reach this "I Am" stage, we become aware of our true identity as part of the divine cosmic consciousness. This provides us with spiritual fulfillment that in turn results in freedom from bondage. The direction of the spiritual journey is from the human to the divine,[41] which was the direction of the spiritual journey of most of the spiritualities at the time. This direction was very different from that of the spirituality offered at Pentecost. As noted in chapter 6, the spirituality of Pentecost was God initiated. It commenced with God and reached humans.

41. Kulathungam, "Christian Meditation," 22–37.
Kulathungam, *Quest*, 158–59.

Wrong Finishing Point

The journey must reach its destination. We have already noted the spirituality offered by Pentecost was a personal relationship with God the Holy Spirit. This relationship empowered those who received the gift and enabled them to continue their spiritual journey, experiencing an intimate fellowship with the triune God. Such spirituality facilitated a personal relationship with God. On the other hand, the spiritualities of the gentile world rendered a spiritual fulfillment that did not facilitate such a relationship. The Epicurean "pleasure," the Stoic "quietude," the Socratic "virtue rendering knowledge," the Hindu *moksha*, and the Buddhist *nirvana* were likely spiritually satisfying to those who adopted such modes. However, none of these ended up in an intimate ongoing personal relationship with God or a fellowship with God as a person. The ardent followers of such modes found the goal of the spirituality of Pentecost both incomprehensible and controversial. They found Pentecost off track in its starting point, in its direction, and in its destination.

The Judeo-Greco-Roman world of the time could not accommodate the spirituality of Pentecost. To the Jew it was blasphemous, while to the gentile it was off track. Such hesitancy still prevails and is indicative of the revolutionary character of Pentecostal spirituality.

9

Until Then

D-DAY

THE JUDEO-CHRISTIAN NARRATIVE ENDS with a grand finale: a D-Day.[1] Some religions accommodate a climaxing final episode, but that typically pertains to the peak experience of the seeker and not to a global occurrence. For Buddhists, it is *nirvana* and for Hindus it is *moksha*. Certain sectors of Hinduism anticipate an ideal age, but time is taken to be cyclical. History for these Hindus has four main epochs. Every epoch begins but ends and may begin again. Even the anticipated ideal age that would supplant the present dark epoch will be transient. The Islamic "day of judgment" comes closest to the Judeo-Christian depiction of the final day. The Quran repeatedly warns people that on the day of judgment, some will enter paradise while others will suffer eternally (Quran 3:106). Warnings like this highlight God's justice but, on the other hand, also cause people to fear that day rather than anticipating it with hope. Interestingly, the father of communism, Karl Marx, believed that history could be geared toward an ideal age of a classless society, attainable through the revolutionary action of the working class. It would be an age orchestrated by humans without the help of the state or

1. "During World War II (1939–1945), the Battle of Normandy, which lasted from June 1944 to August 1944, resulted in the Allied liberation of Western Europe from Nazi Germany's control. The battle began on June 6, 1944, also known as D-Day, when some 156,000 American, British, and Canadian forces landed on five beaches along a 50-mile stretch of the heavily fortified coast of France's Normandy region. The Normandy landings have been called the beginning of the end of war in Europe" (History.com editors, "D-Day," para. 1).

even God. Such a revolution occurred in Russia in October 1917, known as the October or Bolshevik Revolution. However, it did not usher in a classless society but resulted in a dictatorship. It is justified because it was a dictatorship of the proletariat, the working class, to suppress the capitalist sectors in society. Communists believed that the revolution ushering in "the dictatorship of the proletariat" would bring about social and economic justice where one class would not exploit another class. The state would wither away.[2] There is controversy as to whether Marx's dream was ever realized, especially in the context of the performance of communism that Lenin and Stalin articulated in Russia.

Whether Marxism was a success or a failure, Marx becomes relevant for his depiction of human history as leading toward an idyllic age. He presents history as a dynamic narrative that, through revolutionary class conflicts, aims to arrive at an ideal classless society where there is peace and justice. Marx epitomizes the secular, even atheistic, quest for an ideal age.

This depiction of history is relevant to the Judeo-Christian historical perspective, which also anticipates a climax in history that will totally change the tapestry of the world and usher in an endless age of global peace and harmony. This age, unlike the Marxist strategy, will be orchestrated by God. It will complete his quest to relate with and redeem his creation.

Citing certain Old Testament prophets, Jews anticipate a messianic era of global peace and harmony. Orthodox Jews believe that it will be brought about by a God-anointed one, the Messiah. Although Jews do not agree on the necessity of such a Messiah, there seems to be agreement among them regarding the advent of a messianic age that would be preceded by the resurrection of the dead and the day of judgment. When the dead are resurrected, they will enter either everlasting life or everlasting torment (Dan 12:2). Their fate will be decided on the day of judgment that will lead to what the Talmud calls *olam ha ba* (in Hebrew, world to come), when all will worship the one true God. In Jewish theology, *olam ha ba* refers either to "the world after death" or the new creation or restoration of the world that is to follow the messianic millennium. Whatever the interpretation, for Jews it means the end of uncertainty, misery, and strife.[3]

For Christians, the grand finale peaks with the return of Christ. It will be the universal recognition of the lordship of Christ, when everyone in the world will see him in his glory (Rev 1:7). The kingdom of God will finally be established for eternity. On that day, the salvation that commenced with believers' acceptance of Christ as Savior will be fully realized. The warped

2. Marx and Engels, *Manifesto of the Communists*, 10.
3. Editors of Encyclopaedia Britannica, "Judaism: *Olam ha-ba*."

and dilapidated world will become the "new earth" (Rev 21:1). It will be a day of salvation as well as judgment, and will usher in an age of eternal peace and harmony under God in Christ.

However, there are many conflicting views among both Jews and Christians about that anticipated event: what it will be like, when it will come, who or what will figure in it, and how it will be orchestrated. Preoccupation with these controversies would distract us from the core theme of the book: God's relentless quest. The grand finale will be the climax of God's quest, but since it has not yet happened we need to live until then. How can we handle this era that seems as if it will never end? Has God given up his quest?

The escalating and overwhelming problems of our times mean that the grand finale appears to be a vain hope. In our information-packed world where sensational but mostly depressing news is effectively communicated through hyper-technocratic modes, God's quest to relate with and redeem humanity appears to be religious fiction. Not surprisingly, the calamities of our age instill skepticism as to whether the grand finale will ever happen. In the Judeo-Christian context, God is the one who will ultimately orchestrate the grand finale, putting an end to these calamities and catastrophes. Since nothing has yet happened, God becomes the point of controversy. Let us look at some of the ways God becomes the target.

Doubting, excluding, and denying God, or substituting other gods in his place has occurred through history. In our times, these reactions to God occur at unprecedented rates and cause us to question whether the peak point will ever happen, or whether the final manifestation of God's quest is a vain hope.

Doubting God

We live in a sophisticated, science-oriented world where information on any topic is readily available. Although we should be able to discern between the real and the pseudo, ironically we are prone to be gullible. We tend to follow every fad, believe the strangest of dogmas, adhere to theories garbed in pseudoscientific vocabulary, become enthralled by any charismatic figure, or tailgate any political magnate. We laugh at the legends of the past and yet are rabid fans of science fiction films and fables. When it comes to God, however, doubt sets in. In fact, being skeptical of religion has become a matter of pride among the educated elite of society. Why?

Doubting God may not amount to denying his existence, but rather his promises and capabilities. One reason we doubt God is because he seems to turn up late at the very time that we need him urgently. This happened to the prophet Habakkuk who lived in Judah under the dictatorship of King Jehoiakim. The prophet was disturbed that God seemed silent in the face of such cruelty and violence, and cried out to God: "How long, Lord, must I call for help, but you do not listen" (Hab 1:2)? God responded, but only when the panicked prophet settled down and waited for God's response to his complaint (Hab 2:1). God's reply was definitive: "For the revelation awaits an appointed time; it speaks of the end and will not prove false. Though it linger, wait for it; it will certainly come and will not delay" (Hab 2:3). We need to note that lingering does not mean delaying. If our friends tell us that they will meet us on a specific day, but do not turn up on that day, they have delayed. When they tell us that they will meet us later, but do not turn up on the day we expected them to come, they have not delayed but have lingered. They did not specify the date of their coming. We only thought that they would come on the day we had selected in our mind. The prophet Habakkuk took God's lingering as his delaying. God never told Habakkuk the details about when and how he would free the Israelites from the rule of King Jehoiakim. God lingered but did not delay.

Blaming God for being late is not something new. What is new is that in our high-speed, fast-paced, digital world, our patience levels have dwindled so much that we want everything immediately. When there is even a second's delay, we don't have patience to wait, and move on to the next thing. In this hyper-rushed life, reaching the long-anticipated grand finale seems a vain hope. Peter sensed that there would come a time when scoffers would say, "Where is this 'coming' he promised? Ever since our ancestors died, everything goes on as it has since the beginning of creation" (2 Pet 3:3-4). He reminded them that their scoffing arose from measuring delay in a time schedule that is different from God's: "With the Lord a day is like a thousand years, and a thousand years are like a day" (2 Pet 3:8). Peter highlighted that God would keep his promise; he is not slow in keeping his promise, but it will be according to his time schedule (2 Pet 3:9). The author of the book of Hebrews points out, "He who is coming will come and will not delay" (Heb 10:37). The anticipated grand finale will occur as God promised, according to his time schedule, not ours.

The Bible does not mention the day or time when the anticipated event will happen. Jesus told his disciples that no one knows the day or hour when it will occur, not even the angels, or Jesus himself, but only God the Father (Matt 24:36, 25:13).

Jesus further warned his disciples not to try to find out the time or season when the event would occur since God the Father, by his own authority, has set the date (Acts 1:7; Mark 13:32). He warned them of false prophets, spreading pseudogospel messages with deceptive signs and wonders, who would try to attract crowds by claiming to know the date of Christ's return (Matt 24:24–26). The Bible states that this day will come, "like a thief in the night when no one expects it" (Luke 21:34–36, 12:40; 1 Thess 5:1–3; 2 Pet 3:10; Rev 3:3). A thief does not set a time to steal, but visits at an unexpected time. We are asked to be always ready. Attempting to date the dateless turns into a fallacy, just as trying to ask a thief when he plans to visit us!

Over the past 2,000 years, prophetic pundits have been preoccupied with forecasting the date of the end of the world, the second coming of Jesus, the day of judgment, or however we wish to refer to it. These forecasts are recurrent, commencing from the first century CE, and have been made by scientists, biblical scholars, prominent religious leaders, sensational television evangelists, and charismatic prophetic preachers. The Jewish Essene sect, led by Simon bar Giora, thought that the Jewish war against the Romans, from 66 to 70 CE, would usher in the Messiah. Coins were minted declaring the redemption of Israel.[4] However, nothing happened and the coins went out of circulation. Several Catholic clerics, like Pope Sylvester II, predicted that the millennium would commence on January 1, 1000 CE, 1,000 years after the birth of Christ. Since that did not happen, some Vatican clerics predicted that the end would come in 1033 CE, one thousand years after the death of Christ.[5] Sir Isaac Newton also tried his hand at apocalyptic prophecy. Some unpublished documents, supposedly written by Newton, indicate that he believed the world could end in 2060 CE, based on his study of the book of Daniel (12:7). He predicted many other possible dates, such as 2034 CE.[6] John Wesley, the founder of the Methodist denomination, predicted that Christ would come in 1836 based on his study of Revelation 12:14.[7] Popular Baptist preacher William Miller predicted the second coming would occur on October 22, 1844. Thousands gathered that night to await the arrival of Jesus, but obviously nothing happened; it became known as the "great disappointment."[8] In January 1946, the new age writer Alice A. Bailey proclaimed that Christ would return sometime after 2025, incarnated

---

4. Bar Giora coins bore the legend "Redemption of Zion." This does not prove that he was considered the Messiah, but it is likely. The fact that he wore a royal robe in the temple is another indication.

5. Boyett, *Pocket Guide to the Apocalypse*; Strandberg and James, *Are You Rapture Ready?*

6. Whitla, *Sir Isaac Newton's Daniel*.

7. Strandberg and James, *Are You Rapture Ready?*; McIver, *End of the World*, 269. Wesley foresaw the millennium would begin in 1836 based on his belief that Rev 12:14 referred to the years 1058–1836.

8. Strandberg and James, *Are You Rapture Ready?*, 38; Festinger et al., *When Prophecy Fails*.

as the anticipated Buddhist messenger of love (*Maitreya*) to inaugurate the ideal age.[9] In 1994, physicist Frank Tipler's book, *The Physics of Immortality*, claimed to scientifically prove God's existence on the grounds of what he called the Omega Point Theory. His follow-up book of 2007, *The Physics of Christianity*, applied the principles of the Omega Point Theory to predict the second coming of Christ would occur within 50 years, or by 2057.[10] All these predictions—although based on scriptural study, theological dogmas, scientific calculations, and philosophical speculations—seem to commit the fallacy of dating an event that cannot be dated.

Mistaking lingering for delaying and attempting to date what cannot be dated both result in doubting God. Jesus anticipated people losing their faith in the last days when he asked the rhetorical question, "However, when the Son of Man comes, will he find faith on the earth?" (Luke 18:8). Doubting God and his promises leads to excluding him. Why bother with a God who delays and does not keep his promises?

Excluding God

People through the ages have excluded God for various reasons: affluence, self-sufficiency, busy schedules, and life's frustrations. In contemporary times, our science-oriented society is increasingly prone to excluding God. Science is rightfully credited for delivering quality knowledge. Some of its findings—particularly in the areas of the origin of the universe and the nature of human composition—seem to contravene theistic claims. Science turns out to be a pervasive challenge to faith, figuring as a legitimate and even alternate edifice of faith that claims to understand the universe without accommodating God.[11] Science per se is neither pro-God nor anti-God, but some scientific enthusiasts claim that the universe can be adequately understood through scientific theories. For instance, physicist Paul Davies discerns that physics points the way to a novel insight and appreciation concerning the existence of the universe. Questions about existence are not new, but Davies argues that physics is on the verge of answering them in a satisfactory manner. He picks out some questions about existence. Why does the universe consist of the things it does? How did these things arise? How did the universe achieve its organization? Davies concludes that physics offers a better alternative to answer such questions than religion.[12] In Stephen Hawking's final book, *Brief Answers to Big Questions,* he claims "There

---

9. Bailey, *Externalisation of the Hierarchy*; Bailey, *Reappearance of the Christ.*
10. Tipler, *Physics of Christianity.*
11. Kulathungam, "Scientific Understanding and Christian Faith," 161.
12. Davies, *God and the New Physics,* 5.

is no God. No one directs the universe."[13] He comes to this conclusion on the grounds that science provides an adequate explanatory model. Such advocates of the adequacy of scientific explanation tend to dismiss all other modes of explanation, including the theistic. This results in excluding God from one's world view.

Such a maneuver is motivated by the significant success of the scientific method to understand the universe based on a tacit strategy, which may be described as follows:

> In attempting to understand something, say "X," one usually selects and/or constructs a method which seems the most appropriate (in some cases, the only one available) way of understanding "X." When such a strategy turns out to be successful, in that the method, "M," has delivered or could deliver if adequately developed, a satisfactory understanding of "X," call it "U," then a further claim is made: that on the strength of the success of "M," "X" is NOTHING BUT "U"; that "X" is nothing but what one understands or could understand "X" to be through the method "M."[14]

This mode of understanding may be called the reductionist strategy. Adopting this strategy leads to the claim that there is nothing beyond the scientific understanding of the universe. Within such a framework, any other explanation becomes superfluous. This trend is evident particularly in the handling of certain events considered to be miraculous in the religious world. For instance, one recovering from a deadly disease or a blind person regaining sight is acclaimed in religious circles as God's miraculous intervention. These events tend to lose their miraculous flavor when explained through natural causes. Such a stance is legitimate when one acknowledges that something can be explained adequately through natural causes. Does that mean that there are no causes beyond the natural to explain something?

Hawking himself is reported to have acknowledged that certain claims like, "There are forms of intelligent life out there," and "Travel back in time," are not amenable to being scientifically verified or explained.[15] If we can accommodate this type of possibility, why not also leave the question of God open ended, rather than dogmatically excluding him? One is entitled to claim that something, say "X," has been or could be understood or justified through a method, whether scientific or not. But on the grounds of the success of such an accomplishment, to further claim that "X" is "NOTHING

---

13. Picheta, "There is No God," para. 3.
14. Kulathungam, "Scientific Understanding and Christian Faith," 165.
15. Picheta, "There is no God," para. 4.

BUT" what is understood through that method turns out to be restrictive. Moreover, if "X" cannot be explained by a particular method, can we dismiss it as fictitious? For instance, although claims that God exists or that he created the universe may not be scientifically established, does that mean they are invalid? Can one turn to faith to confirm such claims?

Not only those enamored by the success of science, but also some devoted to God are prone to commit the reductionist fallacy. These individuals tend to dismiss any mode that explains something through natural causes as demonic! Can a miracle be miraculous even when it becomes explainable through natural causes? Is it an either-or situation?

The trend to explain through natural causes has penetrated the social and educational sectors of contemporary society. Secular state, secular education, secular moral codes, and human relationships determined exclusively through laws of behavioral psychology are popular contemporary orchestrations that tend to exclude God. Can God be caged within human categories like science and faith, or secular and religious?

Excluding God is only a step away from denying him; secularism leads to atheism.

Denying God

Theism acknowledges God, while atheism denies God. Although modern atheism came out of European enlightenment, when science and secularism started to challenge belief in God, the denial of God has been prevalent from ancient times. Epicureans, who confronted Paul at Athens, were prominent Greek atheists. Their leader, Epicurus, was a radical materialist who claimed that the world was nothing but matter and the human being was merely a physical organism. When death occurs, one dissolves into atoms. Greek gods, manifested through idols and being made of matter, would also die like humans. His stance went against the worship of multiple gods by the Athenians, who branded Epicureans as blasphemous atheists.

The hub of Epicurean atheism was the famous "garden," or "garden of death." Considerable archaeological research is in progress to identify its location. What matters most is not its precise location, but its symbolic significance. As professor Tim Whitmarsh notes, the garden was not a school like Plato's academy, but more a physical manifestation of the ideal of tranquil serenity at which Epicurus aimed, which would enable friendship between people of all backgrounds.[16] Its significance lay in the world in which it appeared. The people of that time were extremely theistic: some worshipped multiple gods and others were enamored by Plato's theistic world

16. Whitmarsh, "Archaeology of Atheism."

view. Plato claimed that there had to be an intelligent being to account for order in the world, and that chaotic matter could not create order on its own. For Plato, that which rendered identity to the human being was the soul and not the body. His philosophy focused on enhancing the soul to free it from the constraints of the body. Death liberated the soul from the bondage of physical existence. Whitmarsh thinks that positioning the garden near the location of Plato's academy might have been a symbolic attempt to hijack the Platonic topography. The garden, covered with material relics, highlighted that nothing survives death except such relics. Since nothing survives death, one need not worry about pleasing or appeasing gods.[17] Whitmarsh argues that the garden was an expression of Epicurean atheistic views about death. His photograph below links Plato's academy to the Epicurean garden of death. The link is symbolic, although speculative.[18] It expressed the opposite of Plato's view of survival after death, which was based on a theistic world view.

The Epicurean Garden of Death (Photo credit: Tim Whitmarsh)

Whitmarsh's book, *Battling the Gods: Atheism in the Ancient World*, highlights the prevalence of atheism in ancient Greece.[19] The Indian school of philosophical skepticism and materialism known as *Charvaka* (originally *Lokayata*) is indicative of the prevalence of atheism in the Hindu world. Atheism has also figured as a reaction against those who deny a particular god. Mesopotamians branded Abraham as an atheist since he viewed their

17. Whitmarsh, "Archaeology of Atheism."
18. Whitmarsh, "Archaeology of Atheism."
19. Whitmarsh, *Battling the Gods*.

gods as mere idols. Early Christians were called atheists because they refused to worship the Greek and Roman gods. There is a distinction between local and global atheism. While local atheism targets the denial of a god of a certain people or locality, global atheism claims that there is no cosmic creator or intelligent designer worthy of worship.[20]

Today, atheism is developing into a sophisticated world view comparable to naturalism and materialism and able to stand on its own without reference to theism. Atheists could exist even if there were no theists, though they would not be called atheists.[21] These atheists do not deny a particular god, but rather totally reject the very idea of God. Eminent Jews like Albert Einstein, Karl Marx, Sigmund Freud, and philosophers like Bertrand Russell and Anthony Flew fall into this category. Karl Marx saw religion as creating a make-believe world that concealed the exploitation of the masses. He claimed, "Religion is the sigh of the oppressed creature, the heart of a heartless world, the soul of soulless conditions. It is the opium of the people."[22] Vinoth Ramachandra notes that during a time of scarcity of medical cures, opium was used as a pain killer.[23] To Marx, religion caused people to cope with the dehumanizing conditions, to tolerate the intolerable, believing that it is all God's will. He felt that such a mindset sapped people's will to change the order of things. Based on his claim, the political structure of Russia excluded God and adopted the policy of *gosateizim*, a policy of expropriation of religious property and promotion of anti-religious propaganda. The Russian communist regime may be the first imperial power in history to function on the maxim that there is no God. Sigmund Freud's theories led him to view religion as psychological deficiency. For Freud, religious people were bound by a guilt complex and turned to a father figure who relieved their fears.[24] According to Bertrand Russell, fear is the foundation of religion: "fear of the mysterious, fear of defeat, and fear of death. Fear is the parent of cruelty, and therefore it is no wonder if cruelty and religion have gone hand in hand."[25] Anthony Flew defined atheism as a psychological state of not be-

---

20. Draper, "Atheism and Agnosticism."
21. Baggini, *Atheism*, 12.
22. Marx, "Contribution to the Critique," 44.
23. Ramachandra, *Gods That Fail*, 32.
24. Sigmund Freud, the renowned Austrian Jewish neurologist and psychologist, presented his theories on the role that the "father complex" played in religion in several of his books, including *Totem and Taboo* in 1913, *The Future of an Illusion* in 1927, *Civilization and Its Discontents* in 1930, and *Moses and Monotheism* in 1938. See Thornton, "Sigmund Freud" for further insight.
25. Russell, "Why I Am Not a Christian," 596.

lieving in the existence of god or gods.[26] Based on the dictum that legitimate statements are falsifiable, he claimed that religious statements are illegitimate since they are not falsifiable.[27] The new atheism propagated by Richard Dawkins, Daniel Dennett, Lewis Wolpert, and Christopher Hitchens is a pungent ridicule of theism. Such atheism ridicules the very concept of God and the religious venture associated with it.[28]

Logical positivism ridicules the religious enterprise, turning to popular scientific methods of verification. The mathematicians and empirical scientists who met in Vienna in the 1920s formulated the *Verifiability Criterion of Meaning*: if a statement cannot be proved mathematically or supported through empirical evidence (observation, experimentation) it is not merely false but meaningless. Therefore, some of the claims of religion, like "there is a God," "God created the universe," and "God is good," were seen as meaningless, since they are not verifiable.[29] Logical positivists view those who make such claims as preoccupied with nonsensical discourse; they need to be ignored rather than persecuted. The religious community is comfortably accommodated, but its voice is never heard. Fools are not to be taken seriously!

Our world continues to deny God, but can he be put to death? The frequently quoted "God is dead" dictum popularized by the German philosopher Friedrich Nietzsche gave birth to the death of God theology, or nihilism. Nietzsche observes:

> God is dead. God remains dead. And we have killed him. How shall we comfort ourselves, the murderers of all murderers? What was holiest and mightiest of all that the world has yet owned has bled to death under our knives: who will wipe this blood off us? What water is there for us to clean ourselves? What festivals of atonement, what sacred games shall we have to invent? Is not the greatness of this deed too great for us? Must we ourselves not become gods simply to appear worthy of it?[30]

Nihilist Nietzsche was also critical of religion and warned about its dangerous consequences. He poses the rhetorical question that, if we can accomplish the task of killing God, are we not ourselves worthy of becoming

26. Flew, "Presumption of Atheism," 29–46.

27. In Flew's debates with C. S. Lewis and Flew, "Theology and Falsification."

28. Dawkins, *God Delusion*; Dennett, *Breaking the Spell*; Wolpert, *Six Impossible Things before Breakfast*; Hitchens, *God is Not Great*.

29. Uebel, "Vienna Circle," provides additional information on logical positivist verifiability criterion.

30. Nietzsche, "Madman," 95–96.

gods? This question takes us to what happens when we kill God. Ironically, we make gods or even become gods.

Making Gods

God-making, as noted in chapter 4, has always been a lucrative industry in the religious market. Idols figure as popular products of god-making, even though idol worship has been forbidden since Old Testament times. Abraham was asked not only to leave Mesopotamia, but also to give up the idol worship that was so prevalent there. Why?

Idols are human constructs. When divinity is invoked to reside in them, they in turn become objects of worship, or gods. These may be physical objects, ideologies, or even emotive fads. Behind every physical idol, there lies a mental construct that gives the physical its alluring hold on those who worship it.[31] Idols do not come from a vacuum, but are birthed in a belief system. People treasure a certain person, thing, or ideology and consider it so worthy that they worship it and it becomes a god. The God of the Judeo-Christian narrative did not evolve through human construction; he was there from the very beginning (Gen 1:1) and revealed himself through history. The Jewish and Christian notions about God came out of divine revelation rather than human conceptualization. Therefore, there is a marked distinction between the Judeo-Christian God and other gods.

Modern-day idols may not be made of wood or metal. Nevertheless, they have turned out to be attractive substitutes for God. The deceptiveness of substitutes is that they are so close to the original. They do not appear as demons, but as attractive ideologies like sophisticated scientism, patriotic nationalism, self-glorifying secular humanism, or accommodative pluralism. Some of them may, in fact, be laudable. When they turn into substitutes for God, they displace God. Science is a blessing to humanity, but when, enthralled by its accomplishments, it claims that it can dictate what one should believe or how one should make critical lifetime decisions, then scientism has stepped outside its borders and has turned into an idol or a god.

Even universally acclaimed virtues, such as reason, can turn into subtle substitutes for God. On April 15, 2019, the world watched and mourned as the Notre Dame Cathedral in Paris was devastated by fire. What the world may not realize was that the cathedral was not always a house of God. In 1793, during the anti-Christian fervor of the French Revolution, Notre Dame was turned into a Temple of Reason and dedicated to the atheistic Cult of Reason. It was France's first state-sponsored atheistic religion, spreading the ideas of the revolution, summarized in its *Liberté, égalité,*

31. Ramachandra, *Gods That Fail*, 107.

fraternité (liberty, equality, fraternity) motto, which was also inscribed on the temple. Here, "atheism was enthroned" and its god was reason.[32] Theologian Thomas Hartwell Horne and biblical scholar Samuel Davidson note that, "churches were converted into 'temples of reason,' in which atheistic homilies were substituted for sermons."[33] It was Napoleon who later rededicated Notre Dame to its original purpose. Reason is God's gift to humans, but when it takes the place of God it turns into an idol.

God may be displaced in today's world, but many other gods are replacing him. Interestingly, they seem to fall within a hierarchical or an inferior-superior order. Among the host of gods, the one at the very top may be identified as the human self, the "I" god. God as almighty director of human destiny may disappear in the religious arena, but he resurfaces himself in the guise of the human self. The God who revealed himself to Moses as the great "I am" (Exod 3:14) now becomes the human "I am!"

In recent times, humanism, in the garb of secular humanism, elevates the human being to almost divine status. The 1973 *Humanist Manifesto II*, authored by Paul Kurtz and Edwin Wilson, claims, "... humans are responsible for what we are or will become. No deity will save us; we must save ourselves."[34] In his book, *Humanist Manifesto 2000: Call for New Planetary Humanism*, Kurtz reiterates and substantiates the core claims of the 1973 Manifesto.[35] Secular humanism designates the human being as key in the task of saving humanity. The Amsterdam Declaration highlights the core principles of secular humanism as formulated by the General Assembly of the International Humanist and Ethical Union (IHEU) at the fiftieth anniversary World Humanist Congress in 2002. This declaration reiterates and expands the basic tenets of secular humanism that the previous manifestos highlighted. It is noteworthy that secular humanism has now evolved into a global phenomenon.

In dismissing God, who has taken his place? While acknowledging the need for humans to be freed from their predicament of existence, secular humanists declare that no deity can help. Instead, they rely on the human being to do the job. They turn to science and secular ethics to articulate the human being as savior, stressing that the solutions to the world's problems depend on human ingenuity rather than divine enablement. They claim that scientific strategies must be tempered by human value and that "science

---

32. Croly, "French Revolution," 57. "The name of the cathedral was thenceforth the Temple of Reason. Atheism was enthroned" (57).

33. Horne et al., *Introduction to the Critical Study*, 30.

34. Kurtz and Wilson, *Humanist Manifesto II*, sec. 1, para. 3.

35. Kurtz, *Humanist Manifesto 2000*.

gives us the means, but human values must propose the ends."[36] Thereby, secular humanism "can be a way of life for everyone everywhere."[37] Not surprisingly, this stance highlighting the human ego is received enthusiastically in our times. In displacing God, the human being becomes the one who does the work of God as the final authority on social and moral issues: the one who determines who should be allowed to be born and who should be killed prior to birth, who determines the sex of a person, and the norms of marital relationships.

The new age movement is a dynamic development taking root in the psyche of today's post-modern humanity. Its concepts arise from religious, scientific, sociological, and philosophical sources. Going a step further than secular humanism, it claims that not only can the human being accomplish what God does, but it is also, at the core, divine in nature. One of its key claims is that all, including humans, are fragments of one reality. The universe is constituted of a single conscious energy that is divine though impersonal. This view is essentially pantheistic and has its roots in Hinduism. In *Vedanta* Hinduism, humans are essentially divine as part of a divine consciousness, even though many are not aware of their identity. Becoming aware of one's true divine identity provides the way of salvation. It exemplifies how an ideology that deifies humans turns into a widespread and popular brand of idol worship. It is a kind of God-making, where the human figures as God. A movement such as this is well received in our egocentric culture.

In a world where God is on a relentless quest to relate with humans, introducing other gods becomes a road block. Is God really threatened by human reactions, like doubting, excluding, denying, and substituting him with other gods? Is such a popular global phenomenon the peak of human wisdom or utter folly?

THE FOLLY OF DENYING GOD

Despite a concerted effort to kill God, he has been replaced by a pantheon of other gods. The Bible depicts the folly of making idols as gods: "Although they claimed to be wise, they became fools and exchanged the glory of the immortal God for images made to look like a mortal human being and birds and animals and reptiles" (Rom 1:22–23). When one makes gods, while at the same time denying God, the result is a glaring inconsistency between dogma and practice. Is this not foolish? The Bible forbids us to call someone

---

36. World Humanist Congress, "Amsterdam Declaration 2002," para. 7.
37. World Humanist Congress, "Amsterdam Declaration 2002," para. 12.

a fool (Matt 5:22), but it also states that: "The fool says in his heart 'There is no God'" (Ps 53:1, 14:1). Why?

Theologian and philosopher St. Anselm of Canterbury (1033–1109 CE) appreciated the validity of the biblical claim that to deny God is foolish, when articulating his argument for God's existence in his *Proslogion* (discourse on the existence of God).[38] He did not attempt to prove God's existence, for he was convinced that it must be accepted on the grounds of faith. He wanted to find out why the Bible stated that denying God was foolish. In his *Proslogion*, he documented how denying God leads to a contradiction.[39] He proposed that if one considers "God" as a "being than which no greater can be conceived" or "the most perfect being, who lacks nothing," it is contradictory to claim that such a perfect being lacks the quality of existence or that the perfect being is at the same time imperfect.[40] Such a claim is self-contradictory and foolish. St. Anselm pointed out that if one rejects an imperfect god, that god is not his god, but a straw god. When one takes God to be perfect in all respects and then states that he lacks existence, it amounts to claiming the perfect being is imperfect. This is self-contradictory and therefore foolish. What we can learn from St. Anselm's stance is that denying God is not smart, but foolish. Such a fool needs our compassion and prayers rather than our condescending condemnation.

Beyond Scripture, God uses his creation to reveal his awesome creativity and power. This is called general revelation. God's plan to relate with humanity encompasses all, not merely those who read the Bible and respond to its message. It is here that general revelation becomes vital, and there are two main channels: the world and human conscience (Rom 2:14–15, 1:20; Ps 19:1–6; Matt 5:45). They both provide occasions for all to know him,[41] but many fail to see God in his creation. In this context, "seeing" is not limited to being captivated by the beauty of nature, but also being impressed by its intricate complexity. The Bible states, "Since the creation of the world God's invisible qualities—his eternal power and divine nature—have been clearly seen, being understood from what has been made, so that people are without excuse" (Rom 1:20). They are caricatured as having eyes but not seeing and having ears but not hearing (Jer 5:21; Mark 8:18). Idols are also portrayed in a similar manner (Ps 115:5, 135:16; Deut 4:28, 5:23; Rev 9:20).

---

38. Anselm of Canterbury, "Anselm's Proslogion or Discourse," para. 6.

39. Anselm of Canterbury, "Anselm's Proslogion or Discourse," para. 7–8. See also McGrath, *Science & Religion*, 89–91.

40. Anselm of Canterbury, "Anselm's Proslogion or Discourse," para. 9–12. See also: Kulathungam, "Why I Am Not an Atheist."

41. For a fuller discussion of the role of general revelation, refer to Kulathungam, *Quest*.

Whether it is peer pressure, stubbornness, mental or spiritual default, or satanic deception, some just do not see God, even when there is sufficient evidence of his work in his creation. That does mean that God has given up on them.

The revolutionary change that occurred in the life of a well-known philosopher and atheist highlights how even a committed atheist can receive sight to view the world in a new light. Throughout his career, Antony Flew rejected God and provided the academic ammunition for his fellow atheists to deny and demolish theism. In several famous Socratic Club debates with C. S. Lewis, Flew claimed that asserting the existence of God is fallacious on the grounds that it is not falsifiable like scientific claims. His major work, *Theology and Falsification*, became the Bible of atheists. In his book *God and Philosophy*—first published in 1966 and later reissued in 1984 as *God: A Critical Enquiry*—Flew formulated a systematic argument for atheism. A decade after this book, he published *The Presumption of Atheism*, where he argued that in any discussion about God the onus of proof must be with theists. Based on these claims, he participated in several debates that drew thousands of people and he fervently proclaimed his convictions:

> "I know there is no God."
>
> "A system of belief about God contains the same 'sort of contradictions' as 'unmarried husbands' or 'round squares.'"
>
> "I myself am inclined to believe that the universe was without beginning and will be without end."
>
> "I believe that living organisms evolved over an immeasurably long period from nonliving materials."[42]

In the last of his debates at a New York University summit in May 2004, to the utter surprise of all, he announced that he accepted the existence of a God. In the video of the symposium, the announcer made an interesting comment that of all the great discoveries of modern science, the greatest was God.[43] What made this atheist change his mind in such a dramatic manner? When asked if a creative intelligence is indicated through research done on the origin of life, he responded:

> Yes, I now think it does . . . almost entirely because of the DNA investigations. What I think the DNA material has done is that it has shown, by the almost unbelievable complexity of the arrangements which are needed to produce (life), that intelligence

---

42. Flew and Varghese, *There is a God*, 68–69.
43. Flew and Varghese, *There is a God*, 74.

must have been involved in getting these extraordinarily diverse elements to work together. The enormous complexity of the number of elements and the enormous subtlety of the ways they work together. The meeting of these two parts at the right time by chance is simply minute. It is all a matter of the enormous complexity by which the results were achieved, which looked to me like the work of intelligence."[44]

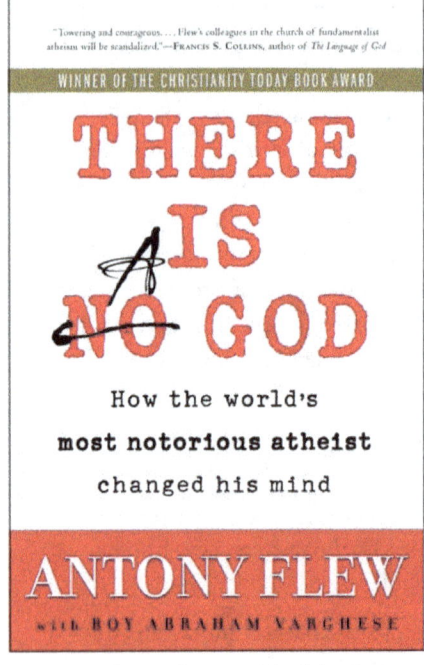

Cover of Antony Flew's book

The title of Antony's Flew's 2007 book, as shown on the cover, effectively describes his journey. Deleting the word "No" just before "God" pinpoints his change of mind.[45] His book argues for the absolute necessity of an intelligent designer to account for the complexity of the DNA structure of the elements of the universe. Antony Flew's metamorphic change from a professed atheist to a convinced theist shows how knowledge about the world could serve as an asset rather than a hindrance to know God. It is ironic that atheists still cite Anthony Flew's claims, even though he has changed his mind.

God is behind the complexity of the DNA of subatomic particles that Flew identified: these are part of God's quest to create order and set in motion the diverse elements and complex processes of the universe. The Bible presents the world as God's handiwork that can enable even atheistic scientists to acknowledge him.

On the other hand, one wonders whether people today will be able to see God's hand at work in this world that seems so out of order and chaotic.

THE WORLD: ITS CHALLENGES AND OUR RESPONSIBILITY

The Judeo-Christian narrative anticipates a grand finale that will occur in this world. One question is whether the earth will last until then. Such a concern is not an outburst of phobic climatologists, but is founded on

---

44. Flew and Varghese, *There is a God*, 75.
45. Flew and Varghese, *There is a God*, cover page.

convincing evidence from reputed and reliable sources. The National Oceanic and Atmospheric Administration, an American scientific agency that tracks billion-dollar disasters, reported that natural calamities caused at least USD $302 billion worth of damage in America in 2017 and that there were 16 separate catastrophes with damages exceeding $1 billion.[46] These catastrophes are not restricted to America but are global. Eco-scientists are loudly warning about the disaster confronting the earth. The United Nations' Intergovernmental Panel on Climate Change (IPCC) warns in definitive terms that the world is not ready for the climate change that will generate extreme weather changes and the likelihood of populated parts of the planet becoming uninhabitable, and that such change will be widespread and consequential.[47] Climate change, global warming, population explosion, industrial pollution, species extinction, and natural resource depletion not only threaten human survival but also place the planet in danger of extinction. This may be attributed to the ruthless exploitation of the earth's resources by humans, arising more out of greed than actual need. Commenting on the tsunami that devastated Southeast Asia in 2004, the Sri Lankan poet Chandra Wickramsinghe insightfully identifies the human factor in such natural disasters poignantly:

> When man plays God,
> Harnessing nature's inner-most secrets
> Destructively, Vaingloriously, Indiscriminately,
> With no cautionary measures taken
> To protect pitifully exposed humankind
> From nature's blindly unleashed backlashes,
> The Devil in nature is riled
> And shows its unimaginable ferocity,
> To make man learn,
> The hard . . . hard way,
> To be humble and wary.[48]

Despite nature's attempt to teach people through such disasters, the human exploitation of nature seems to continue. For human behavior to change, the human mindset needs repair work! It is here that religion clicks in. Ecologists are turning to religions since attitudes that change people's views of nature come primarily from ethical practices and religious world views. The value systems of religions mobilize people to preserve the

---

46. Irfan and Resnick, "Megadisasters Devastated America in 2017," para. 2.
47. Intergovernmental Panel on Climate Change, "IPCC Report," conclusion.
48. Wickramasinghe, "Tsunami," 142–43.

environment.[49] This provides the rationale to consider the Judeo-Christian response to the crisis.

The Judeo-Christian Response to the Ecological Crisis

Jews and Christians have been targeted not only for their indifference to the world's ecological crisis, but also for exploiting the earth's resources. Lynn White points out that in establishing a dualism between man and nature, the Judeo-Christian strategy has traditionally allowed humans to exploit nature for their own ends.[50] White cites Genesis 1:28–30, where God gives the first humans dominion over the earth. It is likely that many have exploited the earth's natural resources, believing that God has granted humans such dominion. To understand the Judeo-Christian stance, we need to consider the whole biblical narrative. We need a comprehensive framework that accommodates both the Old and New Testaments—a narrative approach.[51] As noted in chapter 1, when we adopt such a strategy we see the Bible as depicting a metanarrative: God's story of his commitment to and involvement with his creation. This story exhibits God's protective and redemptive quest through the ages. It does not make sense to think that God has allowed humans to exploit his creation about which he is so concerned.

The Jewish Response

Hava Tirosh-Samuelson identifies some reasons why Jews have had limited interest in environmentalism. She notices that they have been traditionally "people of the Book," who view any preoccupation besides contemplation of the Scriptures as deviation.[52] Even though agriculture was their main mode of livelihood during the Greco-Roman period, for most of their history they have been an urban people. After the rise of Islam, heavy taxation of Jews made agriculture unprofitable, leading them to concentrate on commerce, trade, finance, and money lending. In the post-Holocaust years, their survival dominated their concerns, rather than the care of the earth. They became preoccupied with issues like the Israeli-Arab conflict, and relations between the state of Israel and the diaspora. Taking care of natural resources has not been at the forefront of the Jewish agenda.[53]

However, over the past three decades, there has been a noticeable shift in the Jewish interest in environmental issues. This has been mainly a response to the accusation that the Judeo-Christian tradition is responsible

49. Tucker and Grim, "Overview of World Religions."
50. White, "Historical Roots of Our Ecological Crisis," 1203–7.
51. Srokosz, "God's Story," 163.
52. Tirosh-Samuelson, "Introduction."
53. Tirosh-Samuelson, "Introduction."

for the present environmental crisis. To meet such a criticism, Hava Tirosh-Samuelson edited a volume entitled, *Judaism and Ecology: Created World and Revealed Word*.[54] This work attempts to articulate the discourse on Judaism and ecology by formulating a constructive Jewish theology of nature through clarifying diverse conceptions of nature. The twenty-one contributors, consulting biblical and rabbinic literature, examine the relationship between the doctrine of creation and the doctrine of revelation in the context of natural law, and wrestle with questions of nature and morality. They attempt to face the challenges by highlighting the Jewish stance and commitment to the environment. Such a volume reveals the concerted effort of Jewish scholars to point out that Judaism is committed to being part of the solution of the ecological crisis. Just because problems and pressures force Jews to have higher priorities than ecological issues, it does not mean Judaism is indifferent about the earth.

In appealing to the Jews to pursue the goals of the Paris Climate Accords, Jewish scholar David Kraemer persuades them to take a definitive stand on climate change and be collectively responsible for the planet, since matters of life and death are central within Judaism. He points out that "this is not merely a matter of principle. If scientists are right, this is a matter of life and death for potentially large numbers of creatures, including humans. Matters of life and death are central to the concerns of Jewish thought and religion."[55] Even though some scientists may not concede the threat of global warming, Kraemer comments that: "Because global warming *might* lead to human deaths, it falls into the category of 'safek nefashot,' or occasions when human life might be at risk. And Jewish law is unambiguous when life might be at risk: You are obligated to 'err' in the direction of caution."[56]

Kraemer reminds the Jews that their obligation extends "not just to our own species but to the world as a whole and to all of God's creatures within it,"[57] referencing Psalm 24:1, "The earth is the Lord's, and everything in it, the world, and all who live in it."

Citing Psalm 115:16, Kraemer states that "the heavens belong to the Lord while he gave the earth to the children of men."[58] Citing the Talmud, Kraemer claims that the earth belongs to humans "only after we take responsibility for the earth by recognizing its creator and following the creator's commandments to care for it" (Ber. 6:35a–b).[59] He calls upon the Jews

54. Tirosh-Samuelson, *Judaism and Ecology*.
55. Kraemer, "Judaism Requires Us to Pursue," para. 4.
56. Kraemer, "Judaism Requires Us to Pursue," para. 5.
57. Kraemer, "Judaism Requires Us to Pursue," para. 8.
58. Kraemer, "Judaism Requires Us to Pursue," para. 9.
59. Kraemer, "Judaism Requires Us to Pursue," para. 9. See also "Talmud Berakhot." Composed in Talmudic Babylon (c.450–c.550 CE), *Berakhot* (blessings) is the first

to take care of the earth and to be good stewards; referencing Genesis 2:15, he emphasizes that humans were placed in "this garden . . . to work it *and to guard it*."[60] Kraemer's enthusiastic appeal expresses the Jewish commitment to preserve the planet.

The Christian Response

The Christian responsibility to care for the earth centers on a trinitarian concept of God. God the Father, the Son, and the Holy Spirit are committed to care for and redeem the earth and the people who live in it. It is Jesus who redeems and restores both humanity and the whole creation (John 3:16; Col 1:15–23; Rom 8:18–23). Jesus' death and resurrection highlights God's victory over human sin that brought about creation's corrosion. The rationale for adopting a Christocentric focus to handle the ecological crisis is based on Jesus' identity as God incarnate. The incarnation itself renders dignity to the world, for Jesus lived on this earth for approximately thirty-three years. His redemptive act through the cross covers both humans and the cosmos and his anticipated dominion envisages the new earth. John's prologue (John 3:1–15) to John 3:16 is helpful to understand the Genesis creation story. Here "cosmos" is first the universe, the totality of creation.[61] Jesus' mission was the manifestation of God the Father's love for the cosmos; both humanity and the world fall within the ambit of his care. Moreover, God's universal redemptive plan through Christ includes both the cosmos and humans and is anthropocosmic in scope.[62] The story of the Christian narrative is not over yet. The complete impact of what was accomplished on the cross will be realized in the creation of the new heaven and new earth (Rev 21–22). What are those who anticipate that grand finale to do until then?

First, one needs to stay clear of notions that tend to either degrade the earth or ignore our present life on it. The hope that those who are committed to Jesus would be swept up to heaven in the rapture encourages some to not be too concerned about what they do on earth. Enthralled by sensational prophetic interpretations concerning the last days and captivated by hyper-spirituality, some tend to bypass the challenges and opportunities of the present day. No doubt, one should not be ignorant of the signs of the

---

tractate of the first order, *Zera'im* (seeds), of the Mishnah. It deals with laws related to agriculture, and discusses the rules of prayers and blessings, many associated with partaking of food.

60. Kraemer, "Judaism Requires Us to Pursue," para. 8; emphasis author's. Kraemer cites from the Mishnah Torah and Laws of Shabbat.

61. Srokosz, "God's Story and the Earth's Story."

62. Kulathungam, "Christocentric Anthropocosmic Approach."

times, but to gullibly believe in exciting pronouncements about the future and ignore the earth and its present problems leads us nowhere. Second, the belief that the earth will ultimately be replaced by a new earth tends to lessen one's responsibility for today's earth. Since God will fix it all in the future, why bother about the earth now? Interpreting 2 Peter 3:10 as destruction of the earth could discourage us from looking after it now. This passage speaks about the purging of the sinful world order in which we now live, rather than the obliteration of the earth. Peter points out in 2 Peter 3:6–7 that the flood purged, rather than completely destroyed, the earth. Third, the salvation that Jesus offers depends on individual decision, but sometimes preoccupation with personal salvation tends to dull the breath of God's redemption through Christ that encompasses the whole of creation: people and planet. Fully appropriating the salvation that God provides through Jesus involves taking care of our fellow beings and the earth.

In recent years, deep ecology, also called "ecosophy," has attempted to handle the ecological crisis by glorifying the earth. This strategy refers to a platform of values that some environmental activists share.[63] These values include affirmation of the intrinsic value of nature (biocentrism or egocentrism), even going to the extent of revering the earth as sacred, as "mother earth." Deep ecologists rely on Hindu and indigenous religions, which are founded on the world view that considers the demarcation between nature and divinity as seamless. The Judeo-Christian stance neither degrades the earth nor deifies it. At a time when the worship of nature was prevalent, especially worship of the sun, God sternly warned his chosen people not to be drawn away to worship the sun, the moon, or the stars (Deut 4:19). Job realized that if he had been enthralled by the shining sun and the moon moving in splendor and was enticed to worship them, he would have been unfaithful to God (31:26–28). The Bible never encourages worship of nature. One is called upon to take care of the earth because it is God's creation, but not divine.

"Green Christianity" refers to a group of Christians who are seriously concerned about environmental issues and are actively involved in caring for and protecting the earth. Their stance is founded on the biblical dictum that God created this world and still cares for it. God's quest includes caring for the earth and he calls upon humans to participate in it. Such participation calls for action that goes beyond stewardship of the earth. Stewardship could imply that God serves like an absentee landlord, delegating the responsibility of caring for the earth to humans. He is very involved in the

---

63. Madsen, "Deep Ecology."

caring process and calls on humans to partner with him. Laura Yordy describes the human role as "eco-discipleship."[64]

The Judeo-Christian should be seriously committed to care for the earth and its people.

DOES GOD STILL CARE?

The ever-increasing and unprecedented calamities that affect our world make us doubt whether God still cares. This takes us to a very difficult issue. Why is there so much evil when God is almighty? One way out is to deny him totally or question his ability to destroy evil. When one acknowledges God as almighty and all loving, how could one account for the existence of evil? In the light of the core theme of the biblical narrative—God's quest to relate with his creation—evil could be handled in a different manner. Abraham Heschel, who highlights God's quest in the Jewish narrative, makes an interesting connection between evil and humanity's relationship with God. He points out: "Evil is not man's ultimate problem. Man's ultimate problem is his relation to God." He claims that evil entered into history as a result of man's disobedience to God.[65] From that time onwards, God has used various methods to handle the problem of evil by delving into its core cause: the disrupted relationship between humans and himself. His persistent interventions have been to mend the broken relationship that underlies evil. Although he is on a relentless quest to relate with humanity, he does not impose himself, but gives humans the freedom of choice. Such freedom means that human choices result in consequences, both good and bad. This may account for some of the evil in the world, but not all. The narrative does not provide a theodicy, an explanation for the existence of evil. On the other hand, it highlights God's interventions in the face of evil, mainly caused by human default. Although the narrative does not provide an explanation of evil, it highlights God's acts to protect and redeem his creation from evil. He called on Adam and Eve hiding in sin, called Abraham amidst Babel's blunder, freed the Israelites from Pharaoh's bondage, orchestrated history during the silent years, redeemed his creation on the cross, and empowered the weak through the outpouring of the Holy Spirit at Pentecost. These are just a few instances of God's intervention. The narrative also claims that God's intervention will climax with his final quest when humanity will be fully reconciled with him and the world restored to what he originally intended it to be. When this occurs, evil will be totally and permanently annihilated. Only then will we fully comprehend that it is God alone who

64. Yordy, *Green Witness*, 40–41.
65. Heschel, *God in Search of Man*, 376.

can crush evil to its core. It is through divine actions that Judeo-Christian theodicy is enacted. Actions speak louder than words. Such a pattern of action continues despite the evil that human atrocities and natural disasters bring about. God does not give up on his creation. This takes us to where we began: God's relentless quest.

GOD'S QUEST

The all-encompassing quest to care for his entire creation commenced at the very beginning. The biblical portrayal of the Spirit of God hovering over the stormy waters of a formless, dark, and empty earth (Gen 1:1) depicts such a beginning. The sketch below gives us a glimpse of one interpretation of this event.

Bird hovering over stormy waters (Pencil sketch by Daniel Kulathungam)

This drawing highlights how the bird that here represents the Spirit of God is related to the world; the bird is present in the world but not as part of it. The positioning of the bird may be seen as intentional to differentiate the biblical portrayal of God's care from primitive middle-Eastern mythologies, according to which the universe was hatched out of a primeval cosmic egg.[66] The Bible does not portray the bird hatching the universe, but instead hovering over the stormy waters. "Hovering" or "brooding" gives the picture

---

66. Leeming, *Creation Myths of the World*, 144; Hellborn, "Creation Egg," 63–105.

of a bird spreading its wings over its young in a nest. In the famous song of Moses, which highlights God's faithfulness through the years, his protective care is compared to "an eagle that stirs up its nest and hovers over its young" (Deut 32:11). The verb "hover" here is used in the continuous sense. God's care of his creation is not a one-time event but is continuous and is present even in the darkest of conditions. In *Paradise Lost*, John Milton poetically expresses it this way:

> Thus God the heaven created, thus the earth,
> Matter unformed and void. Darkness profound
> Covered the Abyss; but on the watery calm
> His brooding wings the Spirit of God outspread,
> And vital virtue infused and vital warmth,
> Throughout the fluid mass . . ."[67]

The comparison of the Holy Spirit to a bird continues in the New Testament where the Spirit is portrayed as a dove descending on Jesus at his baptism (Luke 3:22; Matt 3:16).

God, who was at work hovering over the dark and stormy waters to create a beautiful world, continues to hover, especially during dark periods throughout the history of the Judeo-Christian community. When the Israelites fled from Egypt, they faced a terrible roadblock; they faced the Red Sea with Pharaoh's armies pursuing them. They complained to Moses: "Was it because there were no graves in Egypt that you brought us to the desert to die? What have you done to us by bringing us out of Egypt? . . . It would have been better for us to serve the Egyptians than to die in the desert!" (Exod 14:11–12). It is likely that Moses felt a sense of panic as the Egyptian chariots closed in, but God told Moses to raise his staff and stretch it toward the sea, instead of crying out to him (Exod 14:15–16). What followed? When Moses obeyed God and stretched out his hand, God divided the waters and prepared a pathway for the Israelites so they could cross through on dry land throughout the night (Exod 14:21–22). When everything was dark and dismal, God was at work. They crossed through the Red Sea because of what God did during the night. There is another spectacular but desperate moment in history when God was at work while the whole world was immersed in darkness. The Bible records that when Jesus was suffering on the cross, the world was in darkness for three hours (Luke 23:44). During those three hours of complete darkness, God the Father was reconciling sinful humanity to himself through his Son, Jesus, in agony on the cross. God was at work during darkest period of human history.

---

67. Milton, *Paradise Lost*, vii, 234.

In our world today, full of so many calamities, it is natural that many doubt and even dismiss God's care. It is here that we must remind ourselves that God has come to rescue people, even in the darkest of times.

I started this book on a personal note about how my life was changed when God's quest was revealed to me through a dream. Since then, my family and I have experienced God's help in numerous ways. Let me end this book with a personal note referring to an event that shows God's protective care at a difficult time of my life. In 1983, my home country of Sri Lanka was in the middle of a civil war. The communal riots commenced in the capital city of Colombo and soon spread to other parts of the country. In July of that year, the riots spread to the city of Kandy, where I was a professor at the University of Sri Lanka. We lived in a house on the university campus but, due to the riots, were forced to leave our home and flee to the countryside. We took refuge in a rural church-managed orphanage and medical center that catered to the needs of people in that area. On the night of July 25, a police officer informed our pastor that a mob was planning to attack the compound, and asked us to defend ourselves. The police officer could not help a mission outreach center. The pastor met with the adults in the building to inform us of the impending threat. We were all shocked and troubled. We had no weapons with which to defend ourselves, so we turned to our only source of help, God. All those in the building, approximately 150 people, gathered for prayer at about 8:00 p.m. Of course, the young orphaned children were not informed of the threat to prevent them from being frightened. It was a prayer meeting where there was only one prayer request. Surprisingly, the meeting soon turned into a carnival of praise and enthusiastic worship. Our panic turned into praise! Both children and adults rejoiced in prayer and worship that continued well beyond midnight. Some of the young people, including my son, were blessed with the baptism in the Holy Spirit that night. At about 2:00 a.m., the same police officer entered the building and asked us: "What happened here?" He reported that he had seen an angry mob of about 200 people approaching the compound with torches and swords, but they suddenly stopped at the entrance and then turned away. His query was "What weapon did you use to scare them away?" He could not understand, but we knew what our weapon had been. God was our only defense and protector at that critical hour. After a few days, we learned further details as to why the mob had turned away. Some members of the mob saw a fire around the house, while others were overcome with fear. A few of them accepted the God who protected us. Those of us who have experienced this type of ordeal cannot help but accept that God is present and know that he will not forsake us in dark times.

The grand finale that the Judeo-Christian narrative envisages has not yet arrived. Will it ever arrive? Our journey through various events of the biblical narrative has shown how God came to protect and deliver people when they were in desperate situations. Such a God has not given up on humanity. This provides us with the hope that he will complete what he began. It is this hope that our world desperately needs. God's quest to relate with humanity is persistent and relentless despite human reaction and rejection, and this is highlighted throughout the Judeo-Christian narrative. It is a God-given opportunity and privilege to those who have experienced his redemptive quest during dark times to encourage others and to instill hope in an age bereft of hope.

Bibliography

Abhayananda, Swami S. *History of Mysticism: The Unchanging Testament.* 3rd ed. Olympia, WA: Atma, 1996.
"Adam's Peak." https://sacredsites.com/asia/sri_lanka/adams_peak.html.
"Adam's Peak: Myth, Legend and Geography." http://www.hiddenmysteries.org/mysteries/terra/adampeak.html.
Adler, Cyrus, and Israel Abrahams. "Joseph Jacobs." http://www.jewishencyclopedia.com/articles/8475-jacobs-joseph.
Aescoly, Aaron Z. *Jewish Messianic Movements: Sources and Documents on Messianism in Jewish History from the Bar-Kokhba Revolt until Recent Times*, in Two Volumes. Vol. 1, *From the Bar-Kokhba Revolt until the Expulsion of the Jews from Spain.* 2nd ed. Jerusalem: Bialik Institute, 1987.
Alperin, Michele. "Hanukkah: Why Were the Rabbis so Uncomfortable with the Maccabees?" https://www.myjewishlearning.com/article/transforming-hanukkah/.
Ambrose, Alice, ed. *Wittgenstein's Lectures: Cambridge 1932–1935: From the Notes of Alice Ambrose and Margaret Macdonald.* 1979. Reprint. Amherst, NY: Prometheus, 2001.
Anaxagoras. *Fragments of Anaxagoras.* Edited by Taylor Anderson. Translated by John Burnet. Self-published: Createspace, 2017.
Anselm of Canterbury. "Anselm's Proslogion or Discourse on the Existence of God, Chapter 2." In *Internet History Sourcebooks: Anselm on God's Existence*, History Dept of Fordham University. Translated by David Burr. Edited by Paul Halsall. https://sourcebooks.fordham.edu/source/anselm.asp.
Aquinas, Thomas. *Super Evangelium S. Matthaei lectura* (Commentary on Saint Matthew's Gospel). 5th ed. Edited by Raphaelis Cai. Translated by R. F. Larcher. Rome: Marietti, 1951. https://dhspriory.org/thomas/SSMatthew.htm.
Argubright, John. "To the Unknown God." http://www.biblehistory.net/newsletter/the_unknown_God.htm.
Aristotle. "Metaphysics, Book A (1), Chapters 6 & 7." In *Introduction to Aristotle*, edited by Richard McKeon, 238–43. New York: The Modern Library, 1947.
Atkinson, Quentin D. "Phonemic Diversity Supports a Serial Founder Effect Model of Language Expansion from Africa." *Science* 332.6027 (April 15, 2011) 346–49.
Baggini, Julian. *Atheism: A Very Short Introduction.* Very Short Introductions 99. Oxford: Oxford University Press, 2003.
Bailey, Alice A. *The Externalisation of the Hierarchy.* New York: Lucis, 1957.

———. *The Reappearance of the Christ*. New York: Lucis, 1948.
Baker, Mark D., ed. *Proclaiming the Scandal of the Cross: Contemporary Images of the Atonement*. Grand Rapids: Baker, 2006.
Baker, Mark D., and Joel B. Green. *Recovering the Scandal of the Cross: Atonement in New Testament and Contemporary Contexts*. 2nd ed. Downers Grove, IL: IVP Academic, 2011.
Bakon, Shimon. "The Day of the Lord." https://jbqnew.jewishbible.org/assets/Uploads/383/dayofthelord.pdf.
Barmash, Pamela, and W. David Nelson, eds. *Exodus in the Jewish Experience: Echoes and Reverberations*. Lanham, MD: Lexington, 2015.
Barnes, Jonathan. *The Ontological Argument*. London: Palgrave Macmillan, 1972.
Barrett, David B. "The Worldwide Holy Spirit Renewal." In *The Century of the Holy Spirit: 100 Years of Pentecostal and Charismatic Renewal, 1901–2001*, edited by Vinson Synan, 385–414. Nashville: Thomas Nelson, 2012.
Barrett, J. Edward. "Can Scholars Take the Virgin Birth Seriously?" *Bible Review* 4.5 (October 1988) 10–11.
Barth, Karl. *Church Dogmatics*. Vol. 1. Edited by Thomas F. Torrance. Translated by Geoffrey William Bromiley. 5 vols. Edinburgh: T. & T. Clark, 1956.
Basham, Arthur L. *The Wonder that was India*. London: Indian Creation, 1995.
Benedict XVI, Pope. *Jesus of Nazareth: From the Baptism in the Jordan to the Transfiguration*. Vol 1. 3 vols. New York: Bloomsbury, 2007.
ben Elisha, Yishmael. "The 13 Rules of Rabbi Yishmael." https://www.ou.org/torah/gemara-series/the-13-rules-of-rabbi-yishmael/#?.
ben Maimon, Moshe (Maimonides). "The Thirteen Principles of Jewish Faith." https://www.chabad.org/library/article_cdo/aid/332555/jewish/Maimonides-13-Principles-of-Faith.htm.
Berger, David, and Michael Wyschogrod. *Jews and "Jewish Christianity."* New York: Ktav, 1978.
Biddle, Mark E. *Missing the Mark: Sin and its Consequences in Biblical Theology*. Nashville: Abingdon, 2005.
Boyett, Jason. *Pocket Guide to the Apocalypse: The Official Field Manual for the End of the World*. Lake Mary, FL: Relevant Media, 2005.
Brisco, Thomas V. *Holman Bible Atlas*. Nashville: Broadman & Holman, 1998.
Brown, Francis, et al. *A Hebrew and English Lexicon of the Old Testament, with an Appendix Containing the Biblical Aramaic*. Oxford: Clarendon, 1962.
Burnet, John. *Early Greek Philosophy*. 8th ed. Cleveland: Meridian, 1964.
Butler, Ewen H. *Canadian Winds of the Spirit: Holiness, Pentecostal and Charismatic Currents*. The Asbury Theological Seminary Series in World Christian Revitalization Movements in Pentecostal/Charismatic Studies. Lexington, KY: Emeth, 2018.
Charlesworth, James H. "Did They Ever Part?" In *Partings: How Judaism and Christianity Became Two*, edited by Hershel Shanks, 281–300. Washington, DC: Biblical Archaeology Society, 2013.
Chomsky, Noam. *Cartesian Linguistics: A Chapter in the History of Rational Thought*. New York: Harper & Row, 1966.
———. *Language and Mind*. New York: Harcourt Brace Jovanovich, 1972.
———. *Language and Problems of Knowledge: The Managua Lectures*. Cambridge, MA: MIT Press, 1988.

---. *Logical Structure of Linguistic Theory*. New York: Plenum, 1975.
---. *New Horizons in the Study of Language and Mind*. Cambridge: Cambridge University Press, 2000.
---. *What Kind of Creatures are We?* Columbia Themes in Philosophy. New York: Columbia University Press, 2016.
Cision PR Newswire. "Global Nanotechnology Market 2018–2024: Market is Expected to Exceed $125 billion." May 2, 2018. https://www.prnewswire.com/news-releases/global-nanotechnology-market-2018-2024-market-is-expected-to-exceed-us-125-billion-300641054.html.
Craig, William. "Contemporary Scholarship and the Historical Evidence for the Resurrection of Jesus Christ." *Truth* 1.1 (1985) 89–95.
Crawford, Harriet E. W. *Sumer and the Sumerians*. New York: Cambridge University Press, 1993.
Croly, George. "The French Revolution." In *The Literary Emporium: A Compendium of Religious, Literary, and Philosophical Knowledge*, Volumes I and II, edited by J.K. Wellman, 56–59. New York: J. K. Wellman, 1845.
Dale, R. W. *Atonement: The Congregational Union Lecture for 1875*. Charleston, SC: Nabu, 2010.
Dan, Joseph. "Scholem's View of Jewish Messianism." *Modern Judaism* 12.2 (May 1992) 117–28.
Davidson, Donald. "Actions, Reasons and Causes." In *The Philosophy of Action*, edited by Alan White, 79–94. Oxford: Oxford University Press, 1979.
Davies, Paul C. *God and the New Physics*. 1983. Reprint. London: Penguin, 1990.
Dawkins, Richard. *The God Delusion*. 2006. Reprint. Boston: Houghton Mifflin Harcourt, 2008.
Day, John. *From Creation to Babel: Studies in Genesis 1–11*. Library of Hebrew Bible Old Testament Studies 592. London: Bloomsbury, 2014.
Dedopulos, Tim. *Kabbalah: An Introduction to the Esoteric Heart of Jewish Mysticism*. New York: Gramercy, 2005.
Dennett, Daniel C. *Breaking the Spell: Religion as a Natural Phenomenon*. New York: Penguin, 2007.
Dever, William. "An Overview of Biblical Archaeology: History, Aims and Methods." In *How Archaeology Illuminates the Bible: From the Patriarchs to the Babylonian Destruction*. DVD. Lecture #1 in an eight-lecture series presented at Bard College, NY in 2008. https://www.biblicalarchaeology.org/media/video/how-archaeology-illuminates-the-bible-dvd/.
Diels, Hermann, and Walther Kranz. *Die Fragmente der Vorsokratiker* (The Fragments of the Pre-Socratics). 6th ed. Revised by Walther Kranz. Berlin: Weidmann, 1952.
Dimant, Devorah. *From Enoch to Tobit: Collected Studies in Ancient Jewish Literature*. Tübingen: Mohr Siebeck, 2017.
"Discover Messiah in the Prophecy of Genesis 3:15—Rabbinic and Christian Views." https://free.messianicbible.com/feature/messianic-prophecy-genesis-315-jewish-christian-views/.
Dolansky, Shawna. "How the Serpent Became Satan: Adam, Eve and the Serpent in the Garden of Eden." https://www.biblicalarchaeology.org/daily/biblical-topics/bible-interpretation/how-the-serpent-became-satan/.

Draper, Paul. "Atheism and Agnosticism." In *The Stanford Encyclopedia of Philosophy*, edited by Edward N. Zalta, Fall 2017 edition. Stanford: Stanford University, 2017. https://plato.stanford.edu/archives/fall2017/entries/atheism-agnosticism/

Dunner, Pini. "The Reason Why the Jews Accepted the Torah." https://www.algemeiner.com/2016/06/10/the-reason-why-the-jews-accepted-the-torah/.

Editors of Encyclopaedia Britannica. "Judaism: Olam ha-ba." *Encyclopaedia Britannica*. https://www.britannica.com/topic/olam-ha-ba.

Efron, John M., et al. *The Jews: A History*. 2nd ed. New York: Routledge, 2016.

Ekstrand, D. W. "The Intertestamental Period and its Significance upon Christianity." *The Transformed Soul*. http://www.thetransformedsoul.com/additional-studies/spiritual-life-studies/the-intertestamental-period-and-its-significance-upon-christianity.

Eusebius. *Ecclesiastical History, Volume I: Books 1–5*. Translated by Kirsopp Lake. Loeb Classical Library 153. Cambridge, MA: Harvard University Press, 1926.

Faulkner, Raymond O. *The Ancient Egyptian Pyramid Texts*. Oxford: Oxford University Press, 2009.

Federow, Stuart, "Essay #5: People are Born Pure and Without Original Sin." www.whatjewsbelieve.org/explanation5.html.

Feinberg, Joel, and Russ Shafer-Landau. *Reason and Responsibility: Readings in Some Basic Problems of Philosophy*. Belmont, CA: Dickenson, 1969.

Festinger, Leon, et al. *When Prophecy Fails: A Social and Psychological Study of a Modern Group that Predicted the Destruction of the World*. New York: Harper, 1956.

Field, Christopher B., et al., eds. *Climate Change 2014: Impacts, Adaptation, and Vulnerability Report. Contribution of Working Group II to the Fifth Assessment Report of the Intergovernmental Panel on Climate Change*. Cambridge: Cambridge University Press, 2014.

Fitch, W. Tecumseh. "Unity and Diversity in Human Language." *Philosophical Transactions of the Royal Society B: Biological Sciences* 366.1563 (February 12, 2011) 376–88.

Flew, Antony. "The Presumption of Atheism." *Canadian Journal of Philosophy* 2.1 (January 1972) 29–46. doi:10.1080/00455091.1972.10716861.

Flew, Antony, ed. "Theology and Falsification." In *Essays in Logic and Language, First Series*, edited by Antony Flew, 12–13. Oxford: Blackwell, 1951.

Flew, Antony, and Roy Abraham Varghese. *There is a God: How the World's Most Notorious Atheist Changed His Mind*. New York: HarperCollins, 2007.

Freeman, Tzvi. "What's Up With Jewish Spirituality? How is it Unique, and Where Do I Get Some?" https://www.chabad.org/library/article_cdo/aid/4017311/jewish/Jewish-Spirituality.htm.

Fuller, Daniel P. *The Unity of the Bible: Unfolding God's Plan for Humanity*. Grand Rapids: Zondervan, 1992.

Garroway, Joshua D. "Ioudaious." In *The Jewish Annotated New Testament: New Revised Standard Version Bible Translation*, edited by Amy-Jill Levine and Marc Zvi Brettler, 596–98. Oxford: Oxford University Press, 2017.

George, Andrew R. "A Stele of Nebuchadnezzar II (Tower of Babel Stele)." In *Cuneiform Royal Inscriptions and Related Texts in the Schøyen Collection*, edited by Andrew R. George, 153–69. Cornell University Studies in Assyriology and Sumerology, Vol. 17. Bethesda, MD: CDL, 2011.

Gesenius, Wilhelm, et al. *Gesenius' Hebrew Grammar*. Oxford: Clarendon, 1910.

Gilles, Anthony E. *Evolution of Philosophy: An Overview of Western Thought as it Relates to Judeo-Christian Tradition.* New York: Alba House, 1987.
Goodman, Martin. *A History of Judaism.* Princeton, NJ: Princeton University Press, 2018.
———. *Rome and Jerusalem: The Clash of Ancient Civilizations.* 1st ed. New York: Vintage, 2008.
———, ed. "Jews, Greeks and Romans." In *Jews in a Graeco-Roman World*, edited by Martin Goodman, 3–14. Oxford: Oxford University Press, 1998.
Gordis, Robert, and Commission on the Philosophy of Conservative Judaism. *Emet Ve-Emunah: Statement of Principles of Conservative Judaism.* New York: The Jewish Theological Seminary of America, 1988.
Gruber, Yeshaya. "Who is a 'Rabbi?'" *Israel Bible Weekly.* https://weekly.israelbiblecenter.com/who-is-a-rabbi/.
Hallo, William W., and K. Lawson Younger, eds. *The Context of Scripture: Canonical Compositions, Monumental Inscriptions and Archival Documents from the Biblical World.* Leiden: Brill, 2003.
Halton, Charles. *Genesis: History, Fiction, or Neither? Three Views on the Bible's Earliest Chapters.* Counterpoints: Bible and Theology. Grand Rapids: Zondervan, 2015.
Hamilton, Victor P. *The New International Commentary on the Old Testament.* Edited by Robert L. Hubbard, Jr. Grand Rapids: Eerdmans, 1990.
Hardy, Edward R., and Cyril C. Richardson, eds. *Christology of the Later Fathers.* Vol. III. The Library of Christian Classics. London: SCM, 1954.
Harrington, Daniel J. *Invitation to the Apocrypha.* Grand Rapids: Eerdmans, 1999.
Harris, Stephen L. *Understanding the Bible.* 8th ed. New York: McGraw-Hill, 2010.
Hawking, Stephen. "The Beginning of Time." http://www.hawking.org.uk/the-beginning-of-time.html.
———. *Brief Answers to the Big Questions.* London: Hodder & Stoughton, 2018.
Hawking, Stephen, and G. F. R. Ellis. "The Cosmic Black-Body Radiation and the Existence of Singularities in Our Universe." *Astrophysical Journal* 152 (April 1968) 25–36.
Hawking, Stephen, and Roger Penrose. "The Singularities of Gravitational Collapse and Cosmology." *Proceedings of the Royal Society of London* 314.1519 (Jan 1970), 529–48. https://doi.org/10.1098/rspa.1970.0021.
Hazzard, David, and Stacey McKenzie. "The Heresy of Individualism." *Enrich* (Fall 2014) 12–14.
Hellborn, Anna-Britta. "The Creation Egg." *Ethnos* 1 (1963) 63–105.
Heschel, Abraham Joshua. *God in Search of Man: A Philosophy of Judaism.* New York: Farrar, Straus and Giroux, 1983.
———. *Man is Not Alone: A Philosophy of Religion.* Reissue edition. New York: Farrar, Straus and Giroux, 1976.
Hiebert, Theodore. "The Tower of Babel and the Origin of the World's Cultures." *Journal of Biblical Literature* 126.1 (2007) 29–58.
Hillar, Marian. *From Logos to Trinity: The Evolution of Religious Beliefs from Pythagoras to Tertullian.* Cambridge: Cambridge University Press, 2012.
History.com Editors. "D-Day." https://www.history.com/topics/world-war-ii/d-day.
Hitchens, Christopher. *God is Not Great: How Religion Poisons Everything.* New York: Twelve, 2009.

Hoffman, Lawrence. "Circumcision." In *The Jewish Annotated New Testament: New Revised Standard Version Bible Translation*, 2nd ed., edited by Amy-Jill Levine and Marc Zvi Brettler, 673–74. Oxford: Oxford University Press, 2017.

Hoffmeier, James K. "Genesis 1–11 as History & Theology." In *Genesis: History, Fiction, or Neither: Three Views on the Bible's Earliest Chapters*, edited by Charles Halton, 23–163. Grand Rapids: Zondervan, 2015.

Holdcroft, L. Thomas. *The Holy Spirit: A Pentecostal Interpretation*. Abbotsford, BC: Western Pentecostal Bible College Press, 1971.

Homer. *The Odyssey*, Books 10 and 11. Translated by A.T. Murray. Theoi Classical Texts Library. https://www.theoi.com/Text/HomerOdyssey10.html and https://www.theoi.com/Text/HomerOdyssey11.html.

Hopkins, Gerard Manley. "Thou art Indeed Just, Lord." In *Gerard Manley Hopkins: Poems and Prose*, edited by W. H. Gardner, 68. 1953. Reprint. London: Penguin Classics, 1985.

Horne, Thomas Hartwell, et al. *An Introduction to the Critical Study and Knowledge of the Holy Scriptures*. Cambridge: Cambridge University Press, 2013.

Horvat, Robert. "Nebuchadnezzar's Etemananki Ziggurat (Tower of Babel)." https://rear-view-mirror.com/2014/01/05/nebuchadnezzars-etemananki-ziggurat/.

Housden, Roger. "Secular Spirituality: An Oxymoron?" *HuffPost*, March 20, 2012. https://www.huffpost.com/entry/secular-spirituality-an-oxymoron_b_1211837.

Idel, Moshe. *Kabbalah: New Perspectives*. New Haven, CT: Yale University Press, 1988.

———. "Universalization and Integration: Two Conceptions of Mystical Union in Jewish Mysticism." In *Mystical Union and Monotheistic Faith: An Ecumenical Dialogue*, edited by Moshe Idel and Bernard McGinn, 27–58. New York: Macmillan, 1989.

Idel, Moshe, and Bernard McGinn, eds. *Mystical Union and Monotheistic Faith: An Ecumenical Dialogue*. New York: Macmillan, 1989.

"The Importance of the Septuagint." http://www.orthodoxphotos.com/readings/bible2/septuagint.shtml.

Intergovernmental Panel on Climate Change. "IPCC Report: A Changing Climate Creates Pervasive Risks but Opportunities Exist for Effective Responses." https://www.ipcc.ch/2014/03/31/ipcc-report-a-changing-climate-creates-pervasive-risks-but-opportunities-exist-for-effective-responses/.

Irfan, Umair, and Brian Resnick. "Megadisasters Devastated America in 2017. And They're Only Going to Get Worse." https://www.vox.com/energy-and-environment/2017/12/28/16795490/natural-disasters-2017-hurricanes-wildfires-heat-climate-change-cost-deaths.

Jacobs, Joseph, and Judah David Eisenstein. "Sin." http://www.jewishencyclopedia.com/articles/13761-sin

Jacobson, Yosef Y. "The Paradoxes of Oil as a Guide for Life: The Meaning Behind the Chanukah Oil Miracle." https://www.chabad.org/kabbalah/article_cdo/aid/3142705/jewish/The-Paradoxes-of-Oil-As-a-Guide-For-Life.htm.

James, Matthew B. "React vs Respond: What's the Difference?" https://www.psychologytoday.com/ca/blog/focus-forgiveness/201609/react-vs-respond.

Janes, Burton. "Review of *The Quest: Christ Amidst the Quest.*, by Lyman C. D. Kulathungam." *Faith Today* 32.1 (Jan/Feb 2014) 72. http://digital.faithtoday.ca/faithtoday/20140102?pg=72#pg72.

Jaspers, Karl. *The Great Philosophers*. Edited by Hannah Arendt. Translated by Ralph Manheim. 1st American ed. New York: Harcourt, Brace & World, 1962.
———. *The Origin and Goal of History*. New Haven: Yale University Press, 1953.
John Paul II, Pope. *Crossing the Threshold of Hope*. Edited by Vittorio Messori. Translated by Jenny McPhee and Martha McPhee. New York: Knopf, 1994.
Josephus, Flavius. *Antiquities of the Jews. Books I–XX, 92 CE*. Cambridge, MA: Loeb Classics, 1998.
———. *The Wars of the Jews or History of the Destruction of Jerusalem*. http://www.documentacatholicaomnia.eu/03d/0037-0103,_Flavius_Josephus,_De_Bello_Judaico,_EN.pdf
Kaplan, Aryeh. *Maimonides' Principles: The Fundamentals of Jewish Faith*. 2nd ed. New York: National Conference of Synagogue Youth/Union of Orthodox Jewish Congregations of America, 1993.
Kaplan, Aryeh, and Abraham Sutton. *Innerspace: Introduction to the Kabbalah, Meditation and Prophecy*. New York: Moznaim, 1991.
Kautzsch, Emil F., ed. *Gesenius' Hebrew Grammar*. Oxford: Clarendon, 1910.
Keil, Carl Friedrich, and Franz Delitzsch. *Commentary on the Old Testament*. Vol. 1. Grand Rapids: Eerdmans, 1975.
Kertzer, Morris N. *What is a Jew?* 6th ed. New York: Touchstone, 1996.
Keyser, John D. "Yehovah's Shekinah Glory." http://hope-of-israel.org.nz/glory.htm.
Kirsch, Adam. "Why Jewish History is so Hard to Write." https://www.newyorker.com/magazine/2018/03/26/why-jewish-history-is-so-hard-to-write.
Klausner, Joseph. *Jesus of Nazareth: His Life, Times and Teaching*. Translated by Herbert Danby and Sidney B. Hoenig. New York: Macmillan, 1922.
Kogan, Shmuel. "Atonement in the Absence of Sacrifices?" https://www.chabad.org/library/article_cdo/aid/630900/jewish/Atonement-in-the-Absence-of-Sacrifices.htm.
Kohler, Kaufmann, and Samuel Krauss. "Baptism." http://www.jewishencyclopedia.com/articles/2456-baptism.
Kraemer, David C. *Jewish Eating and Identity through the Ages*. Routledge Advances in Sociology. Volume 29. 1st ed. New York: Routledge, 2008.
———. "Judaism Requires Us to Pursue the Goals of the Paris Climate Accords." https://www.jta.org/2017/06/13/opinion/judaism-requires-us-to-pursue-the-goals-of-the-paris-climate-accords.
———. "Leavened or Unleavened: A History." https://forward.com/articles/10411/leavened-or-unleavened-a-history/.
———. *Responses to Suffering in Classical Rabbinic Literature*. New York: Oxford University Press, 1995.
Kramer, Samuel Noah. "The 'Babel of Tongues': A Sumerian Version." *Journal of the American Oriental Society* 88.1 (January 1968) 108–11.
Krauthammer, Charles. "At Last, Zion." *The Weekly Standard*. May 11, 1998. https://www.weeklystandard.com/charles-krauthammer/at-last-zion
Kuhn, Thomas S. *The Structure of Scientific Revolutions*. Vol. 11. International Encyclopedia of Unified Science. 3rd ed. Chicago: University of Chicago Press, 1996.
Kulathungam, Lyman C. D. "Christian Meditation: Doubts and Hopes." *Eastern Journal of Practical Theology* 6.2 (Fall 1992) 22–37.

———. "A Christocentric Anthropocosmic Approach to Ecological Crisis." Paper presented to the Congress of the Humanities and Social Sciences at a seminar organized by the Canadian Society of the Study of Religion, at Brock University, St. Catharines, Canada, May 2014.

———. "Meditation: Doubts and Fears," *Eastern Journal Practical Theology* 1.2 (Fall 1987).

———. *The Quest: Christ Amidst the Quest*. Eugene, OR: Wipf & Stock, 2012.

———. "Reductio-Ad-Absurdum: A Family Feud Between Copi and Scherer." *Notre Dame Journal of Formal Logic* 16.2 (April 1975) 245–54.

———. "Scientific Understanding and Christian Faith." *Faculty Dialogue* 25 (Fall 1995) 23–28.

———. "Why I Am Not an Atheist." Paper presented at meeting organized by the Polish Philosophy and Theology Association, University of Warsaw, Poland, October 12, 2014.

———. "Why Tongues?" *Eastern Journal of Practical Theology* 6.1 (Spring 1992) 22–37.

Kurtz, Paul. *Humanist Manifesto 2000: A Call for a New Planetary Humanism*. Amherst, NY: Prometheus, 2000.

Kurtz, Paul, and Edwin H. Wilson. *Humanist Manifesto II*. Washington, DC: American Humanist Association, 1973.

Kushner, Lawrence. *Jewish Spirituality: A Brief Introduction for Christians*. Woodstock, VT: Jewish Lights, 2002.

Kydd, Ronald A. N. *Finding Pieces of the Puzzle: A Fresh Look at the Christian Story*. Eugene, OR: Wipf & Stock, 2011.

———. "Walking Straight in a Crooked World." *Pentecostal Testimony* (August 1990) 18–19.

Lea, Thomas D., and David Alan Black. *The New Testament: Its Background and Message*. 2nd ed. Nashville: Broadman & Holman, 2003.

Leeming, David Adams. *Creation Myths of the World: An Encyclopedia*. 2nd Edition, Volume I, Parts I and II. Santa Barbara, CA: ABC-CLIO, 2010.

Leff, Barry. "A Jewish View of Jesus." https://neshamah.net/2011/12/a-jewish-view-of-jesus.html.

Levenson, David. "Messianic Movements." In *The Jewish Annotated New Testament: New Revised Standard Version Bible Translation*, edited by Amy-Jill Levine and Marc Zvi Brettler, 622–28. 2nd ed. Oxford: Oxford University Press, 2017.

Levine, Amy-Jill. *The Misunderstood Jew: The Church and the Scandal of the Jewish Jesus*. New York: HarperOne, 2007.

Levine, Amy-Jill, and Marc Zvi Brettler, eds. *The Jewish Annotated New Testament: New Revised Standard Version Bible Translation*. Second edition. Oxford: Oxford University Press, 2017.

Lewis, C. S. *The Last Battle*. London: Bodley, 1956.

Lewis, Solomon. *Jewish Spirituality: Revitalizing Judaism for the Twenty-First Century*. Northvale, NJ: Jason Aronson, 2000.

Livingston, David. "Who Was Nimrod?" http://davelivingston.com/nimrod.htm.

Lizorkin-Eyzenberg, Eli. "Does the Lord's Prayer have Jewish Liturgical Roots?" *Israel Bible Weekly*. January 25, 2019. https://weekly.israelbiblecenter.com/lords-prayer-jewish-liturgy/.

———. *Jewish Insights into Scripture*. Scotts Valley, CA: CreateSpace, 2017.

———. "The Jewish Logos Theology." https://israelstudycenter.com/the-jewish-logos-theology/.
———. "To Pray as a Jew (Blessing #1A)." *Israel Bible Weekly*. August 31, 2018. https://weekly.israelbiblecenter.com/jewish-prayer-our-fathers/.
———. "Why Don't Jews Believe in Jesus?" *Israel Bible Weekly*. April 20, 2017. https://weekly.israelbiblecenter.com/jews-believe-jesus/.
Loewenthal, Naftali. "Schneerson, Menachem M." https://www.encyclopedia.com/environment/encyclopedias-almanacs-transcripts-and-maps/schneerson-menachem-m.
Longenecker, Richard N. *Acts of the Apostles*. Expositor's Bible Commentary Series 9. Edited by Frank E. Gaebelein. Grand Rapids: Zondervan, 1976–1984.
Lupovitch, Howard N. "The Challenge of Hellenism." In *Jews and Judaism in World History*, edited by Peter N. Stearns, 26–48. Themes in World History. London: Routledge, 2010.
MacLeod, Donald. *The Person of Christ*. Contours of Christian Theology. Downers Grove, IL: InterVarsity, 1998.
Madsen, Peter. "Deep Ecology." https://www.britannica.com/topic/deep-ecology.
Magness, Jodi, et al. "The Huqoq Excavation Project: 2014–2017 Interim Report." *Bulletin of the American Schools of Oriental Research* 380 (November 2018) 61–131.
Magonet, Jonathan. "Spirituality and Scripture: A Jewish View." *The Way* Supplement 72 (1991) 91–100.
Martens, John W. "The Menorah and the Cross in Ancient Laodicea: What Does It Mean?" http://www.biblejunkies.com/2012/01/menorah-and-cross-in-ancient-laodicea.html.
Marx, Karl. "Contribution to the Critique of Hegel's Philosophy of Right: Introduction." In *Early Writings*, translated and edited by Thomas B. Bottomore, 57–198. London: Watts, 1963.
Marx, Karl, and Friedrich Engels. *The Manifesto of the Communists*. New York: International Publishers, 1886.
McAllister, Robert E. "The Baptism of the Holy Ghost." *Canadian Pentecostal Testimony* 1 (December 1920) 8–9.
McGee, Gary B. *Initial Evidence: Historical and Biblical Perspectives on the Pentecostal Doctrine of Spirit Baptism*. 1991. Reprint. Eugene, OR: Wipf & Stock, 2008.
McGrath, Alister E. *Science & Religion: An Introduction*. Oxford: Blackwell, 1999.
McIver, Tom. *The End of the World: An Annotated Bibliography*. Jefferson, NC: McFarland, 1999.
"Menachem M. Schneerson." *The Encyclopedia of Hasidism*, edited by Tzvi Rabinowicz. Lanham, MD: Jason Aronson, 1977.
Mendel, Menachem. *Pri ha-Aretz* (Fruit of the Land). Jerusalem: HeMesorah, 1989.
Menner, Robert J. "Nimrod and the Wolf in the Old English 'Solomon and Saturn.'" *Journal of English and Germanic Philology* 37.3 (1938) 332–84.
Merriam-Webster's Collegiate Dictionary. 11th ed. Springfield, IL: Merriam-Webster, 2014.
Milton, John. *The Paradise Lost: With Notes Explanatory and Critical*. Edited by James R Boyd. New York: Baker and Scribner, 1851.
Mishkin, David. *Jewish Scholarship on the Resurrection of Jesus*. Eugene, OR: Pickwick, 2017.

Netanyahu, Benjamin. "Full Text of Prime Minister Benjamin Netanyahu's UN Speech." *The Times of Israel*, September 19, 2017. https://www.timesofisrael.com/full-text-of-prime-minister-benjamin-netanyahus-un-speech/.

Neusner, Jacob. *A Rabbi Talks With Jesus*. Rev. ed. Montreal: McGill-Queen's University Press, 2000.

Newman, Peter. *Pentecostal Experience: An Ecumenical Encounter*. Eugene, OR: Pickwick, 2012.

Nietzsche, Friedrich. "The Madman." In *Nietzsche: Philosopher, Psychologist, Antichrist*, translated and edited by Walter Kaufmann, 95–96. 4th ed. Princeton, NJ: Princeton University Press, 1974.

Oppenheim, Adolf Leo. *Ancient Mesopotamia: Portrait of a Dead Civilization*. Chicago: University of Chicago Press, 1977.

Orr, James. "Definition for 'Shekinah.'" *International Standard Bible Encyclopedia*. https://www.biblestudytools.com/encyclopedias/isbe/shekinah.html.

———, ed. "The Apostles' Creed." *International Standard Bible Encyclopedia*. https://www.biblestudytools.com/encyclopedias/isbe/apostles-creed-the.html.

Orwell, George. "Politics and English Language." *Horizon* 13.76 (April 1946) 252–65.

"Overview: Jews and Judaism in the Greco-Roman Period." http://315.eof.myftpupload.com/overview-_jews_and_judaism_in_the_greco-roman_period/.

Owens, Robert. "The Azusa Street Revival: The Pentecostal Movement Begins in America." In *The Century of the Holy Spirit: 100 Years of Pentecostal and Charismatic Renewal, 1901–2001*, edited by Vinson Synan, 24–33. Nashville: Thomas Nelson, 2012.

Patrick, G. T. W. *The Fragments of Heraclitus of Ephesus On Nature*. Baltimore: N. Murray, 1889.

Peterson, Eugene H. *Reversed Thunder: The Revelation of John and the Praying Imagination*. 1st ed. San Francisco: Harper & Row, 1988.

Picheta, Rob. "'There is No God,' Says Stephen Hawking in Final Book." *CNN*. October 17, 2018. https://www.cnn.com/2018/10/16/health/stephen-hawking-final-book-intl/index.html.

Pinnock, Clark H. *A Wideness in God's Mercy: The Finality of Jesus Christ in a World of Religions*. Grand Rapids: Zondervan, 1992.

Polkow, Dennis. "Andrew Lloyd Webber: From Superstar to Requiem." https://www.religion-online.org/article/andrew-lloyd-webber-from-superstar-to-requiem/.

Pollock, Algernon J. *Modern Pentecostalism, Four Square Gospel, "Healings" and "Tongues": Are They of God?* London: Central Bible Truth Depot, 1945.

Provan, Iain W., et al. *A Biblical History of Israel*. 1st ed. Louisville: Westminster John Knox, 2003.

Purves, Dale, et al., eds. *Neuroscience: Third Edition*. Sunderland, MA: Sinauer, 2004.

Puskas, Charles B., and C. Michael Robbins. *An Introduction to the New Testament: 2nd Edition*. Eugene, OR: Cascade, 2011.

Rabinowicz, Tzvi, ed. *The Encyclopedia of Hasidism*. Lanham, MD: Jason Aronson, 1977.

Radner, Ephraim. *Chasing the Shadow—The World and its Times: An Introduction to Christian Natural Theology, Volume 2*. Eugene, OR: Cascade, 2018.

———. *The World in the Shadow of God: An Introduction to Christian Natural Theology*. Eugene, OR: Cascade, 2010.

Ramachandra, Vinoth. *Gods That Fail, Revised Edition: Modern Idolatry and Christian Mission*. Eugene, OR: Wipf & Stock, 2016.

Reinhartz, Adele. "Introduction to the Gospel According to John." In *The Jewish Annotated New Testament: New Revised Standard Version Bible Translation*, edited by Amy-Jill Levine and Marc Zvi Brettler, Second edition, 168–74. Oxford: Oxford University Press, 2017.

Rosenthal, Herman, and Peter Wiernik. "Eisenstein, Julius (Judah David)." http://www.jewishencyclopedia.com/articles/5491-eisenstein-julius-judah-david.

Rubin, Barry, ed. *The Complete Jewish Study Bible: Insights for Jews and Christians*. Translated by David Stern. Peabody, MA: Hendrickson, 2016.

Rudin, A. James. *Christians & Jews—Faith to Faith: Tragic History, Promising Present, Fragile Future*. Woodstock, VT: Jewish Lights, 2010.

Rudman, Zave. "Chumash Themes #3: In the Garden of Eden: Reconstructing the Drama of the Tree and the Snake." https://www.aish.com/jl/b/chumash/Chumash-Themes-3-In-the-Garden-of-Eden.html.

Russell, Bertrand. "Why I Am Not a Christian." In *The Basic Writings of Bertrand Russell: 1903–1959*, edited by Robert E. Enger and Lester E. Denonn, 585–97. New York: Simon and Schuster, 1961.

Rutherfurd, Edward. *New York: The Novel*. 1st United States ed. New York: Doubleday, 2009.

Ryvchin, Alex. "Not Yet: Why Jews Remain a People of Hope." https://www.abc.net.au/religion/not-yet-why-jews-remain-a-people-of-hope/10095932.

Sarna, Nahum M. *Genesis=Be-reshit: The Traditional Hebrew Text With New JPS Translation*. 1st ed. The JPS Torah Commentary. Philadelphia: Jewish Publication Society, 1989.

Satyavrata, Ivan. *The Holy Spirit: Lord and Life-Giver*. Christian Doctrine in Global Perspective. Downers Grove, IL: IVP Academic, 2009.

Saunders, Jason L. *Greek and Roman Philosophy after Aristotle*. New York: Collier Macmillan, 1966.

Schiffman, Lawrence H. "Pharisees." In *The Jewish Annotated New Testament*, by Amy-Jill Levine and Marc Zvi Brettler, 619–22. New York: Oxford University Press, 2017.

Scholem, Gershom. *Major Trends in Jewish Mysticism*. Reissue ed. New York: Schocken, 1995.

———. *The Messianic Idea in Judaism and Other Essays on Jewish Spirituality*. New York: Schocken, 1972.

Schonfield, Hugh J. *The Passover Plot*. London: Hutchinson, 1965.

Schøyen, Martin. "Tower of Babel Stele." https://www.schoyencollection.com/history-collection-introduction/babylonian-history-collection/tower-babel-stele-ms-2063.

Schwartz, Stephen. *The Other Islam: Sufism and the Road to Global Harmony*. 1st ed. New York: Doubleday, 2008.

Seitz, Christopher R. *Word Without End: The Old Testament as Abiding Theological Witness*. Grand Rapids: Eerdmans, 1998.

Shanks, Hershel, ed. *Ancient Israel: From Abraham to the Roman Destruction of the Temple*. Revised and expanded edition. Washington, DC: Biblical Archaeology Society, 1999.

Shanks, Hershel, and Géza Vermès. *Partings: How Judaism and Christianity Became Two*. Washington, DC: Biblical Archaeology Society, 2013.

Smart, Ninian. *The Religious Experience of Mankind*. New York: Scribner, 1969.

Smith, James K. A. *Thinking in Tongues: Pentecostal Contributions to Christian Philosophy*. Grand Rapids: Eerdmans, 2010.

Solomon, Lewis D. *Jewish Spirituality: Revitalizing Judaism for the Twenty-First Century*. Northvale, NJ: Jason Aronson, 2000.

Sparks, Kenton I. "Genesis 1–11 as Ancient Historiography." In *Genesis: History, Fiction, or Neither: Three Views on the Bible's Earliest Chapters*, edited by Charles Halton, 110–50. Grand Rapids: Zondervan, 2015.

Spurgeon, Charles H. "The Friend of God." In *The Complete Works of C.H. Spurgeon, Volume 33: Sermons 1938 to 2000*, edited by Peter J. Carter, 78–84. Harrington, DE: Delmarva, 2013.

Srokosz, Meric A. "God's Story and the Earth's Story: Grounding Our Concern for the Environment in the Biblical Metanarrative." *Science & Christian Belief* 20.2 (October 2008) 163–74.

Stone, Barton W. "Piercing Screams and Heavenly Smiles: An Eye Witness Account of Signs and Wonders at Early Camp Meetings." *Christian History* 45 (1995) 3–4. https://christianhistoryinstitute.org/magazine/article/piercing-screams-and-heavenly-smiles.

Stott, John R. W. *The Cross of Christ*. 20th anniversary ed. Downers Grove, IL: IVP, 2006.

Strandberg, Todd, and William T. James. *Are You Rapture Ready?: Signs, Prophecies, Warnings, Threats, and Suspicions That the Endtime is Now*. New York: Dutton, 2003.

Strawn, Brent A. "Holes in the Tower of Babel." https://global.oup.com/obso/focus/focus_on_towerbabel/.

Stronstad, Roger. *A Pentecostal Biblical Theology: Turning Points in the Story of Redemption*. Cleveland, TN: CPT, 2016.

Studebaker, Steven. *From Pentecost to the Triune God: A Pentecostal Trinitarian Theology*. Grand Rapids: Eerdmans, 2012.

Studebaker, Steven M., ed. *Defining Issues in Pentecostalism: Classical and Emergent*. McMaster Divinity College Press Theological Studies Series, Vol. 1. Eugene, OR: Pickwick, 2008.

Synan, Vinson. *The Century of the Holy Spirit: 100 Years of Pentecostal and Charismatic Renewal, 1901–2001*. Nashville: Thomas Nelson, 2012.

———. *The Holiness-Pentecostal Movement in the United States*. Grand Rapids: Eerdmans, 1971.

Tabor, James D. "Who Wrote the Dead Sea Scrolls?" http://reply.biblicalarchaeology.org/dm?id=18E590FAE4F32AC69BF13C85FF16EB7B900DD0DB29C490F6.

"Talmud Berakhot." https://www.sefaria.org/Berakhot?lang=bi.

Taylor, Charles. *The Language Animal: The Full Shape of the Human Linguistic Capacity*. Cambridge, MA: Belknap, 2016.

Taylor, Cheryl A. "Deaf and the Initial Physical Evidence." *Paraclete* 29/3 (Summer 1995) 37–45.

Telushkin, Joseph. *Jewish Literacy: The Most Important Things to Know about the Jewish Religion, its People, and its History*. New York: Morrow, 1991.

Thompson, Thomas L. *The Mythic Past: Biblical Archaeology and the Myth of Israel.* New York: Basic, 2000.
Thonnard, François-Joseph. *A Short History of Philosophy.* Edited and translated by Edward A. Maziarz. 2nd ed. New York: Desclee & Cie, 1956.
Thornton, Stephen. "Sigmund Freud: Religion." https://www.iep.utm.edu/freud-r/.
Tillich, Paul. "The God of History." *Christianity and Crisis* 4.7 (May 1944) 5–6.
Tipler, Frank J. *The Physics of Christianity.* New York: Doubleday, 2008.
Tirosh-Samuelson, Hava, ed. "Introduction: Judaism and the Natural World." In *Judaism and Ecology: Created World and Revealed Word.* Religions of the World and Ecology. Cambridge, MA: Harvard University Press, 2002.
———. *Judaism and Ecology: Created World and Revealed Word.* Religions of the World and Ecology. Cambridge, MA: Harvard University Press, 2003.
Tolstoy, Leo Nikolaivitch. "What is a Jew?" In *A Book of Jewish Thoughts*, edited by Joseph Herman Hertz, 135–36. London: Oxford University Press, 1926.
Tucker, Mary Evelyn, and John Grim. "Overview of World Religions and Ecology." http://fore.yale.edu/about-us/overview-of-world-religions-and-ecology/.
Tunks, George P., and David Kitz. *Tunks on Tongues.* Winnipeg, MB: Forever, 2010.
Uebel, Thomas. "Vienna Circle." *The Stanford Encyclopedia of Philosophy.* (Spring 2019 Edition), edited by Edward N. Zalta. https://plato.stanford.edu/archives/spr2019/entries/vienna-circle/
VanderKam, James C. "The Dead Sea Scrolls and the New Testament." *Biblical Archaeology Review* 41.2 (March/April 2015) 43–44.
Van Ness, Peter H., ed. *Spirituality and the Secular Quest.* World Spirituality: An Encyclopedic History of the Religious Quest. Volume 22. 25 vols. New York: Crossroad, 1996.
Vosper, Gretta. *With or Without God: Why the Way We Live is More Important than What We Believe.* Toronto: HarperCollins, 2008.
Voss, Rebekka. "Messianic Thought and Movements." *Oxford Bibliographies in Jewish Studies.* https://www.oxfordbibliographies.com/view/document/obo-9780199840731/obo-9780199840731-0032.xml.
Walton, John H. *The Lost World of Adam and Eve: Genesis 2–3 and the Human Origins Debate.* Downers Grove, IL: IVP Academic, 2015.
Walvoord, John F. "The Holy Spirit and Spiritual Gifts." *Bibliotheca Sacra* 143 (April–June 1986) 109–22.
Warfield, Benjamin B., and John E. Meeter. *Selected Shorter Writings of Benjamin B. Warfield.* Vol. 1. 2 vols. Phillipsburg, NJ: Presbyterian and Reformed, 1970.
Wellhausen, Julius, J. *Prolegomena to the History of Ancient Israel.* 1878. Reprint. Eugene, OR: Wipf & Stock, 2003.
Wenham, Gordon. "Genesis 1–11 as Proto-History." In *Genesis: History, Fiction, or Neither? Three Views on the Bible's Earliest Chapters*, edited by Charles Halton, 73–97. Counterpoints: Bible and Theology. Grand Rapids: Zondervan, 2015.
Went, Katy Jon. "Difficult Sayings: The Seed, the First Messianic Prophecy, Genesis 3:15." https://www.studylight.org/language-studies/difficult-sayings.html?article=456.
White, Lynn. "The Historical Roots of Our Ecologic Crisis." *Science* 155.3767 (March 10, 1967) 1203–7. doi:10.1126/science.155.3767.1203.
Whitla, William. *Sir Isaac Newton's Daniel and the Apocalypse.* London: Murray, 1922

Whitmarsh, Tim. "The Archaeology of Atheism in Ancient Athens: Locating the Garden of Epicurus." https://www.biblicalarchaeology.org/daily/ancient-cultures/daily-life-and-practice/the-archaeology-of-atheism-in-ancient-athens/.
———. *Battling the Gods: Atheism in the Ancient World*. New York: Knopf, 2015.
Wickramasinghe, Chandra. *Eyes, Winds, Seas, Skies*. Sri Lanka: Ranik Technologies, 2014.
Wolpert, Lewis. *Six Impossible Things before Breakfast: The Evolutionary Origins of Belief*. London: Faber & Faber, 2007.
World Humanist Congress. "The Amsterdam Declaration 2002." https://humanists.international/what-is-humanism/the-amsterdam-declaration/.
"The World's Youngest Countries." https://www.worldatlas.com/articles/which-are-the-youngest-countries-of-the-world.html.
Wright, N. T. *The Day the Revolution Began: Reconsidering the Meaning of Jesus's Crucifixion*. 1st Ed. San Francisco: HarperOne, 2016.
———. "Jesus' Resurrection and Christian Origins." *Gregorianum* 83.4 (2002) 615–35.
Wright, Paul. *Understanding Biblical Kingdoms & Empires: An Introductory Atlas and Comparative View*. Jerusalem: Carta, 2010.
Yerushalmi, Yosef Hayim. *Zakhor: Jewish History and Jewish Memory*. The Samuel and Althea Stroum Lectures in Jewish Studies. Seattle: University of Washington Press, 1996.
Yordy, Laura Ruth. "Ecology, Eschatology, and Christian Ethics." PhD diss., Duke University Divinity School, 2005.
———. *Green Witness: Ecology, Ethics, and the Kingdom of God*. Eugene, OR: Cascade, 2008.

www.ingramcontent.com/pod-product-compliance
Lightning Source LLC
Chambersburg PA
CBHW051519230426
43668CB00012B/1669